INTERMEDIATE BUSINESS ENGLISH COURSE BOOK

NEW EDITION

MARKET LEADER

David Cotton   David Falvey   Simon Kent

PEARSON
Longman

FINANCIAL TIMES
World business newspaper.

Map of

	Discussion	Texts	Language work	Skills	Case study
Unit 1 Brands page 6	Talk about your favourite brands Discuss two authentic product promotions	Reading: Outsourcing production – *Financial Times* Listening: An interview with a brand consultant	Words that go with brand and product Present simple and present continuous	Taking part in meetings 1	Caferoma: Solve the problems of a leading brand Writing: e-mail
Unit 2 Travel page 14	Talk about your travel experiences	Reading: Air rage – *Guardian* Listening: A business traveller's priorities	British and American travel words Talking about the future	Making arrangements on the telephone	Work, rest and play: Choose a suitable hotel for a seminar in France Writing: e-mail
Unit 3 Organisation page 22	Rank status symbols in order of importance	Reading: Flexibility in the workplace – *Fast Company* Listening: An interview with the partner of a management consultancy	Words and expressions to describe company structure Noun combinations	Socialising: introductions and networking	Auric Bank: Choose the best way to reorganise customer services. Writing: report
Unit 4 Change page 30	Discuss attitudes to change in general and at work Rank stressful situations	Reading: Change in retailing – *Financial Times* Listening: An interview with a business transformation director	Words for describing change Past simple and present perfect	Taking part in meetings 2	Acquiring Metrot: Agree on changes at a company that has been taken over Writing: action minutes
Unit 5 Money page 38	Do a quiz and discuss attitudes to money	Reading: Two financial reports – *Financial Times* Listening: An interview with the founder of a finance firm	Words and expressions for talking about finance Describing trends	Dealing with figures	Angel Investments: Choose a company to invest in Writing: e-mail
Unit 6 Advertising page 46	Discuss authentic advertisements Discuss good and bad advertising practices	Reading: Successful advertising – *Guardian* Listening: An interview with the head of planning at an advertising agency	Words and expressions for talking about advertising Articles: *a, an, the*, zero article	Starting presentations	Focus Advertising: Create and present an advertising campaign Writing: summary
Unit 7 Cultures page 54	Discuss the importance of cultural awareness in business	Reading: Advice for doing business across cultures Listening: An interview with a trainer in cultural awareness	Idioms for talking about business relationships Modals of advice, obligation and necessity	Social English See also: the social-cultural game on pages 138 and 139	Visitors from China: Plan a visit by a Chinese manufacturer Writing: e-mail
Revision unit A page 62					

Writing file: page 132   **Activity file:** page 140   **Grammar reference:** page 150

	Discussion	Texts	Language work	Skills	Case study
Unit 8 Employment page 68	Choose the most important qualities for getting a job Describe best and worse experiences at work	Reading: Retaining good staff – *Financial Times* Listening: An interview with an executive search consultant	Words to describe the recruitment process and personal character Indirect questions and statements	Managing meetings	Slim Gyms: Choose the best candidate for the job of General Manager Writing: letter
Unit 9 Trade page 76	Discuss ideas about globalisation	Reading: Fair trade – *Guardian* Listening: An interview with an expert on negotiating	Words for talking about international trade Conditions	Negotiating	Ashbury Guitars: Negotiate a deal with an overseas guitar manufacturer Writing: e-mail
Unit 10 Quality page 84	Discuss ideas of quality	Reading: Old-fashioned quality – *Financial Times* Listening: An interview with the Senior Vice President of a prestigious hotel chain.	Words for talking about quality control and customer service Gerunds and infinitives	Complaining on the telephone	Brookfield Airport: Work out an action plan following complaints from passengers Writing: report
Unit 11 Ethics page 92	Discuss questions of ethics at work Rank a list of unethical activities	Reading: Business ethics – *Financial Times* Listening: An interview with a bank executive	Words to do with *honesty* or *dishonesty* Narrative tenses	Problem-solving	Profit or principle? Decide if a manager has acted unethically and what action to take Writing: letter
Unit 12 Leadership page 100	Discuss the qualities of good leadership	Reading: Profile of a leading Chief Executive – *Financial Times* Listening: An interview with an expert in leadership training	Words to describe character Relative clauses	Decision-making	Orbit Records: Discuss ideas to save a failing music retailer Writing: e-mail
Unit 13 Innovation page 108	Talk about innovations in your daily life and in the twentieth century	Reading: In-company innovation – *Fortune magazine* Listening: An interview with an expert on presentations	Words and expressions to describe innovations Passives	Presentation techniques	Style is everything: Prepare a product presentation for a competition Writing: short article or press release
Unit 14 Competition page 116	Do a quiz on how competitive you are	Reading: Losing competitive edge – *Financial Times* Listening: An interview with the Marketing Manager of a credit card business	Idioms from sport to describe competition Modals of probability	Negotiating	Beverley Watches: Choose the best supplier Writing: e-mail
Revision unit B page 124					

Introduction

What is Market Leader and who is it for?

Market Leader is a multi-level business English course for businesspeople and students of business English. It has been developed in association with the *Financial Times*, one of the leading sources of business information in the world. It consists of 14 units based on topics of great interest to everyone involved in international business.

This new edition of the Intermediate level features new authentic texts and listenings throughout, reflecting the latest trends in the business world. If you are in business, the course will greatly improve your ability to communicate in English in a wide range of business situations. If you are a student of business, the course will develop the communication skills you need to succeed in business and will enlarge your knowledge of the business world. Everybody studying this course will become more fluent and confident in using the language of business and should increase their career prospects.

The authors

David Falvey *(left)* has over 20 years' teaching and managerial experience in the UK, Japan and Hong Kong. He has also worked as a teacher trainer at the British Council in Tokyo, and is now Head of the English Language Centre and Principal Lecturer at London Metropolitan University.

Simon Kent *(centre)* has over 15 years' teaching experience including three years as an in-company trainer in Berlin at the time of German reunification. He is currently a Senior Lecturer in business and general English, as well as having special responsibility for designing new courses at London Metropolitan University.

David Cotton *(right)* has over 35 years' experience teaching and training in EFL, ESP and English for Business, and is the author of numerous business English titles, including *Agenda*, *World of Business*, *International Business Topics*, and *Keys to Management*. He is also one of the authors of the best-selling *Business Class*. He is a Senior Lecturer at London Metropolitan University.

What is in the units?

Starting up

You are offered a variety of interesting activities in which you discuss the topic of the unit and exchange ideas about it.

Vocabulary

You will learn important new words and phrases which you can use when you carry out the tasks in the unit. A good business dictionary, such as the *Longman Business English Dictionary* will also help you to increase your business vocabulary.

Discussion

You will build up your confidence in using English and will improve your fluency through interesting discussion activities.

Reading

You will read authentic articles on a variety of topics from the *Financial Times* and other newspapers and books on business. You will develop your reading skills and learn essential business vocabulary. You will also be able to discuss the ideas and issues in the articles.

Listening

You will hear authentic interviews with businesspeople. You will develop listening skills such as listening for information and note-taking.

Language review

This section focuses on common problem areas at intermediate level. You will become more accurate in your use of language. Each unit contains a Language review box which provides a review of key grammar items.

Skills

You will develop essential business communication skills such as making presentations, taking part in meetings, negotiating, telephoning, and using English in social situations. Each Skills section contains a Useful language box which provides you with the language you need to carry out the realistic business tasks in the book.

Case study

The Case studies are linked to the business topics of each unit. They are based on realistic business problems or situations and allow you to use the language and communication skills you have developed while working through the unit. They give you the opportunities to practise your speaking skills in realistic business situations. Each Case study ends with a writing task. A full writing syllabus is provided in the Market Leader Practice File.

Revision Units

Market Leader Intermediate new edition also contains two revision units, based on material covered in the preceding seven Course book units. Each revision unit is designed so that it can be completed in one session or on a unit-by-unit basis.

LONGMAN ON THE **WEB**

Longman.com offers classroom activities, teaching tips and online resources for teachers of all levels and students of all ages. Visit us for course-specific Companion Websites, our online catalogue of all Longman titles, and access to all local Longman websites, offices and contacts around the world.

*Join a global community of teachers and students at **Longman.com.***

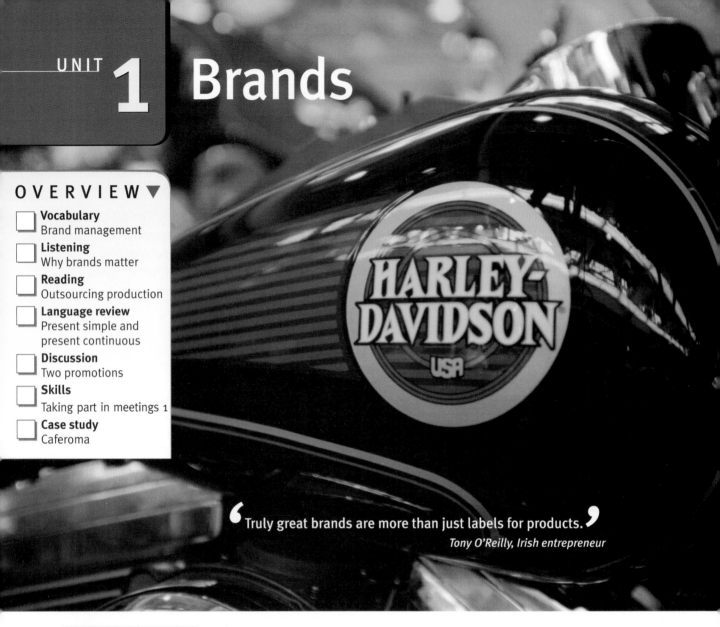

UNIT 1 Brands

OVERVIEW ▼

☐ **Vocabulary**
Brand management

☐ **Listening**
Why brands matter

☐ **Reading**
Outsourcing production

☐ **Language review**
Present simple and
present continuous

☐ **Discussion**
Two promotions

☐ **Skills**
Taking part in meetings 1

☐ **Case study**
Caferoma

'Truly great brands are more than just labels for products.'

Tony O'Reilly, Irish entrepreneur

Starting up

A List some of your favourite brands. Then answer these questions.

1 Are they international or national brands?

2 What image and qualities does each one have? Use the following words and phrases to help you.

value for money	luxurious	timeless	well-made
top of the range	durable	inexpensive	cool
reliable	stylish	fashionable	sexy

3 Why do people buy brands?

4 Why do you think some people dislike brands?

5 How loyal are you to the brands you have chosen?
For example, when you buy jeans, do you always buy Levi's?

B A recent survey named the brands below as the world's top ten. Which do you think is number one? Rank the others in order.

Marlboro	Nokia	Mercedes	General Electric	Intel
IBM	Microsoft	Coca-Cola	McDonald's	Disney

Check your answer on page 144. Are you surprised?

C 🎧 1.1 Listen to two speakers talking about brands. What reasons does each person give for liking or disliking brands?

Vocabulary
Brand management

(A) Match these word partnerships to their meanings.

B R A N D	
1 loyalty	a) the name given to a product by the company that makes it
2 image	b) using an existing name on another type of product
3 stretching	c) the ideas and beliefs people have about a brand
4 awareness	d) the tendency to always buy a particular brand
5 name	e) how familiar people are with a brand

P R O D U C T	
6 launch	f) the set of products made by a company
7 lifecycle	g) the use of a well-known person to advertise products
8 range	h) when products are used in films or TV programmes
9 placement	i) the introduction of a product to the market
10 endorsement	j) the length of time people continue to buy a product

(B) Complete these sentences with word partnerships from Exercise A.

BRAND

1 The creation of Virgin Cola, Virgin Air, Virgin Rail and Virgin Bride is an example of ..*brand stretching*.. .

2 Consumers who always buy Levi's when they need a new pair of jeans are showing ....

3 Not enough people recognise our logo; we need to spend a lot more on raising ....

PRODUCT

1 David Beckham advertising Vodafone is an example of .*product endorsement*. .

2 A .... consists of introduction, growth, maturity and decline.

3 The use of BMW cars and Nokia phones in James Bond films are examples of ....

(C) Make sentences of your own using the word partnerships in Exercise A.

Listening
Why brands matter

▲ Sandra Greaves

(A) 🎧 1.2 Sandra Greaves is a consultant at Wolff-Olins, a leading international brand consultancy based in London. In the first part of the interview she talks about why we need brands. Listen and complete these extracts.

1 Brands are all about ....

2 You know what a brand is .... , what it .... , what it's going to ....

3 You actually trust it to .... again.

4 One thing about brands is they add a lot of .... and .... and .... , as well as giving you the power to .... things.

(B) 🎧 1.3 Listen to the second part of the interview and tick the points below which Sandra makes.

1 People are very loyal to successful brands.

2 Even successful brands are seen as just a product or a service.

3 Apple was popular because it wasn't a big corporation.

4 Apple customers felt that the Mac was an easy product to use.

(C) 🎧 1.4 Listen to the example Sandra gives of how Wolff-Olins helped a company with its branding and answer these questions.

1 What was the company?

2 What is its business sector?

3 What advice did they receive?

Reading
Outsourcing production

A Why do some companies make luxury products abroad rather than at home?

B Read the article and answer these questions.

1 Which brands are mentioned? Do you know which country each is from?

2 Which companies make all of their products in their own country?

Made in Europe

By Jo Johnson, Fred Kapner and Richard McGregor

Almost every fashion label outside the top super-luxury brands is either already manufacturing in Asia or 5 thinking of it. Coach, the US leather goods maker, is a classic example. Over the past five years, it has lifted all its gross margins by 10 manufacturing solely in low-cost markets. In March 2002 it closed its factory in Lares, Puerto Rico, its last company-owned plant, and 15 outsources all its products.

Burberry has many Asian licensing arrangements. In 2000 it decided to renew Sanyo's Japanese licence for 20 ten years. This means that almost half of Burberry's sales at retail value will continue to be produced under licence in Asia. At 25 the same time however, Japanese consumers prefer the group's European-made products.

Sanyo is now reacting to 30 this demand for a snob alternative to the Burberry products made in its factories across Asia by opening a flagship store in 35 Tokyo's Ginza, where it sells Burberry products imported from Europe.

In interviews with the FT, many executives say the top 40 luxury brands will continue to be seen, particularly in Asia, as European. Domenico De Sole of Gucci says: 'The Asian consumer 45 really does believe – whether it's true or not – that luxury comes from Europe and must be made there to be the best.'

Serge Weinberg, Chief 50 Executive of Pinault Printemps Redoute, which controls Gucci, says it will not move Gucci's production offshore. Yet some in the 55 industry recognise that change may be round the corner even for the super-luxury brands. Patrizio Bertelli, Chief Executive of 60 Prada, says: 'The "Made in Italy" label is important but what we are really offering is a style, and style is an expression of culture.' He 65 therefore recognises that quality fashion items may not always need to be produced in Italy.

Amitava Chattopadhyay, 70 Professor of Marketing at Insead, the business school, says: 'A brand is a set of associations in the mind of the consumer and one of 75 these is the country of origin. For luxury goods, the role of the brand is crucial. To damage it is a cardinal sin and no brand manager will 80 want to get the balance between manufacturing location and the brand image wrong.'

From the *Financial Times*

FINANCIAL TIMES
World business newspaper.

▲ Mother, baby and pushchair in Burberry.

C Which of these statements are true? Correct the false ones.

1 Coach no longer has a factory in Puerto Rico.

2 Coach, like many other companies, is outsourcing its products to reduce costs.

3 Some Japanese people choose to buy Burberry products made in Europe rather than in Japan.

4 Sanyo's store in Tokyo sells Burberry products made only in Asia.

5 According to Domenico De Sole, the best luxury products are made in Japan.

6 Gucci is planning to outsource some of its products.

7 Patrizio Bertelli believes that luxury fashion products should always be made in Europe.

8 Amitava Chattopadhyay says that companies need to pay careful attention to where they manufacture their products.

D Choose the best summary of the article.

a) Most manufacturers of luxury brands do not wish to produce their goods in low-cost countries because they believe that it will damage their brand image.

b) Most manufacturers of top brands now produce their goods in low-cost countries. Consumers no longer care about where the products are manufactured.

c) Asian consumers think that European luxury goods are of high quality. The current trend of making such goods in Asia could damage the reputation of these luxury brands.

 Vocabulary file page 170

Language review
Present simple and present continuous

The present simple and the present continuous have several uses.

- We use the present simple to give factual information, for example about company activities.
  *Coach **outsources** all its products.*
  *Does Burberry **outsource** its products?*
- We use the present simple to talk about routine activities or habits.
  *I always **buy** Armani suits. **Do** you usually **buy** designer brands?*
- We use the present continuous to talk about ongoing situations and projects.
  *Sanyo **is** now **reacting** to this demand.*
- We use the present continuous to talk about temporary situations.
  *We **are testing** a new brand at the moment.*

➡ page 150

A Which of the time expressions below do we usually use with the present simple? Which of the time expressions do we usually use with the present continuous? Which are used with both?

usually	this year	every day	now
often	nowadays	once a month	
currently	at the moment	these days	

B Complete these sentences with the present simple or the present continuous forms of the verbs in brackets.

1 **a)** This year we .... (try) to develop a brand with personality.

   b) We usually .... (develop) brands that say something.

2 **a)** Powerful brand names .... (create) strong consumer loyalty.

   b) At the moment we .... (look) for a new brand name that suggests something about the product's benefits and qualities.

3 **a)** L'Oréal .... (sell) cosmetics and toiletries to consumers around the world.

   b) This year L'Oréal .... (invest) over £180m in R & D .

4 **a)** The marketing department always .... (keep) within its budget.

   b) Because the company made a loss last year, the marketing department .... (try) to reduce costs.

C Complete the text below with the present simple or the present continuous forms of the verbs in brackets.

At the moment I .... [1] (work) for a cosmetics company. We offer a full range of cosmetic products and .... [2] (sell) cosmetics and toiletries around the world. Our main cosmetics brand .... [3] (dominate) the French market and it .... [4] (do) well in the rest of Europe at the moment, too. In fact, the brand .... [5] (become) more and more popular throughout the world and our market share .... [6] (grow) every day.

We usually .... [7] (develop) and .... [8] (extend) products under our existing brand name. The brand is distinctive and .... [9] (stand) out from the competition. However, this year we .... [10] (create) a completely new brand of cosmetics.

Discussion

Two promotions

A Work in pairs. Student A reads Case 1 and answers the questions. Student B reads Case 2 and answers the questions.

Case 1 Harley Davidson

In 2003 the Harley Davidson brand was 100 years old. Although its brand image is based on the spirit of wild and rebellious youth such as Marlon Brando in the film *The Wild One* (1954), the typical consumer is very different. They are likely to be rich, middle-aged accountants trying to recapture their youth. The average age of Harley Davidson customers is 46 compared with 36 for the rest of the motorbike industry. At the party to celebrate the centenary, the surprise performer was actually Elton John, rather than the Rolling Stones who many people had expected. This caused many of the 150,000 riders and dealers to leave the event very unhappy. Although sales and earnings for Harley Davidson have been increasing for the past 18 years, many people see trouble on the road ahead. The problem is Harley Davidson's typical customers come from the baby-boom generation (1946–1964) and, as these customers get older, Harley Davidson may find its market shrinking.

1 What is the brand image of Harley Davidson?
2 Why were many people unhappy about the music at the party?
3 What problem could Harley Davidson have in the future?
4 What can Harley Davidson do to preserve its sales? Should it change its brand image? Should it look for new market segments? Should it stretch its brand?

Case 2 JCB

1 Where does the name JCB come from?
2 What was surprising about JCB's customer research?
3 What sort of products do you think JCB developed as a result of its research?
4 Can you think of a similar example of brand-stretching in your country?

JCB is a world-famous engineering company. It was founded in 1945 by Joseph Cyril Bamford. He began his business working alone in a small garage. JCB makes construction and agricultural equipment such as tractors, earth-moving vehicles and loading machines. Now its world headquarters in England is one of the finest engineering factories in Europe. The company produces over 130 different models on four different continents and sells a full range of equipment in over 150 countries. It is truly a global brand.

JCB's research showed that its customers associated the company with the following brand values: 'yellow', 'digger' and 'durable'. Adults saw the brand as being very British, and suggesting an image of quality and being functional. Children, on the other hand, saw the brand as 'big', 'muddy' and 'fun'. JCB made a decision to stretch its brand.

B Share information about your case with your partner.
• What was the original brand image of the product in your case study?
• Who does the brand appeal to now?

Skills
Taking part in meetings 1

A 🎧 1.5 **Four marketing executives at a cosmetics company, Marvel Plc, are talking about licensing their 'Luc Fontaine' product range to an Asian manufacturer. Listen to the conversation and answer the questions.**

1 Why do the marketing executives at Marvel Plc want to license their 'Luc Fontaine' product range?

2 What advantages does Susan Li offer to Marvel?

3 According to Barbara, what is the disadvantage of offering a licence to Susan Li?

4 What suggestion does Barbara make to her colleagues?

B 🎧 1.5 **Listen again and complete the extracts.**

Marcia	Alain, how .... ¹ about this? Is she the right person for us?
Alain	Definitely. In my opinion, she's ideal.
Marcia	Right. Valerie, what .... ² ?
Valerie	I .... ³ because she's very good at marketing. I've met her several times.
Marcia	Barbara, you're shaking your head. .... ⁴?
Barbara	I'm .... ⁵ agree. I don't think she's suitable at all.
Marcia	So what do you suggest then?
Barbara	.... ⁶ find someone else. I do have someone in mind.
Barbara	In my opinion, his company has a lot to offer. .... ⁷ meet him and see if he's interested?

C **Which of the phrases in Exercise B are:**

1 asking for opinions?   3 agreeing or disagreeing?

2 giving opinions?   4 making suggestions?

D **Role play this situation.**

Jonson, a large department store in Chicago, USA, is losing money. Its main product areas are food, clothing and household furniture. Seventy percent of its revenue comes from clothing, twenty-two percent from food and eight percent from furniture. Three directors of the company meet to discuss the company's problems and how to solve them.

Work in groups of three. Student A: turn to page 141. Student B: turn to page 147. Student C: turn to page 149. Read your role cards then role play the discussion.

 Vocabulary file pages 170 and 174

Useful language

Asking for opinions
How do you feel about ... ?
What do you think?
What's your opinion?
What's your view?

Giving opinions
I think ... / I don't think ...
In my opinion ...

Agreeing
That's true.
I agree.
Absolutely / Exactly.
I think so too.

Disagreeing
I see / know what you mean, but ...
I'm afraid I can't agree.
Maybe, but ...

Making suggestions
I think we should ...
How about ... ?
Why don't we ... ?
Maybe / Perhaps we could ...

CASE STUDY

Caferoma

Background

Caferoma, a well-known brand of coffee, is owned by PEFD, a company based in Turin, Italy. It is promoted as an exclusive product for people who love ground coffee. Its image is of an Italian-style coffee. It has a strong and slightly bitter taste, and costs more than almost every other ground coffee product on the market.

Problems

In the last two years, Caferoma's share of the quality ground coffee market has declined by almost 30% (see chart). There are several reasons for this:

a) *Brand loyalty*: Consumers have become less loyal to brands and more price conscious. They are willing to buy lower-priced coffee products.

b) *Price*: Supermarkets are selling, under their own label, similar products to Caferoma at much lower prices.

c) *'Copycat' products*: Competing products of Italian-style ground coffee are selling at prices 30 to 40% lower than Caferoma.

d) *Brand image*: the Caferoma brand no longer seems to be exciting and up-to-date.

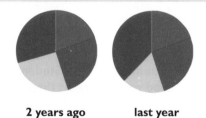

2 years ago	**last year**

Market share European quality ground coffee

- ■ **Top five European coffee brands**
- ■ **Supermarket own label brands**
- ■ **Other brands**
- ■ **Caferoma**

Sales outlets as a percentage of Caferoma sales

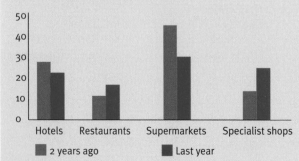

Hotels Restaurants Supermarkets Specialist shops

■ 2 years ago   ■ Last year

Focus group results

Do you think Caferoma is…	% of people answering 'yes'
expensive?	60
value for money?	43
good quality?	70
old-fashioned?	80
exciting?	23
exclusive?	55

Possible solutions

Repositioning the product

Change Caferoma's image to appeal to a different market segment. (Which segment? What changes to taste, quality, packaging, logo, labelling, distribution?)

Pricing

Reduce the price by, say, 20% to 30% so that it is in the medium range of prices.

Advertising

Develop a new advertising campaign to relaunch the brand.

Multiple brands

Sell Caferoma, with small changes to product, under different brand names at lower prices.

Task

As members of PEFD's marketing team, hold an informal meeting. Consider the advantages and disadvantages of each solution. Then decide what to do to stop the decline in the product's market share and to increase profits.

Writing

Write an e-mail to Caferoma's Managing Director, Mario Cumino. Summarise what action you agreed to take at the meeting to solve Caferoma's problems. Explain your reasons.

 Writing file page 133

Own brand label products

Allow supermarkets and hypermarkets to sell Caferoma under the supermarkets' own brand labels. Continue to market the Caferoma brand at the same time.

A new product

Bring out an instant coffee or decaffeinated product under the Caferoma brand as soon as possible.

Stretching the brand

Allow some makers of coffee equipment (cafetieres, percolators, coffee machines, etc.) to use the Caferoma brand on their goods, for a licensing fee.

1.6 Claudia, Caferoma's Marketing Manager, has some recent news from one of Caferoma's biggest customers, Majestic Hotels, a major European hotel chain. She discusses the news with Caferoma's Sales Director, Pietro. Listen to their conversation. How does this new information affect your decisions?

OVERVIEW▼

☐ **Vocabulary**
British and American English

☐ **Listening**
A business traveller's priorities

☐ **Language review**
Talking about the future

☐ **Reading**
Air rage

☐ **Skills**
Making arrangements on the telephone

☐ **Case study**
Work, rest and play

Starting up

(A) **Answer these questions individually. Then compare your answers with a partner.**

1 How often do you travel by air, rail, road and sea?

2 What do you enjoy about travelling? What don't you enjoy?

3 Put the following in order of importance to you when you travel.

comfort	safety	price	reliability	speed

4 Does the order change for different types of travel?

(B) **Choose the correct word from the box to complete the following list of things which irritate people when flying.**

seats	trolleys	queues	luggage
room	cancellations	food	jet

1 not enough leg ....

2 lost or delayed ....

3 long .... at check-in

4 poor quality .... and drink

5 no baggage .... available

6 overbooking of ....

7 flight delays and ....

8 ....- lag

(C) 🎧 **2.1 Listen to three people talking about their travel experiences. Tick the problems in Exercise B that they mention.**

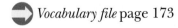 *Vocabulary file page 173*

(D) **Which of the things in Exercise B irritate you most? Which irritate you least? Discuss your ideas with a partner.**

' *He travels fastest who travels alone.* '
Proverb

Vocabulary
British and American English

A Match the words and phrases below which have the same meaning. For each pair decide which is British English and which is American English.

1 subway
2 city centre
3 carry-on baggage
4 one way
5 return
6 freeway
7 rest room
8 elevator
9 coach class
10 timetable
11 car park

a) motorway
b) lift
c) public toilet
d) schedule
e) economy class
f) single
g) parking lot
h) underground
i) hand luggage
j) round trip
k) downtown

 Vocabulary file page 172

B Work in pairs. Use words or phrases in American English from Exercise A to complete the text below.

My last overseas business trip was a nightmare from start to finish. First of all there was a delay on the way to the airport as there was an accident on the ...._freeway_...... ¹. When I got there I found the lower level of the airport .... ² was flooded. Next my .... ³ was too big and heavy so I had to check it in. When we arrived the .... ⁴ was closed and there were no cabs at all. After a long time trying to read the .... ⁵ and waiting for forty minutes, we finally got a bus .... ⁶ and found the hotel, but the .... ⁷ wasn't working and our rooms were on the fifth floor.

C 🎧 2.2 Listen to the recording and check your answers.

Listening
A business traveller's priorities

▲ Stephanie Taylor

A 🎧 2.3 Stephanie Taylor is a businesswoman who travels regularly as part of her job. Listen to the first part of the interview and choose the three priorities she mentions from the list below.

- Good organisation
- Easy booking
- Regular transport
- Balancing cost with comfort
- Being patient
- Airline food

B Why does Stephanie think it is still important for businesspeople to travel regularly?

C 🎧 2.4 Listen to the second part of the interview and list the best and worst travel experiences that Stephanie describes.

Best: 1 .... Worst: ....

2 ....

D In pairs discuss what developments you expect to see in future business travel.

E 🎧 2.5 Listen to what Stephanie says about future business travel and complete her prediction below.

Perhaps, particularly in the area of .... ¹, I think hotels will need to improve .... ² in general. There are some very good hotels already, but I think more hotels will provide .... ³ for businesspeople ... perhaps some .... ⁴ facilities for .... ⁵ .

Reading
Air rage

A Answer these questions before you read the article.

1 What was your worst experience when travelling by air?

2 Why do some people get angry when they are travelling on a plane?

➡ *Vocabulary file* page 173

B Now read the article. Which of these statements are true about the article? Correct the false ones.

1 People in groups are more likely to behave badly on planes.

2 Drink is often the cause of problems on board.

3 Airlines can do little to improve air quality.

4 Travellers are using new technology to express their dissatisfaction with airlines.

5 Airlines have taken no action to address travellers' concerns.

C Which of the following reasons are given for air rage in the article?

1 poor service
2 flights not leaving on time
3 poor quality of food
4 too many passengers on a plane
5 not feeling safe
6 people drinking alcohol
7 poor air quality
8 noisy passengers
9 not being able to smoke
10 not enough cabin crew

D Which of the following words from the article have a negative meaning? Use a good dictionary to help you.

rage	misbehaviour	quality	frustration
concern	harm	optimum	valuable
irritability	disorientation	complaints	criticise
disruptive	dangerous	dissatisfactio	

Road ragers in the sky

By Derek Brown

Airlines and their long-suffering customers are reporting a steep climb in air rage incidents. Some incidents are apparently caused by
5 problems which are familiar to many regular travellers. One case reported from America stemmed from an interminable delay in takeoff, when passengers were
10 cooped up in their aircraft on the tarmac for four hours, without food, drink or information. Mass unrest is less common than individual misbehaviour, as in the case of the
15 convict who recently went crazy on a flight, attacked the crew and tried to open a door in mid-flight.

The psychology of air rage is a new area of study, and there are
20 almost as many explanations as examples. Most analysts of the phenomenon blame alcohol, but many people now think that the airlines are at fault. To cut costs,
25 they are cramming ever more passengers into their aircraft, while reducing cabin crew, training and quality of service, all of which increase passenger frustration. In
30 addition, there is increasing concern in the US about another cost-cutting exercise, which could seriously harm passengers' health: cabin ventilation.

35 Modern aircraft are equipped with sophisticated air conditioning devices – but running them at optimum capacity burns up valuable aviation fuel. Many
40 airlines routinely instruct their flight crews to run the systems on minimum settings. Campaigners for improved air quality claim that this can lead to irritability and
45 disorientation.

In the US, the soaring number of passenger complaints across a wide range of issues is reflected in a number of new Internet sites which
50 criticise the airlines and demand better service. One of the sites is demanding an air passengers' Bill of Rights.

Cabin and flight crews, who are
55 in the front line of the battle against disruptive and dangerous in-flight behaviour, have called for stiffer penalties against the offenders. Management have also called
60 for legislation – while denying that its cost-cutting practices have contributed to the problem. But there are some signs, in the US at least, that the airlines are at last
65 attempting to respond to customer dissatisfaction. Some major lines have announced concessions to the most frequent complaint of all, and are removing seats to make more
70 room for their customers.

From *The Guardian*

Language review

Talking about the future

> **We can use different language forms to talk about the future.**
>
> 1 We use *going to* to talk about what we intend to do and have already decided to do. *We're going to attend the seminar in France next week.* **Are** *you* **going to** *book the tickets for the flight?*
>
> 2 We use *will* or *'ll* to talk something we have decided to do at the time of speaking: *The flight's late. I'll call the office to cancel the meeting.*
>
> 3 We use the present continuous to talk about a fixed arrangement. *I'm travelling to Germany next week.* **Are** *you* **flying** *on the same flight as your boss?*
>
> 4 We use the present simple to talk about a timetable or programme. *The train **leaves** Rome at 2 p.m. tomorrow. It **doesn't stop** at Milan.*
>
> page 150

A **Complete each dialogue with the correct form of *going to* or *will*.**

1 **A** I'm really sorry, I can't take you to the station. Something has just come up.

   B Oh, don't worry. I .... (take) a taxi.

2 **A** We've chosen a name for our new low-cost airline.

   B Really. What .... (you / call) it?

3 **A** Have you decided how to increase the number of passengers?

   B Yes, we .... (offer) a family discount at weekends.

4 **A** I can't send an e-mail to the travel agent; my computer's just crashed.

   B Write down your details and I .... (fax) them over for you.

5 **A** How's your daughter?

   B She's fine. She .... (learn) to be a pilot for the flying doctor service next year!

B **Use the present continuous or the present simple to complete the sentences below.**

1 His flight *arrives / is arriving* at 9 o'clock tomorrow morning.

2 We*'re staying / stay* at the Hilton Hotel for next month's sales conference.

3 The next seminar *is beginning / begins* at 3 p.m.

4 I *travel / am travelling* by train from Paris to London next time.

5 The boat *is departing / departs* at midday so you have the whole morning to get ready.

6 The delegation from China *are seeing / see* the Chairman the following Monday.

C **Work in pairs. Take turns to complete the sentences below. Use *going to*, *will*, the present continuous or the present simple.**

1 I'm sorry, I can't attend the sales meeting tomorrow. ....

2 The marketing department have decided on their travel plans for the next month. ....

3 The trains are delayed because of bad weather, so ....

4 Don't worry if you can't drive me to the airport, ...

5 I've got the details of your flight to Turkey. ....

6 Oh no! There's been an accident and the traffic is very heavy on the motorway. ....

7 Did I give you the departure time? It ....

8 I've made up my mind, ...

Skills
Making arrangements on the telephone

A 🎧 2.6, 2.7 **Philippa Knight, Sales Director at The Fashion Group in New York, makes two telephone calls to Maria Bonetti, a fashion buyer in London. Listen and note: a) the purpose of each call and b) the result.**

B 🎧 2.6 **Listen to the first call again and complete the extract below.**

Philippa	I'm calling because I'll be in London next week and .... [1] to see you. I want to tell you about our new collection.
Maria	Great. What .... [2]? I'm fairly free next week, I think.
Philippa	.... [3]? In the afternoon? Could .... [4] then?
Maria	Let me look now. Let .... [5]. Yes, that'd be no problem at all. .... [6] 2 o'clock? Is that OK?

C 🎧 2.7 **Listen to the second call again and complete the extract below.**

Receptionist	Thank you. I'm putting you through. Hello, I'm afraid she's engaged at the moment. .... [1] or can I take a message?
Philippa	I'll leave a message, please. The thing is, I should be meeting Ms Bonetti at 2 p.m, ... [2]. My plane was delayed, and I've got to reschedule my appointments. If possible, ... [3] tomorrow. .... [4] in the morning. .... [5] here at the hotel, please?
Receptionist	Certainly. What's the number, please?
Philippa	It's .... [6].

D **Role play these two telephone situations.**

1 Student A is a company employee who has arranged to meet Student B, a colleague from one of your subsidiaries. Explain that you cannot keep the appointment, and give a reason. Suggest an alternative day.

2 Student B is on a business trip to Sydney, Australia and wants to stay an extra day. Telephone the Qantas airline office. Talk to the representative, Student A, to arrange a different flight.

Useful language

Answering the phone
Hello, Erik Halse speaking.
Good morning, Madison Ltd.

Making contact
I'd like to speak to Anna Schilling, please.
Could I have the sales department, please?

Identifying yourself
This is / My name's Marta Blanco.
Marta Blanco speaking.

Stating your purpose
I'm calling about …
The reason I'm calling is …

Making arrangements
Could we meet on Monday at 10.30?
How / What about April 10th?
Is 11.15 convenient / OK?

Changing arrangements
I'm afraid I can't come on Friday.
We've got an appointment for 11.00, but I'm afraid something's come up.
Could we fix another time?
I can't make it on …

Responding
That's fine / OK for me.
Sorry, I can't make it then.
No problem.

Closing
Good. So, I'll see you on the 8th.
Thank you. Goodbye.
Right. / OK then.
That's great, I'll see you …

Work, rest and play

Background

ICON is a computer software company based in Los Angeles, USA. The Manager of its company travel service is making arrangements for some senior managers to attend a seminar in France.

The seminar starts on Friday July 5th and ends on Sunday July 7th. It will include meetings to discuss work problems and executive games to encourage teamwork. This is important because the participants are of different nationalities. The participants will expect to work hard, then relax, enjoy the amenities of the hotel, explore the surrounding area and have a really good time. The Manager of ICON's travel service wants to book a hotel which is both stylish and value for money.

Stage 1

The Manager of ICON's travel service phones the Account Manager for Corporate Travel at Universal Airlines. He asks Universal to propose three hotels in France for the seminar. The Account Manager of Corporate Travel asks for more details about the seminar and its participants. Manager, ICON's travel service: turn to page 140. Account Manager, Universal Airlines: turn to page 147.

Read your information files. Then role play the telephone conversation and arrange to meet one day the following week.

Stage 2

The Manager of ICON's travel service has to change the date of the meeting. Read your information files and role play the telephone call. Manager, ICON's travel service: turn to page 142. Account Manager, Universal Airlines: turn to page 149.

Task

You are either:
Manager, ICON's travel service
or
Account Manager for Corporate Travel, Universal Airlines
You should keep these roles throughout the case study.

Château Monfort ✳✳✳

Description:	18th century castle; 35 rooms
Location:	In the countryside. Bordeaux – 30 km; airport – 25 km; railway station – 20km
Restaurant:	French cuisine. Excellent vegetarian food.
Price:	€200 per room per night. Cost of meals per day: €50 Group discount: 20%
Conference facilities:	1 large room, 3 small rooms. Basic equipment.
Other facilities:	Swimming pool, Gym, Bar Disabled facilities on the ground floor only. No smoking
Entertainment:	Free visits to a nightclub (Sat evening).

Hotel Marine ✳✳✳

Description:	Modern hotel; 68 rooms
Location:	On the seafront in the Bay of Arcachon; Bordeaux – 60 km; airport – 50 km; railway station – 1.5 km
Restaurant:	International cuisine. Vegetarian menu available
Price:	€150 per room per night. Cost of meals per day: €80. No discount for groups
Conference facilities:	2 large rooms, 2 smaller rooms. High-tech equipment.
Other facilities:	Bar, Satellite TV, Modem point, Air conditioning Smoking areas in hotel lounge only. Disabled facilities on ground floor only. Outdoor activities including golf, horse-riding, wind-surfing, fishing and boat trips.

Hotel Splendide ✳✳✳

Description:	Modern hotel (built in 1992); 120 rooms
Location:	In Bordeaux city centre in a large pedestrian zone. Airport – 15 km; railway station – 15 km; hotel shuttle bus to and from the airport
Restaurant:	French and Italian cuisine. Vegetarian menu available.
Price:	€220 per room per night. Cost of meals per day: €80. Group discount: 10%
Conference facilities:	1 large rooms, 3 small rooms. Basic equipment.
Other facilities:	Bar, Satellite TV, Modem point, Air conditioning No smoking. Disabled facilities on all floors.

Stage 3

The Account Manager at Universal Airlines sends information about three possible hotels for the seminar to the Manager, ICON's travel service. They are all in Bordeaux, or in the surrounding area. At the meeting they discuss the three proposals and choose one of the hotels for the seminar. Role play the discussion.

Writing

As the Account Manager for Corporate Travel at Universal Airlines, write an e-mail to the manager of the hotel chosen for the seminar. Confirm the booking, giving details of the number of participants, arrival and departure times, meals, equipment and any other special requirements.

 Writing file page 133

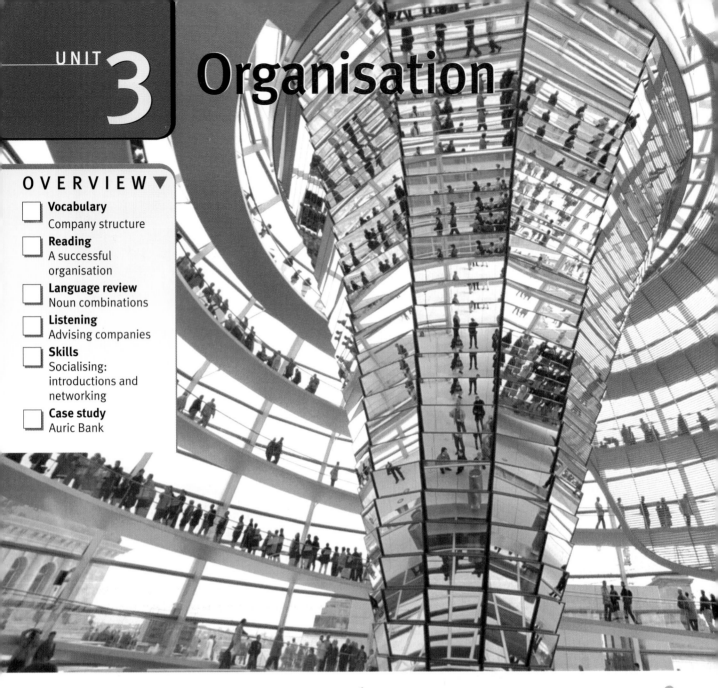

UNIT 3 Organisation

OVERVIEW ▼

☐ **Vocabulary**
Company structure

☐ **Reading**
A successful organisation

☐ **Language review**
Noun combinations

☐ **Listening**
Advising companies

☐ **Skills**
Socialising: introductions and networking

☐ **Case study**
Auric Bank

How many people work in your office? About half.

Anonymous

Starting up

A Discuss these questions.

1 Would you like to work in the building in the photo above? Explain why or why not.

2 Which people in your organisation have their own office? Do they have their own office because of a) seniority; b) a need for confidentiality; c) the type of work they do?

B How important are the following in showing a person's status in an organisation? Give each one a score from 1 (not important) to 5 (very important).

- a reserved parking space
- an office with a window
- a uniform
- a personal business card
- your own office
- a company car
- your name on your door

- having a secretary
- taking holidays when you like
- the size of your desk
- more than one seat in your office
- flying business class
- a company credit card
- having fixed working hours

Company structure

A Match the words and phrases below to the correct place on the diagram.

subsidiary *8*	head office
factory / plant	distribution centre
call centre	warehouse
service centre	branches / outlets

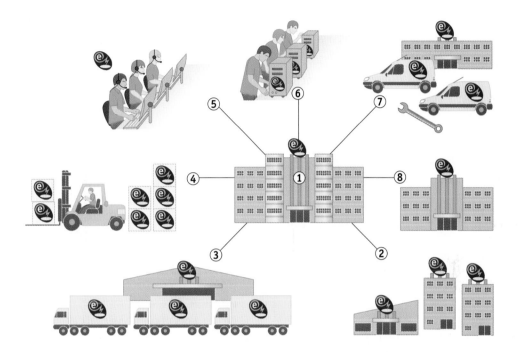

B 3.1 Listen to the comments from different places in the organisation and write them down. Then match them to the places shown in Exercise A.

1 *Stock levels have been low for two weeks now. – warehouse*

C Think about the organisation you work for, or one you know well. How is it organised?

D Discuss these questions.

1 Which of the words below can describe:

   a) good qualities of an organisation?

   b) bad qualities of an organisation?

bureaucratic	caring	centralised	conservative
decentralised	democratic	dynamic	hierarchical
impersonal	market-driven	professional	progressive

2 Can you add any others?

3 Which of the words describe your own organisation or an organisation you know well?

 *Vocabulary file page 172*

Reading
A successful organisation

A Read paragraph 1 of the article and answer these questions.
1 Where is SOL located?
2 What is unusual about the company?
3 What does SOL do?

B Read the article and match the headings below to paragraphs 2, 3, 4, 5 and 6.
A People set their own targets
B Hard work has to be fun
C Loose organisations need tight systems
D Great service requires cutting-edge technology
E There are no low-skill jobs

Dirty Business, Bright Ideas

By Gina Imperato

1 A headquarters with a difference

Walk into SOL City, headquarters of one of northern Europe's most admired companies, and it feels like you've entered a business playground. Located in a renovated film studio in the heart of Helsinki, the office explodes with
5 colour, creativity and chaos. The walls are bright red, white and yellow; the employees wander the halls talking on yellow portable phones. Liisa Joronen developed SOL Cleaning Service 11 years ago, out of a 150-year-old industrial empire owned by her family. SOL's competitive
10 formula has five key ingredients.

2 ....

Few people dream about becoming a cleaner. But that doesn't mean cleaners can't find satisfaction in their work. The keys to satisfaction, Joronen believes, are fun and individual freedom. Its cleaners wear red-and yellow
15 jumpsuits that reinforce the company's upbeat image. SOL's logo, a yellow happy face, is on everything from her blazer to the company's budget reports. Freedom means abolishing all the rules and regulations of conventional corporate life. There are no titles or secretaries at SOL, no
20 individual offices or set hours of work. The company has eliminated all perks and status symbols.

3 ....

SOL's training programme consists of seven modules, each of which lasts four months and ends with a rigorous exam. Of course, there are a limited number of
25 ways to polish a table or shampoo a carpet. That's why SOL employees also study time management, budgeting and people skills.

4 ....

Lots of companies talk about decentralising responsibility and authority. At SOL it''s a way of life.
30 The real power players of the company are its 135 supervisors, each of whom leads a team of up to 50 cleaners. These supervisors work with their teams to create their own budgets, do their own hiring and negotiate their own deals with customers.

5 ....

35 Liisa Joronen believes in autonomy, but she's also keen on accountability. SOL is fanatical about measuring performance. It does so frequently and visibly, and focuses on customer satisfaction. Every time SOL lands a contract, for example, the salesperson works at the new
40 customer's site alongside the team that will do the cleaning in the future. Together they establish performance benchmarks. Then, every month, the customer rates the team's performance based on those benchmarks. 'The more we free our people from rules,'
45 Joronen says, 'the more we need good measurements.'

6 ....

Laptops and cell-phones are standard equipment for all supervisors at SOL, freeing them to work where they want, how they want. Inside the offices there's almost no room for paper. So the company stores all critical budget
50 documents and performance reports on its Intranet, along with training schedules, upcoming events and company news.

From *Fast Company*

C **Which of these statements are true? Correct the false ones.**

1 Everyone has their own office.

2 Liisa Joronen believes cleaners can feel good about their job.

3 At the end of the training course there is an exam.

4 The training course takes 28 months to complete.

5 At SOL giving responsibility to employees is important.

6 SOL thinks measuring performance restricts freedom.

7 Every month Liisa Joronen measures each team's performance.

8 All the information is stored in filing cabinets.

D **Match these phrases from paragraph 5 of the article to their meanings.**

1 keen on accountability

2 fanatical about measuring performance

3 establish performance benchmarks

4 rates the team's performance

   a) assesses how the group have done

   b) extremely interested in judging achievements

   c) interested in people being responsible for what they do

   d) set up standards of achievements

E **Discuss these questions.**

1 Would you like to work in a company like SOL? Explain why or why not.

2 Would Liisa Joronen's ideas work in your own company or organisation?

Language review

Noun combinations

We can combine two or more nouns in several ways.

1 *'s* possessive
   Julia's desk

2 one noun used as an adjective
   head office

3 phrases with *of*
   Director of Communications

4 compound nouns forming one word
   boardroom

Match these examples from the article on page 24 with the categories above.

a) *customer satisfaction*

b) *way of life*

c) *SOL's logo*

d) *salesperson*

→ page 151

A **Find noun combinations in the article on page 24. Write them under these four headings:**

's possessive	one noun used as an adjective	phrases with *of*	compound nouns forming one word

B **Underline the most suitable noun combination in each group.**

1 **a)** the meeting of today
   b) today's meeting
   c) today meeting

2 **a)** a letter of credit
   b) a credit's letter
   c) a letter's credit

3 **a)** a business card
   b) a card of business
   c) a businesses' card

4 **a)** a data's base
   b) a base of data
   c) a database

C Nouns used as numerical adjectives are singular. For example, *a plan which lasts for 10 years = a ten-year plan*. Change the following phrases in the same way.

1 a hotel with five stars
2 a budget worth 3 million dollars
3 a presentation that lasts 20 minutes
4 a contract worth 200,000 pounds
5 an industrial empire which is 150 years old

D Match each noun in column 1 to two of the nouns in column 2 to make word partnerships.

1 business	a) virus	b) cards	c) plan
2 management	a) style	b) technology	c) policy
3 sales	a) campaign	b) department	c) trade
4 labour	a) force	b) technology	c) market
5 company	a) house	b) headquarters	c) logo
6 trade	a) union	b) technology	c) fair
7 consumer	a) goods	b) logos	c) awareness
8 research	a) project	b) findings	c) knowledge
9 information	a) technology	b) force	c) desk
10 computer	a) union	b) program	c) virus

E Make sentences with the noun combinations in Exercise D. For example:
*It is common practice to exchange **business cards** when meeting new clients.*

Listening

Advising companies

▲ Richard Brown

A 🎧 3.2 Richard Brown is the managing partner of Cognosis, a management consultancy in London which advises companies on organisation and change. Listen to the first part of the interview and answer these questions.

1 What four approaches does Cognosis use to analyse a business?
2 How many different business 'character types' does Cognosis recognise?
3 What three things do companies deal with differently, according to Richard?

B 🎧 3.3 Listen to the second part of the interview. Tick the sentences below which are true, according to Richard, and correct those which are false.

1 The hardest way to change the character of a business is to merge it with another company.
2 When Guinness and Grand Metropolitan merged, they wanted to create a business culture which was different from the two companies.
3 The senior managers spent a lot of money training staff in the new business methods.
4 The new culture was only partly successful.

C 🎧 3.4 In the third part of the interview, Richard Brown describes three ways in which successful companies are similar. Complete the description below.

First, they're ………. ……….. [1] : they have a very clear sense of ………. ………. ………. ………. [2]. Second, they're ………. - ………. [3] : they invest much time and energy in understanding and ………. ………. ………. ………. [4]. And third, they are ………. - ………. [5]. By that I mean that people inside the organisation are very clear about the values that should ………. ………. ………. [6] and behaviours.

Skills

Socialising: introductions and networking

A 🎧 **3.5, 3.6, 3.7 Listen to the three conversations. Choose the correct description from the list for each one.**

Greeting someone and talking about the past

Introducing another person

Introducing yourself and giving information about your company

B 🎧 **3.5 Listen to the first conversation again and answer these questions.**

1 Which of these expressions do you hear in the dialogue?
   a) Nice to see you again.   **d)** How about you?
   b) Fine, thanks.   **e)** I changed my job last year.
   c) Wonderful!   **f)** I'm in banking now.

2 Who is head of data processing?

3 Who now works in marketing?

C 🎧 **3.6 Listen to the second conversation again and complete the chart below.**

Name	Company	Activity
Don Larsen Erika Koenig		

D 🎧 **3.6 Listen again and complete this extract from the second conversation.**

Don   Well, we're basically an .... [1] business. We supply large companies with various services including payroll, ... [2] and human resources.

Erika   Is Atsource Solutions a new company?

Don   No, we're well established. The company was .... [3] in 1978. It's organised into three .... [4]. We have over 6,000 .... [5]; we've got our .... [6] in Frankfurt and .... [7] in over 20 countries – we're pretty big.

E 🎧 **3.7 Listen to the third conversation again and answer these questions.**

1 What expression does John use to introduce Miriam?

2 Why could Miriam be helpful to Heinz in his work?

3 What interest do they share?

 *Vocabulary file page 172*

Useful language

Greetings
Hello ... . Nice to see you again.
Hi ... . How are you?
How's everything going?

Introducing yourself
I'm from ... / I'm with ... / I work for ...
I'm in sales / finance / marketing.
I'm in charge of ...
I'm responsible for ...

Introducing someone else
I'd like you to meet Miriam.
Can I introduce you to Miriam?
Robert, have you met Vladimir?

Talking about your company
The company was founded in ...
We make / manufacture / sell / distribute ...
We have subsidiaries / factories / branches in ...
We have a workforce of 2,000.
Our main competitors are ...

Responding
Fine, thanks.
Not too bad, thanks.
Nice / Pleased to meet you.
It's a pleasure.

Talking about common interests
You and Heinz have something in common.
You both like / enjoy / are interested in ...

Networking
We're very interested in ...
Do you know anyone who could help us?
Could you let me have their contact details?
Could I call him and mention your name?
Let me give you my business card.

CASE STUDY

Auric Bank

Background

'We constantly review our business in order to provide customers with excellent service at competitive prices. As part of our major reorganisation, we've been looking at the cost of customer services. We have a range of options. We can make changes in-house, outsource call centres to areas within the UK or outsource off-shore to low-cost countries such as India.'

Graham Hammond, Chief Executive, Auric Bank.

The Chief Executive made the statement above to a group of investors three weeks ago. Auric Bank (AB) lost £1.5 billion last year because it invested in unprofitable areas of business. Since then AB has carried out a major review of its operations. It has concluded that:

1 customers believe AB is charging too much for its services;

2 AB no longer has the image of a 'caring' bank which is close to its customers and understands their needs;

3 the bank needs to reduce costs to boost its profits and share price.

To cut costs and increase efficiency, AB is now considering a number of options concerning the location of its call centres.

The call centres

AB has approximately 2,500 employees working in three large call centres located in cities in the South of England. The company's headquarters are in London. There are four options that the directors of the bank are considering.

Option 1: Keep the call centres in-house

Keep the call centres in their present locations but try to reduce costs by:

- using more part-time employees
- reducing the hours of business of the centres
- increasing the targets for the number of calls handled per hour

Estimated cost of running the centres for the next five years: £16 million. Estimated savings by introducing changes above: £3 million.

Option 2: Outsource the call centres to a company based in South Africa

Use Resource Plc, a Cape Town firm. They can set up the call centres in Cape Town and run them.

- the firm has an excellent reputation for reliability and good service
- it has a lot of experience in running centres

Cost of the contract with Resource Plc to run the call centres for the next five years: £8 million.

Option 3: Outsource the call centres to a company based in Scotland

Use Orion Plc, a Scottish firm

- the firm is new; its managers are young
- it has several contracts with big companies
- it is experienced in running call centres
- some customers have complained in newspapers that the lines are always busy

Cost of the contract with Orion Plc to run the call centres for the next five years: £10 million.

Option 4: Outsource the call centres to a company based in India

Use X-source India, a company based in Bangalore.

- X-source India is expanding fast
- it has contracts with several large US companies
- it has no problems hiring staff and its costs are low

Cost of the contract with X-source India to run the call centres for the next five years: £5.5 million.

Task

Work in groups of four. You are directors of AB.

1 Choose a role card (pages from 140, 141, 147, 149). Read your role card and prepare for a meeting to consider the four options.
2 Discuss the advantages and disadvantages of each option.
3 Try to persuade the other directors that your option is the right one for AB.

Writing

Write a short report to the Chief Executive giving both a summary of the four options and your recommendations.

 Writing file page 136

UNIT 4 Change

OVERVIEW ▼

Reading
Change in retailing

Vocabulary
Describing change

Listening
Managing change

Language review
Past simple and present perfect

Skills
Taking part in meetings 2

Case study
Acquiring Metrot

It's not the strongest species that survive, nor the most intelligent, but the most responsive to change.

Charles Darwin (1809–1882), British scientist

Starting up

A **Which of these situations would you find the most difficult to deal with?**

1 Losing a lot of money
2 Moving house
3 Moving to another country
4 Losing your job
5 A new boss
6 New neighbours
7 Driving abroad
8 Getting married

B **What has been the most significant change in your life?**

C **Which of these business situations would worry you most? Why?**

1 You read in the paper that your company will probably be merging with another company.
2 You keep your job after a merger, but you are in a less powerful position.
3 Your company has to relocate to the other side of the city.
4 You are asked to relocate to a dangerous foreign country.
5 You are promoted but are now in charge of a hostile workforce.
6 You have to move from an open plan office to sharing your boss's office.
7 You have to work with a completely new computer system.
8 You have to decide who to make redundant in your new department after a merger.

Reading
Change in retailing

A Discuss these questions. Which department stores have you visited in your own country or abroad?

1 What were your impressions?

2 What in your view should a 21st century department store look like?

3 What should it offer its customers?

B Now read the article. What are the names of the two US department stores mentioned in the article?

US department stores launch counter-attack

By Lauren Foster

As consumers demand better value and a more interesting and stimulating experience while shopping, department stores face a clear choice: adapt or die.

'My concern is that they will become retail museums,' says Britt Breemer, chairman of America's Research Group. 'The bottom line is that they have to admit they are in trouble and figure out some way to reinvent themselves.'

This may help to explain why four times as many households visit discount stores as department stores.

Department stores face mounting competition from speciality retailers and discounters, such as Wal-Mart and Target. Their steady loss of market share may be partly because the concept was born in a different era, a time when, for families, a trip to the stores combined shopping with entertainment.

What is needed, say retail experts, is a new approach. A typical example of this approach working is seen at Selfridges. This UK group has recast itself from a 'sleepy 1970s-style department store' into a retailing experience fit for the 21st

▲ Selfridges, Oxford Street, London

▲ Selfridges, Birmingham

century, says Wendy Liebmann, President of WSL Strategic Retail.

One of the main changes is that more floor space is rented to vendors, in what is sometimes referred to as the showcase business model: vendors design their own booths and are encouraged to be creative.

The Selfridges model, says Peter Williams, CEO of Selfridges, is about creating an experience that is 'new, interesting and different' where it is not just the product that is different. He says the problem with US department stores is that they all look the same.

Arnold Aronson, a management consultant, believes Selfridges could be a prototype for failing US department stores: 'It has brought back excitement and novelty and is really seducing customers by developing the right merchandise, in the right quantities at the right time.'

Federated, which owns Macy's and Bloomingdale's, appears to be moving in the right direction. Forty-two stores are being upgraded with the latest components of its 'reinvent' strategy, including enhanced fitting rooms, convenient price-check devices, comfortable lounge

areas, computer kiosks and shopping carts.

The challenge department stores face is how to develop in a sector that is, essentially, not growing. But if they adapt, many industry observers believe they will survive. 'The department store is not dead, it will live on,' said Robert Tamilia, Professor of Marketing at the University of Quebec. 'But it will not be the same animal it was before.'

From *The Financial Times*

FINANCIAL TIMES
World business newspaper.

C Match these people to their views.

1 Britt Breemer
2 Wendy Liebmann
3 Peter Williams
4 Arnold Aronson
5 Robert Tamilia

a) This is not the end of department stores but in the future they will be different.

b) American department stores are not different enough from each other.

c) Selfridges has changed into an up-to-date store.

d) Department stores need to recognise their problems and have to change.

e) Selfridge's new approach works.

D What changes have taken place at:

a) Selfridges?　　**b)** Macy's?　　**c)** Bloomingdale's?

E Which of these groups of people are mentioned in the article?

1 agents	**5** discounters	**9** vendors
2 clients	**6** manufacturers	**10** wholesalers
3 consumers	**7** retailers	
4 customers	**8** shoppers	

F Which of the groups of people in Exercise E:

1 are buyers? ....

2 are sellers? ....

3 are intermediaries? ....

4 offer goods at reduced prices? ....

5 sell directly to the public? ....

G What are the differences between the types of retail outlet in the box? Consider the following factors: size, prices, product range, length and frequency of shopping visits, customer service level.

> supermarket　department store　kiosk　convenience store　discount store

Listening
Managing change

▲ Maggie Miller

A 🎧 4.1 Maggie Miller is the Business Transformation Director of Sainsbury's, one of the largest supermarket groups in the UK. She is talking about the programme of change at Sainsbury's. Listen to the first part of the interview. Match these phrases to their meaning.

1 'supply chain' means:

　a) warehousing and delivery systems　　**b)** customers and clients

　c) supermarket stores and retail outlets

2 'a third party' here means:

　a) in-house staff　**b)** an external company　**c)** another company in the group

3 'people see the barriers eliminated' means:

　a) that it is easier for people to do things than it was before

　b) that it is harder for people to do things than it was before

　c) that there is no difference in the way people do things

B 🎧 4.1 Now listen to the first part again and answer these questions.

1 Why did the new Chief Executive want to change things at Sainsbury's?

2 In which three areas was new investment necessary?

3 What changes have there been in people's attitudes?

4 What evidence of benefits has there been so far?

C 🎧 4.2 Listen to the second part of the interview. What do the following numbers refer to?

a) 14,000　**b)** 50　**c)** 22　**d)** 100,000

D Which three areas does Maggie say are important to focus on when planning change?

Vocabulary
Describing change

A Write the verbs from the box under the correct prefix to make words connected with change. Use a good dictionary to help you. Some of the words can be used with more than one prefix.

centralise	organise	train	grade	regulate
size	develop	launch	locate	structure

down-	de-	up-	re-
	centralise		

B Complete these sentences with the correct form of the verbs from the box in Exercise A. Use a good dictionary to help you.

1 It is now so expensive to rent offices in the city centre that many companies are ...*relocating*.... to the suburbs.

2 The company has recently had to down...................... its workforce. Reducing the number of employees is the best way to stay profitable in the current economic climate.

3 Excellent customer service is vital to keep up with the competition. The company has introduced new working practices and is re...................... all part-time staff.

4 The seating plan in our office has been re...................... to accommodate new staff.

5 Our product hasn't been selling well recently. The marketing team has decided to re...................... the product with a more up-to-date image.

6 The company has noticed that too many decisions are made at Head Office. It is de...................... the decision-making process so that branch managers are more involved at an earlier stage.

7 The company has finalised the plans to re...................... the disused car park site. It is going to become a modern three-storey office block.

8 The most successful change in our company was the decision to re...................... the company hierarchy. Now there is more opportunity for promotion.

C Underline the nouns in Exercise B that make partnerships with the verbs.

D Work in pairs. Describe the changes that have happened in a workplace you know well.

 *Vocabulary file* page 172

Language review

Past simple and present perfect

We use the past simple for actions at a particular point in the past.
*Last year only 18% of US consumers **visited** a leading department store.*

We use the present perfect for actions linking the present to a point in the past.
*We **have made** a lot of changes since 2003.*

 page 151

A Which of the following expressions are used with the past simple and which are used with the present perfect? Which are used with both?

in 2003	since 2003	yet
this week	yesterday	ever
recently	last year	six months ago

B Complete this report about the history of Joie de Vivre. Use the past simple or the present perfect forms of the verbs in brackets.

I ..*received*.. [1] (receive) the year's results yesterday and I am delighted to announce that our company .... [2] (have) another fantastic year. We .... [3] (start) in 1970 in a small factory in Shatin, Hong Kong, and we only .... [4] (employ) four people. That number .... [5] (grow) to around 2,000 today.

In the early years we .... [6] (face) strong competition from our competitors and in 1982 we nearly .... [7] (go) bankrupt. But from that difficult period until now, we .... [8] (hold) out and we .... [9] (not make) the mistake of becoming typecast as a label for the changeable junior market.

Things .... [10] (improve) considerably since we .... [11] (move) from Shatin to China. In 2000 we .... [12] (buy) the international operations of our partner company Joie de Vivre Holdings and we now do business in more than 30 countries.

In recent years we .... [13] (expand) our product range and we have carved out a sizeable niche in the same market as Benetton and Zara.

Last year we .... [14] (have) our fifth consecutive year of growth with $98 million in net profit and in January of this year we .... [15] (deliver) the first retail stock to be included in Hong Kong's Hang Seng index.

A lot of change .... [16] (take) place recently. This is because last year most of our sales .... [17] (come) from the Asian market. So, in January this year, we .... [18] (decide) to try and break into the US market. Just recently, we .... [19] (enter) into negotiations with Macy's department stores.

In conclusion, our company so far this year .... [20] (prosper) and that is down to all your hard work. Congratulations to you all.

C Talk about recent changes that have happened in your life.

Skills
Taking part in meetings 2

A 🎧 **4.3 Four executives are discussing changes to company working practices. Listen to the meeting and answer these questions.**

1 Why does Nancy think the open-plan office is a good idea?
2 Why are two of the people against introducing an open-plan office?
3 What proposal does Carl make to deal with the problem mentioned?
4 Why is Max against hot-desking?
5 What change in working practices does Nancy want?

B 🎧 **4.3 Listen again and tick the expressions in the Useful language box that you hear.**

Useful language

Interrupting
Could I just say something?
Excuse me, but could I just say …

Asking for clarification
How do you mean, …?
What exactly are you saying?
What exactly do you mean?
Are you saying we need to … ?
Sorry, I don't follow you.
Can you explain in more detail?

Clarifying
What I mean is …
What I'm saying is …
No, I was thinking of …
To be more specific …
To clarify …

Dealing with interruptions
Hold on. Can I finish the point?
Let Stefan finish, please.
I'd like to finish if I may.
Just a moment …

Making proposals
I suggest …
I propose that …
How about …
We could…

Rejecting proposals
Sorry, I don't think it's / that's a good idea.
I'm not sure I agree with you there.
It / That just won't work.
Well, I'm not happy about it/that.

TAX

AFTER YOU...

'There are three things you can predict in life: tax, death and more meetings.'

Mike Moore,
Sydney Morning Herald

C **Role play this situation. You are managers of a television production company, Zoom International. You are discussing these two proposals for changes to company policy.**

1 Zoom International (ZI) could reduce costs by offering staff a 10% increase in salary instead of a company car. If ZI makes the change, staff will have to provide their own car for business use, using their own money.

2 ZI could increase security at their head office. At present, a security guard checks staff who enter the building. In future, staff will have to go through a barrier where they insert an identity card. If they do not have an identity card, they cannot enter the building. In addition, they must, at all times, wear an identity card with their photograph on it. There will be two female receptionists behind the barrier.

Student A: Turn to page 146.

Student B: Turn to page 144.

Acquiring Metrot

Background

Last June, readers of the business magazine *Investor International* were given some information about the Cornerstone Group

COMPANY PROFILE

Company:	**Cornerstone Group**
Workforce:	**35,000**
Turnover:	**$4.1bn**
Located:	**Dallas, US**
Net profit:	**11% of turnover (approx.)**

Main activities

Providing services and products for the oil industry.

Recent developments

Cornerstone has recently bought the French company, Metrot. Metrot produces a wide range of household goods. Their head office is in Paris, and they have two factories in northern France.

Reasons for Cornerstone's acquisition

1. Cornerstone will expand sales of Metrot products in Europe.
2. It will use Metrot as a base for launching its own products in Europe.
3. Metrot's biggest asset is its valuable land. Cornerstone could use this to grow the company or may sell off some of the land to finance the acquisition.

Comment

Metrot is an excellent acquisition for the Cornerstone Group. However, there may be some problems when a different style of management is introduced into the French company. Metrot has always been a family-owned company and its Chief Executive, Jean Metrot, has always taken a personal interest in all his employees' welfare.

The new Chief Executive will be Hugh Whitman. He is in his early 30s and was educated at Harvard University. Whitman used to be Executive Vice President of the Cornerstone Group. Jean Metrot will remain on the board as an adviser.

Hugh Whitman   Jean Metrot

🎧 **4.4** Hugh Whitman, the new Chief Executive, gave a television interview for European Business News. He was asked about Cornerstone's plans for Metrot. Listen and note what he says.

Problems

It is now nine months later. The change of ownership and new management style at Metrot have caused many problems. The e-mail below illustrates some of the difficulties.

To...	Dan Johnson, Personnel Director
From...	Jacques Lafont, Union Organiser
Subject:	Staff morale

Date: March 18

Staff are very unhappy with the present changes. Productivity has fallen and staff turnover is high. These are some of the reasons for the staff's low morale.

1. Factory inspections
   The new managers are always checking up on us and taking notes. No one knows why they are doing this.

2. Redundancies
   Since June, about 60 employees from the R & D Department have lost their jobs. They were given no reasons. Everyone thinks this is very unprofessional.

3. Further changes
   Many members of staff are looking for new jobs. They want to move before they are made redundant. People are afraid that the new management will relocate the factories.

4. Management style
   Staff complain about the changes the new management are making. I enclose a list of comments made by staff.

   • 'They're trying to do everything too fast – a new computer system, making us learn English, selling in new European markets and bringing out new products.'

   • 'There was a family atmosphere before. The management really cared about us. Everything was more informal.'

   • 'We don't know where the company is going. We've no idea what our strategy is.'

   • 'We get e-mail messages from Head Office telling us what to do. Surely they can trust the management over here to make the policies and decisions?'

Task

A meeting of senior managers is called to resolve the problems. There are two groups at the meeting.
Group A: new managers led by Hugh Whitman.
Group B: senior executives of Metrot who have kept their jobs since the takeover.
Each group prepares separately for the meeting. Then hold the meeting as one group. The agenda is as follows:
1 Background: Why are staff resisting the changes?
2 Practical suggestions for improving the situation.
3 What can be learned from this experience to manage change more effectively in the future?

Writing

Write the action minutes for the above meeting.

➡ *Writing file page 135*

Money

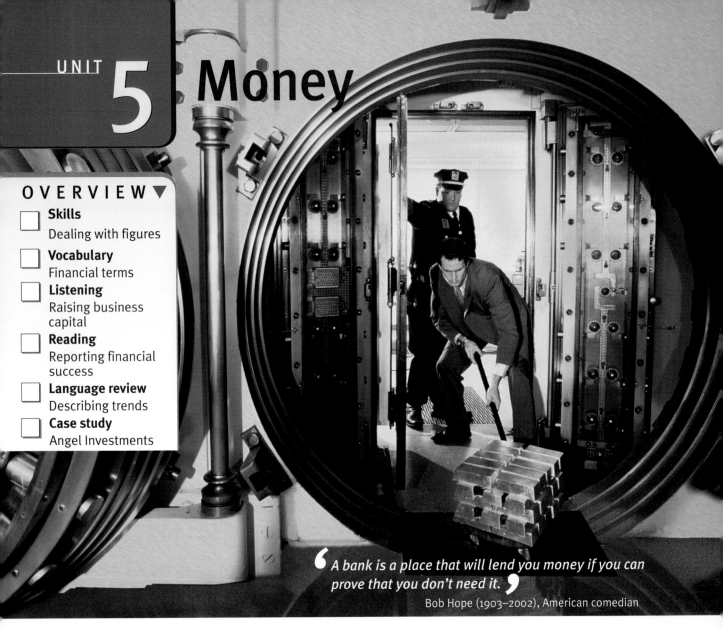

OVERVIEW ▼

☐ **Skills**
Dealing with figures

☐ **Vocabulary**
Financial terms

☐ **Listening**
Raising business capital

☐ **Reading**
Reporting financial success

☐ **Language review**
Describing trends

☐ **Case study**
Angel Investments

> ❛ *A bank is a place that will lend you money if you can prove that you don't need it.* ❜
>
> Bob Hope (1903–2002), American comedian

A Answer these questions individually. Then compare your answers with a partner.

QUIZ

1 How much cash do you have with you at the moment? Do you:
   a) know exactly?
   b) know approximately?
   c) not know at all?

2 Do you normally check:
   a) your change?
   b) your bank statements and credit card bills?
   c) restaurant bills?
   d) your receipts when shopping?
   e) prices in several shops before you buy something?

3 Do you:
   a) give money to beggars?
   b) give money to charities?
   c) give away used items, such as clothing?

4 If you go for a meal with someone you don't know well, do you:
   a) offer to pay the whole bill?
   b) suggest dividing the bill into equal parts?
   c) offer to pay the whole bill but expect them to pay next time?
   d) try to avoid paying anything?

5 What do you think about people who do not pay the correct amount of tax? Is this:
   a) a serious crime?
   b) morally wrong but not a crime?
   c) excellent business practice?

6 If you lend a colleague a small amount of money and they forget to pay it back, do you:
   a) say nothing?
   b) remind them that they owe you money?
   c) arrange to go for a drink with them and say you've forgotten your wallet or purse?

B What do your answers to the questions in Exercise A say about your attitude to money? What do they say about your culture?

Useful language

Saying numbers

Years

| 1984 | nineteen eighty-four |
| 2006 | two thousand and six |

Decimals

16.5	sixteen point five
17.38%	seventeen point three eight percent
0.185	(nought / zero) point one eight five

Currencies

£3.15	three pounds fifteen
$7.80	seven dollars eighty
€250	two hundred and fifty euros
¥125	one hundred and twenty-five yen

Bigger numbers

3,560	three thousand five hundred	**and** sixty (BrE) sixty (AmE)
598, 347	five hundred	**and** ninety-eight thousand, three hundred **and** forty-seven (BrE) ninety-eight thousand, three hundred forty-seven (AmE)
1,300,402	one million three hundred thousand, four hundred	**and** two (BrE) two (AmE)

1m	one /a million (1,000,000)
3bn	three billion (3,000,000,000)
$7.5bn	seven point five billion dollars
€478m	four hundred	**and** seventy-eight million euros (BrE) seventy-eight million euros (AmE)

A Work in pairs.
Student A: turn to page 144 and read the text aloud to Student B. Student B: listen to Student A while reading the article below. Correct any incorrect information.

BUSINESS IN BRIEF

Yahoo has strengthened its European presence with the €375m ($578m) acquisition of Kelkoo, the French-based on-line shopping service. The European
5 on-line retail market is forecast to grow to €116bn in the next three years.

The Nikkei 225 Average climbed 0.7 percent to 10,364.99 while the Topix index rose 1.2 percent to 1,145.90. Banking
10 shares benefited most, with Mizuho jumping 5.7 percent to ¥437,000, SMFG rising 4.7 percent to ¥852,000, MTFG gaining 7.9 percent to close at ¥1,019,000 and UFJ up 4.2 percent to ¥656,000.

From The Financial Times

FINANCIAL TIMES
World business newspaper.

B 🎧 5.1 Listen and check your answers.

C Write all the numbers and symbols in full, according to the way they are pronounced. For example, €3.1m: *three point one million euros.*

Vocabulary
Financial terms

(A) Match the definitions 1 to 6 with the financial terms a) to f).

1 money owed by one person or organisation to another person or organisation

2 a period of time when business activity decreases because the economy is doing badly

3 difference between the selling price of a product and the cost of producing it

4 a place where company shares are bought and sold

5 money which people or organisations put into a business to make a profit

6 equal parts into which the capital or ownership of a company is divided

a) gross margin
b) recession
c) shares
d) debt
e) stock market
f) investment

(B) Match the sentence halves.

1 Earnings per share are

2 A forecast is

3 Bankruptcy is

4 A dividend is

5 Pre-tax profits are

6 Revenues are

a) a part of the profits of a company paid to the owners of shares.

b) a company's profits divided by the number of its shares.

c) a description of what is likely to happen in the future.

d) money which businesses receive from selling goods or services.

e) when a person or organisation is unable to pay their debts.

f) the money a business makes before payment to the government.

(C) Complete this report with the terms from Exercises A and B.

In our home markets it has been another excellent year. *Pre-tax profits* [1] are up by £23 million, and the .... [2] for the next quarter is equally good. Profits from abroad are down because of a .... [3] in Japan. However, our performance overall has been good, and the .... [4] have increased to 26.4p and the .... [5] will be increased to 4.3p per share, which will please our shareholders*.

We plan to issue new .... [6] in order to finance expansion in Asia. We also plan to increase our.................... [7] in plant and equipment before entering the Chinese market. We are particularly pleased with our performance in France and Germany where.................... [8] have increased. As a result of using a new distributor, our costs fell giving us a.................... [9] of 40 percent on our main product line. We will use any extra cash to reduce the level of our .... [10].

Our performance in Italy should improve significantly following the .... [11] of our biggest competitor. However, we should not become too satisfied with our share price as economic conditions remain uncertain and the .... [12] will continue to reflect this. Share prices will not rise in the short term.

*Shareholders: the people who own shares in a business

Listening
Raising business capital

A 🎧 **5.2 Hugh Campbell is the founder of GP Capital, a London-based finance firm which raises money for entrepreneurs. Listen to the first part of the interview and complete the chart.**

Type of business	Type of investor
Business set up by new entrepreneurs	....
Business borrowing up to ...	....
Business borrowing more than ...	....

B 🎧 **5.3 Listen to the second part of the interview and answer these questions.**

1 According to Hugh, which three areas do venture capitalists look at when selecting companies to invest in?
2 What type of market is good to invest in and why?
3 What helps some businesses to win against other companies?
4 What three questions would Hugh ask the management team?

C 🎧 **5.4 Listen to the third part of the interview. What kind of company does Hugh describe? Why did he like this type of company?**

D 🎧 **5.5 Listen to the final part of the interview. Which of these statements are true? Correct the false ones.**

1 Hugh was offered the chance to buy fifty percent of an Internet business.
2 He didn't invest because he thought the management team was weak.
3 The business did very well for a couple of years.
4 It was sold for twenty times its original value.

Reading
Reporting financial success

A **Before you read the articles decide which of these statements are true.**

1 Both Wal-Mart and Target Stores are based in the UK.
2 Wal-Mart is the world's largest retailer.
3 Target is not a competitor of Wal-Mart.

B **Work in pairs. Student A read Article 1 below and Student B read Article 2 on page 42. Complete the parts of the chart on page 42 which relate to your article.**

Article 1

Wal-Mart

WAL★MART
ALWAYS LOW PRICES.
Always

By Lauren Foster

Wal-Mart yesterday really surprised investors when it sounded a strong note of optimism. This optimism is ⁵a marked turnaround from three months ago when Wal-Mart warned about the strength of the recovery in US consumer spending.
¹⁰Lee Scott, the CEO, said: 'I am more optimistic about the year we have just started than I have been in several years. I am not ¹⁵only optimistic about the economy and the continuing strength of the housing market but also encouraged about Wal-²⁰Mart's position.'
Mr Scott was also encouraged by consumer spending, which he said was driven by higher tax ²⁵refunds and 'eventually improvements in the jobs picture'.

The world's largest retailer by revenues said ³⁰fourth-quarter profits rose 11 percent to $2.7bn, or 63 cents a share, compared with $2.5bn, or 56 cents a share over a year ³⁵ago. Revenues for the quarter increased 12.2 percent to $74.5bn.
For the full year, Wal-Mart's profits jumped 13.3 ⁴⁰percent to $8.9bn or $2.03 a share, up from $7.8bn. Revenues increased 11.6 percent from $229.6bn to $256.3bn. International ⁴⁵sales were strong, contributing about $7bn to the near $27bn gain in overall sales.

Mr Scott said Wal-Mart ⁵⁰had a good year but the international division had an excellent year.
He stressed that, while gross margin was better ⁵⁵than originally forecast, the improvement was thanks to the mix of merchandise, not higher prices. 'We are not raising ⁶⁰prices and have no intention of doing so,' Mr Scott said.

From the *Financial Times*

FINANCIAL TIMES
World business newspaper.

Article 2

Target Stores

By Lauren Foster

Target yesterday beat Wall Street expectations when it delivered a 21.1 percent rise in quarterly earnings.

Gains in Target's credit card business, as well as both its Target Stores division and Marshall Field's stores, offset a small drop in pre-tax profit at the Mervyn's department store chain.

Target has cultivated a more upmarket and style-conscious image than other discount retailers. It is the third-largest general retailer in the US by revenues.

Target yesterday said it saw continued price pressure from rival Wal-Mart. For the fourth quarter, Target's profit rose to $832m, or 91 cents a share, compared with $688m, or 75 cents a share, a year ago. Analysts had expected Target to earn 87 cents a share, according to Reuters Research.

Revenues for the quarter rose 10.7 percent to $15.57bn from $14.06bn, while same-store sales – from stores open at least a year – rose 4.9 percent.

Target said pre-tax profit soared 18.5 percent at Target Stores. At the department stores, which have been ailing, pre-tax profit jumped 15.6 percent at Marshall Field's but fell 0.3 percent at Mervyn's.

Credit card operations added $168m to pre-tax profit in the recent quarter, up 11.7 percent from a year ago.

For the full year, Target's profits were $1.84bn, or $2.01 a share, up 11.4 percent from $1.65bn, or $1.81 a share, the year before. Revenues rose 9.7 percent to $48.16bn from $43.91bn, driven by new stores, a 2.9 percent rise in same-store sales and growth in credit revenues.

From the *Financial Times*

FINANCIAL TIMES
World business newspaper.

	Wal-Mart 4th quarter	Target 4th quarter	Wal-Mart Full year	Target Full year
Total profits				
% increase in profits / earnings				
Earnings per share				
Sales revenues				

C Exchange information with a partner and complete the chart.

D Read both texts and answer the questions. Which company:

1 feels confident about the future?
2 has developed a more fashionable image?
3 had particularly good results overseas in the last 12 months?
4 is not planning to increase prices?
5 did better than the American stock market forecast?
6 feels its success is due to the variety of its goods?

E Match the words to make word partnerships from the text.

1 consumer   **a)** division
2 tax   **b)** pressure
3 international   **c)** refunds
4 quarterly   **d)** spending
5 price   **e)** earnings

F Read the articles again and check your answers.
Now match the word partnerships in Exercise E to their definitions.

1 the money people spend on goods and services
2 money given back at the end of the financial year
3 company profits for a three-month period
4 part of a company which deals with or is located overseas
5 decreasing or freezing the price of goods or services in order to gain an advantage over competitors

Language review
Describing trends

We can describe trends in English in different ways. For example:

1 Verbs of change
Profits **soared** *18.5%.*
Profits are **falling.**
Sales **plummeted** *in January.*

2 Prepositions
Profits rose 11% **to** *$2.7 billion.*
Profits have gone up **from** *3 million* **to** *4 million euros.*
Our business grew **by** *10% last year.*
There's been a decrease in annual sales **of** *1 million euros.*
Last year profits stood **at** *2.5 million pounds.*

3 Different verb forms
The figures **show** *a positive trend.* (present simple)
We're **watching** *the trends carefully.* (present continuous)
Last year we **made** *a loss.* (past simple)
In recent months our profits **have risen** *dramatically.* (present perfect)
If sales **drop** *further, we'll be in serious financial difficulty.* (first conditional)

➡ page 152

A What kind of movement do the verbs below describe? Match them to the symbols 1 to 11. Then compare your answers with your partner. (Use some symbols more than once.)

decline	gain	drop	increase	rocket	plummet
double	fall	halve	level off	triple	recover
decrease	fluctuate	improve	peak	rise	jump

B Which of the above verbs also have noun forms? What are they? For example, *to increase – an increase.*

C Complete these sentences about the graphs below with appropriate prepositions.

1 Sales have increased .... €5m .... €7m.
2 Sales have increased .... €2m.
3 There has been an increase .... €2m in our sales.
4 Sales now stand .... €7 million.
5 Sales reached a peak .... €7 million in July.
6 Sales reached a low point .... €1 million in April.

D Write two more sentences about each of the graphs below.

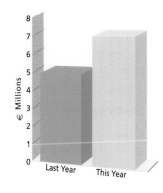

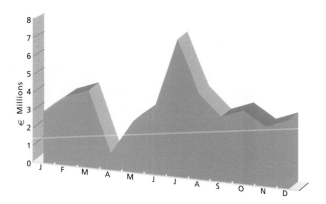

Angel Investments

Background

Angel Investments (AI) is based in Warsaw, Poland. It is run by a group of rich people who invest money in companies. It is willing to take risks by buying stakes in start-up or small companies, but also puts money into larger companies which have good prospects for growth.

AI makes money by selling shares in companies when their share price is high, then re-investing the money in companies which it expects to do well in the future.

At present, it has €10 million to spend and it has chosen four companies as potential investments.

TECHNOPRINT

Technoprint is a manufacturer of office equipment, based in Frankfurt, Germany. Its main products are inkjet and laser printers.

Present share price:	€4.14
High (last year):	€5.42
Low (last year):	€3.59

Extract from business analyst's report

Technoprint's performance has been good. They are a reliable company and are exceeding their sales targets. Increased competition in the inkjet sector will affect sales. The new laser printer could be a market leader, but outsourcing components is unpopular with the unions who are threatening industrial action.

Technoprint share price – last 18 months

	Turnover (€ millions)	Pre-tax profit (€ millions)	Earnings per share (cents)	Dividend per share (cents)
Last year	90.8	10.9	51	5.7
2 years ago	88.3	9.9	42	3.9
3 years ago	69.4	4.8	24	0.6
Turnover for first 6 months of this year: €64.5 million				

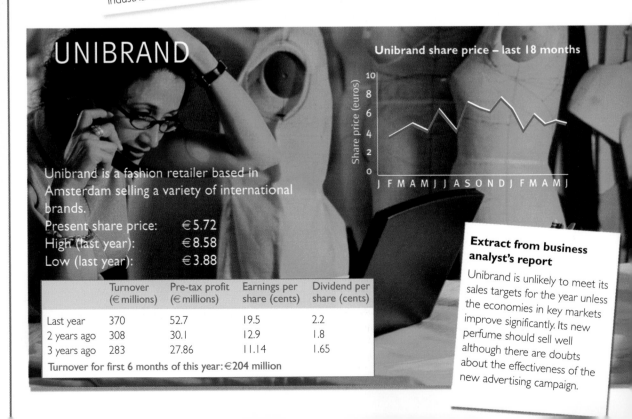

UNIBRAND

Unibrand share price – last 18 months

Unibrand is a fashion retailer based in Amsterdam selling a variety of international brands.

Present share price:	€5.72
High (last year):	€8.58
Low (last year):	€3.88

	Turnover (€ millions)	Pre-tax profit (€ millions)	Earnings per share (cents)	Dividend per share (cents)
Last year	370	52.7	19.5	2.2
2 years ago	308	30.1	12.9	1.8
3 years ago	283	27.86	11.14	1.65
Turnover for first 6 months of this year: €204 million				

Extract from business analyst's report

Unibrand is unlikely to meet its sales targets for the year unless the economies in key markets improve significantly. Its new perfume should sell well although there are doubts about the effectiveness of the new advertising campaign.

On-line Fashions

Extract from business analyst's report

On the surface this seems to be an impressive performance, but there are major problems. OLF are finding it difficult to meet the demand for their goods. Customers complain of late or incorrect deliveries. The new warehouse in Spain is not efficient. Are they expanding too fast or do they lack management skills?

OLF is based on its website www.OLF.com. Its target audience is fashion-conscious women aged between 30 and 45 who want to keep up with the latest trends in clothing and accessories.

Present share price:	€5.73
High (last year):	€8.96
Low (last year):	€2.71

On-line Fashions share price – last 18 months

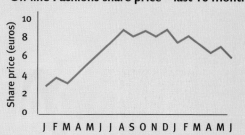

	Turnover (€ millions)	Pre-tax profit (€ millions)	Earnings per share (cents)	Dividend per share (cents)
Last year	19.3	2.1	0.38	nil
2 years ago	9.1	−2.561	3.8	nil
3 years ago	4.9	−2.862	−5.6	nil
Turnover for first 6 months of this year: €14.8 million				

AMAZON VENTURES (AV)

Based in Milan, Italy, AV was founded two years ago. It is searching for diamonds in two areas (each about 2,000 hectares), near the Amazon river.

Present share price:	€7.84
High (last year):	€9.20
Low (last year):	€1.80

Amazon Ventures share price – last 18 months

Extract from business analyst's report

An interesting company but unfortunately it has heavy debts. Early this year, AV found six large reserves of diamonds. This lead to increased sales but also a bill for €750,000 for increased security. Costs will rise sharply in the next quarter because heavy rains are predicted and the plant must be moved to higher ground. Environmental groups and their protests are a major problem. Unfavourable news stories have appeared attacking foreign companies working in the area.

	Turnover (€ millions)	Pre-tax profit (€ millions)	Earnings per share (cents)	Dividend per share (cents)
Last year	1,027	87	0.38	nil
2 years ago	378	-1,340	3.8	nil
Turnover for first 6 months of this year: €57 million				

Task

1 Work in small groups. You are directors of Angel Investments. Read the reports and note down the key points concerning each company.

2 🎧 5.6 Listen to the CEOs' comments to investors for the four companies. Note down the key points concerning each company.

3 Discuss the advantages and disadvantages of investing in each company. Then decide what proportion of the €10 million you will invest in each company. (You may decide not to invest in one or more of the companies – it is up to you.)

4 Compare your decisions with those of the other groups.

Writing

Write an e-mail to the CEO providing a list of your recommendations. Give reasons for your recommendations.

 Writing file page 133

Advertising

> *Half the money I spend on advertising is wasted. The trouble is I don't know which half.*
>
> William Hesketh Lever (1851–1925), English industrialist

OVERVIEW ▼

☐ **Discussion**
Good and bad advertisements

☐ **Vocabulary**
Advertising media and methods

☐ **Reading**
Successful advertising

☐ **Listening**
Planning advertising campaigns

☐ **Language review**
Articles

☐ **Skills**
Starting presentations

☐ **Case study**
Focus Advertising

Starting up

Discuss the advertisements above.

1 Which do you like best? Why?

2 What kind of advertisement do you like?

Discussion
Good and bad advertisements

A What makes a good advertisement? Use some of the words below.

clever	interesting	funny	inspiring	eye-catching
powerful	humorous	shocking	informative	sexy

B Do you think that the advertising practices described below are acceptable? Are any other types of advertisement offensive?

1 Using children in advertisements
2 Using nudity in advertisements
3 Promoting alcohol on TV
4 Comparing your products to your competitors' products
5 An image flashed onto a screen very quickly so that people are influenced without noticing it (subliminal advertising)
6 Exploiting people's fears and worries

C Which of the following statements do you agree with?

1 People remember advertisements not products.
2 Advertising raises prices.
3 Advertising has a bad influence on children.

Vocabulary
Advertising media and methods

A Newspapers and TV are advertising media. Can you think of others?

B Look at the words in the box below. Label each item 1 for advertising media, 2 for methods of advertising or 3 for verbs to do with advertising.

directories *1*	persuade	publicise	sponsorship
run	mailshots	promote	cinema
commercials	public transport	place	free samples
exhibition	billboards/ hoardings	launch	leaflets
point-of-sale	posters	word of mouth	radio
target	endorsement	research	sponsor
press	Internet	slogans	television

C Choose the most suitable word from the words in brackets to complete these sentences.

1 Viacom Outdoor is an advertising company that specialises in placing adverts on (*billboards / public transport / television*) such as buses.
2 Some perfume companies provide (*leaflets / commercials / free samples*) so that customers can try the perfume on their skin before they buy.
3 Advertising companies spend a lot of money on creating clever (*slogans / directories / mailshots*) that are short and memorable such as the message for the credit card, Access: 'Your flexible friend'.
4 Celebrity (*exhibition / research / endorsement*) is a technique that is very popular in advertising at the moment.
5 If news about a product comes to you by (*word of mouth / press / Internet*), someone tells you about it rather than you seeing an advert.
6 If you have something to sell, you can (*target / place / launch*) an advert in the local newspaper.

Give examples of:

1 outdoor advertising on the buses or trains in your country.
2 clever slogans that you remember from advertising campaigns.

Reading
Successful advertising

A Discuss with your partner.

1 Which celebrities from your country are used in advertising?

2 Which products or types of products do they advertise?

3 Do you think this kind of advertising is effective?

B Read the article. Match the celebrities mentioned to their sport.

What makes Nike's advertising tick?

By Stefano Hatfield

Phil Knight, the co-founder and former Chief Executive of Nike, prefers to let his superstar athletes and advertisements do his talking for him. Named Advertiser of the Year at the 50th Cannes International Advertising Festival, he is the first person to win the award twice.

Knight has an absolutely clear and committed strategy to use celebrity athlete endorsement. He describes it as one part of the 'three-legged stool' which lies behind Nike's phenomenal growth since the early 1980s, with the other two being product design and advertising.

He has built Nike's expansion into sport after sport from its athletics roots on the back of sporting masters: Carl Lewis on the track; tennis's Jimmy Connors and John McEnroe; Tiger Woods, who led Nike into golf; Ronaldo and the Brazilian national football team; and the basketball star, Michael Jordan, who famously rescued the company.

From the beginning Nike has been prepared to take a gamble on sporting bad boys others would not touch: Andre Agassi springs to mind. It was a strategy that began with Ilie Nastase, the original tennis bad boy. The Romanian had the quality that has come to represent Nike and its advertising: attitude.

After extraordinary growth, Nike became number one trainer manufacturer in the US. But Knight admits the company then lost its way as it failed to cope with its success. It experimented unsuccessfully with expansion into non-athletic shoes, and lost its number one position to Reebok in 1986.

Knight bet the future of the company on a new feature: a new air technology inside the trainer. He launched the product with a David Fincher-directed ad which used the Beatles track Revolution, and then marketed the Air Jordan brand on the back of Michael Jordan. Sales took off and the rest is history.

This brings us to the subject of globalisation and the question of how American the brand can be. Nike uses a mix of global ad campaigns such as 'good v evil' and local advertising such as its famous poster campaigns in the UK.

During a 21-year partnership with the agency Wieden and Kennedy, Nike has created some of the world's most attention-grabbing advertising: for example the Nike 'good v evil' campaign and two advertisements both for World Cups and the ad 'tag', last year's Cannes grand prix winner. Other famous ads star Pete Sampras and Andre Agassi playing in the streets of Manhattan; Tiger Woods playing 'keepy-uppy' with a golf ball; and Brazil's team playing soccer at the airport terminal.

It is a remarkable body of work, both in its variety, daring and consistent originality. At Nike there is a streamlined decision-making process that gives marketing directors real power. They do not rely on market research pre-testing which often reduces the impact of more experimental commercials. There is also the long relationship with one of the world's best ad agencies, and what Wieden describes as 'an honesty about sport'. Things only happen in Nike ads that sportsmen and women can really do.

'My number one advertising principle – if I have one – is to wake up the consumer,' concludes Knight, with an absolute conviction that is unique among modern-day chief executives. 'We have a high-risk strategy on advertising. When it works, it is more interesting. There really is no formula.'

From The Guardian

C Now answer these questions.

1 According to Phil Knight, what are the three factors which have led to the huge success of Nike?

2 Why did Nike lose market share in the mid 1980s?

3 Which innovation saved the company?

4 Which celebrity saved the company?

5 What is Phil Knight's key idea about advertising?

D Which of these statements are true? Correct the false ones.

a) Nike has been Advertiser of the Year three times.

b) Nike uses only worldwide advertising.

c) Nike believes market research pre-testing is very important.

d) A lot of computer tricks are used in Nike ads.

E What are the advantages and disadvantages for a company of using celebrity endorsement in its advertising?

F The article mentions an attention-grabbing advertisement. This type of phrase is common in advertising. Match the words 1 to 6 to the words a) to f) to make word partnerships.

1 energy   a) teasing
2 eye   b) saving
3 thirst   c) watering
4 money   d) catching
5 mouth   e) quenching
6 brain   f) saving

G Which of the word partnerships in Exercise F would you use to describe these products?

1 a soft drink   4 a low-power light bulb
2 a fruit bar   5 a range of smart clothing
3 a computer quiz game   6 a range of supermarket own-brand products

Listening
Planning advertising campaigns

A 🎧 6.1 Jeremy Thorpe Woods, Head of Planning at Saatchi and Saatchi, a leading advertising agency based in London, talks about advertising campaigns. Listen to the first part of the interview and answer these questions.

1 What does Jeremy say is the most important thing about advertising nowadays?

2 What are the key elements of a good advertising campaign, according to Jeremy?

B 🎧 6.2 Listen to the second part of the interview and complete the flow chart.

Planning and launch stages of an advertising campaign
Stage 1 **Discussion with** .... [1]   Talk about their .... [2] and .... [3]   Develop a .... [4]
Stage 2 .... [5] **stage**   Observe the target audience, get to know them through .... [6]
Stage 3 **Develop a** .... [7]   Talk to your creative partners about .... [8]   Discuss the communication idea with your .... [9]   Go back to your .... [10]
Stage 4 **Make the** .... [11]   Use .... [12] to track how it is working.

Language review
Articles

a/an	We use *a* or *an* before singular countable nouns. *He works for **an** advertising agency.* We use *a* or *an* to introduce new information. *I saw **a** humorous advert on the way to work this morning.* We often use *a* or *an* to refer to people's jobs. *She's **an** architect.*
a	We use *a* before consonants. ***a** commercial*
an	We use *an* before vowel sounds. ***an** advert*
the	We use *the* when we think our listener will know what we are talking about. ***The** International Advertising Festival will be held at Cannes as usual.* We use *the* when it is clear from the context what particular person, thing or place is meant because it has been mentioned before. *Let's change **the** campaign.*

'zero article' We do not use an article before:
- mass nouns used in general statements. *Information is power.*
- the names of many places and people. *Japan, Phil Knight*

 page 152

A Put *a* or *an* before the words in the box.

advert	commercial	strategy	USP (Unique Selling Point)	university
VIP	hour	European	account	MBA	employee	endorsement

B Tick the correct sentences. Add *the* where necessary in the other sentences. You may need to add *the* more than once.

1 Knowledge of advertising code of practice is vital to those wishing to work in advertising industry.
2 We want to film a TV commercial in Kingdom of Saudi Arabia.
3 Wales, Scotland, England and Northern Ireland make up UK.
4 The 'Think small' Volkswagen Beetle advert was one of most successful advertising campaigns of the twentieth century.
5 We are going to Czech Republic this summer.
6 Four major brands, AOL, Yahoo!, Freeserve and BT, all achieve awareness of over 40% amongst the UK adult population.
7 This year the sales conference is in Netherlands.
8 Next year I am going to work for an advertising agency in US.

C The text below is about the filming of a television advertisement using a famous Brazilian football star. There are no articles in the text. Write in the articles *a*, *an* or *the* where appropriate. Give a reason for your choice.

Ronaldinho smashed window in centuries-old cathedral of Santiago de Compostela while filming advert for television today. Luckily for Barcelona star, window was only small, modern addition to Spain's famous cathedral in Galicia. Brazilian blundered after being asked to try scissor-kick beneath cathedral's 12th century Portico de la Gloria (Portal of Glory). 'I asked Ronaldinho to hit ball as hard as he could and he had bad luck to hit window,' said advert's director Emil Samper. 'It was my fault.'

From the *Evening Standard*

Skills
Starting presentations

A Decide whether each expression in the Useful language box is *formal* or *informal*. Write F (formal) or I (*informal*). Underline the key words which helped you to decide. Then compare your answers.

Useful language

Introducing yourself
- On behalf of myself and *Focus Advertising*, I'd like to welcome you. My name's Sven Larsen.
- Hi everyone, I'm Dominique Lagrange. Good to see you all.

Introducing the topic
- I'm going to tell you about the ideas we've come up with for the ad campaign.
- This morning, I'd like to outline the campaign concept we've developed for you.

Giving a plan of your talk
- I've divided my presentation into three parts. Firstly, I'll give you the background to the campaign.

Secondly, I'll discuss the media we plan to use. Finally, I'll talk you through the storyboard for the TV commercial.
- My talk is in three parts. I'll start with the background to the campaign, move on to the media we plan to use, and finish with the storyboard for the commercial.

Inviting questions
- If there's anything you're not clear about, go ahead and ask any questions you want.
- If you have any questions, please don't hesitate to interrupt me.

B 🎧 6.3 Listen to these two presentations and check your answers to Exercise A.

C 🎧 6.4 Presenters can use different techniques to get their audience's attention at the start of a presentation. Listen to the start of five presentations and match them to the techniques below.

a) tell a personal story **d)** ask a question
b) offer an amazing fact **e)** state a problem
c) use a quotation

D Choose one of the presentation situations below. Prepare five different openings using the techniques in Exercise C. Practise the openings with a partner.

1 Your company is developing a small car aimed at city workers.
   Audience: a group of distributors.

2 Your bank wishes to encourage young people to save money.
   Audience: a group of students.

3 Your firm has produced a type of torch which has unique features.
   Audience: a group of buyers at a trade fair.

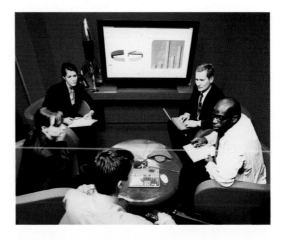

CASE STUDY

Focus Advertising

Background

Focus, a large advertising agency based in Paris, has a reputation for creating imaginative and effective campaigns.

At present, Focus is competing for several contracts. It has been asked to present ideas for advertising campaigns to the managements of the companies concerned. Concepts are required for the following advertising campaigns.

A chain of eight restuarants in your country

- The restaurants are in prime locations.
- Low fat and vegetarian dishes served in a clean, simply furnished, non-smoking environment.
- Reasonably priced, but not attracting enough customers.
- Target consumer: health-conscious people of all ages.

Aim: A creative campaign to improve sales.

A perfume

- An upmarket perfume.
- Produced by a well-known fashion house.
- Will be endorsed by a famous personality.
- Target consumer: aged 25–40 who enjoy luxury and sophistication.

Aim: Launch the perfume in an English-speaking country.

A sports car

- A high-priced, hand-finished model with a classic design.
- Originally popular in the 1950s and 60s.
- Available in both coupé and soft-top versions.
- Target consumer: high-income executives with a sense of fun and style.

Aim: An international press and TV campaign.

Task

You are members of an advertising team at Focus. Prepare an advertising campaign for one of the products or services. Use the *Key questions* below to help you. Then present your campaign to the management of the company concerned. When you are not presenting your campaign, play the role of the company's management. Listen and ask questions. Use the *Assessment sheet* below to choose:

a) the best campaign concept

b) the most effective presentation.

KEY QUESTIONS (ADVERTISING TEAM)

- What is the campaign's key message?
- What special features does the product or service have?
- What are its USPs (Unique Selling Points)?
- Who is your target audience?
- What media will you use? Several, or just one or two?
  If you use:
  an advertisement — write the text and do rough art work.
  a TV commercial — use a storyboard to illustrate your idea.
  a radio spot — write the script, including sound effects and music.
  other media — indicate what pictures, text, slogans, etc. will be used.
- What special promotions will you use at the start of the campaign?

ASSESSMENT SHEET (MANAGERS)

Give a score of 1–5 for each category: 5 = outstanding, 1 = needs improvement

Campaign concept	Presentation
1 Will it get the target audience's attention?	1 Was it interesting?
2 Will it capture their imagination?	2 Was it clear?
3 Does it have a clear, effective message?	3 Was it loud and clear enough? Was it varied in pitch or monotonous?
4 Will it differentiate the product or service?	4 Was the pace too quick, too slow, or just right?
5 Will it persuade the target audience to buy the product or service?	5 Was the language fluent, accurate and appropriate?
6 Will the target audience remember the campaign?	6 Did it impress you? Was there enough eye contact?
TOTAL: 30	**TOTAL: 30**

Writing

As the leader of one of Focus's advertising teams, prepare a summary of your concept for your Managing Director. The summary will be used as a discussion document at a forthcoming board meeting.

 Writing file page 137

Cultures

Share our similarities, celebrate our differences.

M Scott Peck, American author

OVERVIEW ▼

- **Listening**
  Cultural awareness
- **Vocabulary**
  Idioms
- **Reading**
  Cultural advice
- **Language review**
  Advice, obligation and necessity
- **Skills**
  Social English
- **Case study**
  Visitors from China

Starting up

A What do you miss most about your own country or culture when you go abroad?

B Why is cultural awareness important for businesspeople? Give examples.

What is culture? Choose the four factors which you think are the most important in creating a culture. Give your reasons.

climate	language	historical events
institutions	arts	social customs and traditions
ideas and beliefs	religion	ceremonies and festivals
cuisine	geography	architecture

C Do you think cultures are becoming more alike? Is this a good thing or a bad thing? Give reasons for your answers. Think about:

- improved communications
- global business
- cheap foreign travel
- trading groups (such as the EU, ASEAN)

D How important are the following things when doing business in your country? Are they: a) important b) not important or c) best avoided?

- exchanging business cards
- being formal or informal
- shaking hands
- punctuality
- kissing
- humour
- socialising with contacts
- giving presents
- small talk before meetings
- being direct (saying exactly what you think)
- accepting interruption
- using first names

**Cultural
awareness**

A 🎧 **7.1** Listen to the first part of an interview with Jeff Toms, Marketing
Director at the International Briefing Centre at Farnham Castle, Surrey. He
talks about training courses which prepare people for doing business
internationally. Complete the list of issues that he mentions.

Issues covered by the training course

- .... [1] awareness
- Practical issues of .... [2] and .... [3] overseas
- Dealing with .... [4]
- Schooling; .... [5] care; international security
- How to negotiate .... [6]
- Communication
  – telephone – e-mail – the .... [7]

- Presentation skills
  – the words you use
  – the .... [8] you use
  – how to deal with .... [9]
    and answers
  – managing your .... [10]

B 🎧 **7.2** Listen to the second part of the interview. Jeff talks about the
personality traits that help in doing business internationally. Which three
personality traits does he consider to be important?

C 🎧 **7.3** Listen to the third part of the interview. Which two cultural aspects
does Jeff mention and what does he say about them?

- Entertaining   • Gift-giving   • Hierarchy
- Time   • Greetings   • Dress

D Which country would you like to visit on business? What would you like to
know about the culture of this country before visiting? Think of some questions
to ask. Use the topics listed above to help you. Add some others of your own.

Vocabulary
Idioms

A Choose the most appropriate word in the box to complete the idioms in the sentences below.

eye	eye	foot	water	water	fire	ice	~~end~~

1 I was *thrown in at the deep* .....*end*...... when my company sent me to run the German office. I was only given two days' notice to prepare.

2 We *don't see eye to* .... about relocating our factory. The Finance Director wants to move production to the Far East, but I want it to remain in Spain.

3 I *got into hot* .... with my boss for wearing casual clothes to the meeting with our Milanese customers.

4 Small talk is one way to *break the* .... when meeting someone for the first time.

5 I really *put my* .... *in it* when I met our Japanese partner. Because I was nervous, I said 'Who are you?' rather than 'How are you?'

6 I *get on like a house on* .... with our Polish agent; we like the same things and have the same sense of humour.

7 When I visited China for the first time I was *like a fish out of* .... Everything was so different, and I couldn't read any of the signs!

8 My first meeting with our overseas clients was *a real* .... *-opener.* I had not seen that style of negotiation before.

B 🎧 7.4 **Listen to eight people using the idioms from Exercise A and check your answers.**

C **Consider the context of each idiom in Exercise A and write down those which have:**

a) a positive meaning. ....

b) a negative meaning. ..*1*.. , ...

D **Match the idioms in Exercise A to the correct meanings a) to h).**

a) given a difficult job to do without preparation ....*1*............

b) quickly have a friendly relationship with someone ....

c) feel uncomfortable in an unfamiliar situation ....

d) say or do something without thinking carefully, so that you embarrass or upset someone ....

e) to disagree with someone ....

f) an experience where you learn something surprising or something you did not know before ....

g) make someone you have just met less nervous and more willing to talk ....

h) to get into trouble ....

E **Work in pairs or small groups. Discuss the following.**

1 What tips do you have for *breaking the ice* at meetings with new clients?

2 Talk about a place you have visited which was *a real eye-opener*.

3 Describe a situation when you

   a) *put your foot in it.*   **c)** *got into hot water.*

   b) *felt like a fish out of water.*   **d)** *were thrown in at the deep end.*

Reading
Cultural advice

A Work in pairs. Student A: read the articles A and B on this page. Student B: read the articles C and D on pages 142 and 146. Choose the two most interesting points about each country and tell your partner.

B Read your articles again and answer as many of the following questions as you can.

In which country or countries:

1 do people talk in a lively way? ....

2 do people ask questions about your personal life? ....

3 does the host invite you to comment on a previous conversation? ....

4 do the hosts like to hear praise about their country? ....

5 do people like gifts with your company logo? ....

6 is it important to give a more expensive gift to the most senior person? ....

7 does your host open your gift immediately? ....

8 is it a mistake to offer an expensive gift? ....

9 is it bad manners to refuse an invitation to a meal? ....

10 is it rude to refuse to sing when asked? ....

11 is it important to be punctual for lunch or dinner? ....

12 is it important not to offer food with your left hand? ....

C In pairs, share your information with your partner so you can answer all the questions.

D What advice would you give a business visitor to your country? Give a short presentation. You could mention conversation, gifts, entertainment, appointments and business dress.

Article A: Italy

Conversation

Lively conversation is common in Italy. Welcome topics of conversation include Italian architecture, art and films, sports (especially football), opera and praising the hospitality of the country! It is best to avoid criticising Italian culture, even if your Italian counterparts are doing so.

Gift-giving

Don't give a business gift until you receive one. Your gift should be a well-known brand name. Gifts of alcohol or crafts from your own country are often good choices. Other possible gifts are fine pens, a framed print or picture, silver key rings or calculators. Avoid giving gifts showing your company's logo.

Entertaining

Hospitality plays a key role in Italian business culture. Regardless of how you feel, refusing an invitation of any kind may give offence. The business breakfast is almost unheard of. Rare exceptions may be found in the major cities. Business dinners involve only a small, exclusive group. If you are the host, check with your Italian contact before making any invitations. Lunch is still the main meal of the day in most areas of the country. It is usually served after 12:30 p.m. and often has many courses.

Article B: United Arab Emirates

Conversation

The hosts usually set the subject of conversation. They will normally begin with polite enquiries (How are you? How are you enjoying your visit? etc.). If others arrived before you, your hosts will often tell you the subject of the previous conversation and invite you to contribute.

Gift-giving

Giving gifts in the UAE is more complex than in other countries. This is partly because of the mixture of nationalities: each nationality has different tastes and customs. Also, nearly everything can be purchased in the UAE less expensively than elsewhere in the world. As a gesture of respect, your host is likely to open and carefully examine your gift in your presence. It is important that your gift is the best you can afford to avoid embarrassment.

Entertaining

Sharing a meal is considered the best way for people to get to know one another. Locals often entertain at home but they will accept a foreigner's invitation to a hotel or restaurant. Hospitality in the UAE is very important but should not be interpreted as future commercial success. There are local customs to be aware of, for example, it is considered bad manners to either eat or offer something with the left hand. Adapted from www.executive.com

Language review
Advice, obligation and necessity

1 **Advice**

- We can use *should* and *shouldn't* to give or ask for advice.
  You should learn a song to sing before going to Korea.

- For strong advice we can use *must* or *mustn't*.
  You mustn't refuse an invitation to dinner in Italy. It may cause offence.

2 **Obligation / Necessity**

- We often use *must* when the obligation comes from the person speaking or writing.
  We must buy a gift for our visitor.

- We use *mustn't* to say something is prohibited or is not allowed.
  You mustn't use a mobile phone in an aeroplane.

- We often use *have to* to show that the obligation comes from another person or institution, not the speaker.
  You have to get a visa to enter the country. (This is the law.)

3 **Lack of obligation / Lack of necessity**

- *don't have to* and *mustn't* are very different:
  don't have to = it is not necessary

 page 153

A Choose the most appropriate verb. There are some situations where both verbs are possible. Can you say why?

1 Visitors *must / should* carry an identity card at all times when travelling.

2 Passengers *mustn't / don't have to* smoke anywhere on the aircraft.

3 All personnel *should / must* wear their badge while in the building.

4 The visitors *don't have to / mustn't* enter the radioactive zone unless authorised.

5 I think you *should / must* learn how to negotiate in Chinese. It would be a good skill if you had the time to learn it!

6 My boss *doesn't have to / shouldn't* travel so much – he is looking ill.

7 When going to a new country to do business, you *should / must* do some research on the etiquette and taboos of the host country.

8 Monday is a public holiday. I *mustn't / don't have to* work.

B Read these notes on US business protocol. How does each piece of advice compare with the situation in your country?

US business protocol

Timing
- You must arrive at business meetings on time. Only a 15-minute delay because of traffic problems is allowed.

Greetings and polite conversation
- You must shake hands during introductions.
- You don't have to make a lot of small talk. Americans like to get down to business quickly.
- You mustn't ask about a businesswoman's marital status. It is considered rude.

Business cards
- You don't have to exchange business cards unless there is a reason to get in contact later.

Smoking
- You mustn't smoke in many public spaces. Most businesses, cabs and many restaurants nowadays have a no-smoking policy.

Gift-giving
- Business gifts shouldn't be given until after the business negotiations are over.
- You mustn't give an expensive business gift. It may cause embarrassment.

Entertaining at home
- You should write a short thank you note to your host and hostess if you are entertained at their home. You don't have to give a gift but flowers or wine are appreciated.

From *Do's and taboos around the world*, edited by Roger E. Axtell

Skills
Social English

A 🎧 7.5 **Listen to the conversation between two people who have recently met. What is wrong? How can it be improved?**

B **In what business situations would you use the words and expressions below? Discuss your ideas with a partner.**

Congratulations!	I don't mind.	I'm afraid ...
Cheers!	Excuse me.	Please ...
Make yourself at home.	Sorry.	Could you ... ?
Help yourself.	It's on me.	That sounds good.

C **What would you say in the following situations?**

1 You don't hear someone's name when you are introduced to them.
2 You have to refuse an invitation to dinner with a supplier.
3 You are offered food you hate.
4 You want to end a conversation in a diplomatic way.
5 You have to greet a visitor.
6 You have to introduce two people to each other.
7 You offer to pay for a meal.
8 You have to propose a toast.
9 Your colleague has been made redundant.
10 You arrive half an hour late for a meeting.

D 🎧 7.6 **Listen and check your answers to Exercise C.**

E **What can you say in the first five minutes of meeting someone? Choose the best answer a) to l) for each of the questions 1 to 10.**

1 Is this your first visit to the Far East?
2 Oh really. What do you do?
3 How long have you been there?
4 Have you been to Hong Kong before?
5 Business or pleasure?
6 How long have you been here?
7 How long are you staying?
8 Where are you staying?
9 What's the food like?
10 So, what do you think of Hong Kong?

a) At the Peninsula Hotel.
b) Nearly ten years.
c) No, I come here quite often.
d) No. This is my first trip.
e) I'm the Marketing Director for a small import–export company.
f) Business, I'm afraid.
g) Till tomorrow night.
h) A week.
i) I really like it. There's so much to do.
j) It's very good, but eating in the Peninsula can be quite expensive.

F 🎧 7.7 **Listen and check your answers to Exercise E.**

G **In your opinion, which of these items of advice for a successful conversation are useful and which are not?**

1 Listen carefully
2 Give only yes or no answers
3 Interrupt a lot
4 Be polite
5 Ask questions
6 Stay silent
7 Keep eye contact
8 Be friendly

• **Turn to pages 138 and 139 to play The social-cultural game.**

CASE STUDY

Visitors from China

Background

Toyworld is a profitable toy retailer based in Seattle, US, with subsidiaries in over 30 countries. Toyworld buys its products from suppliers all over the world.

Mr Lee Chung, head of a toy manufacturing firm based in Guandong, China, is going to visit the Toyworld subsidiary in your country. Mr Chung will be accompanied by his Export Manager, John Wong. The purpose of the visit is to get to know Toyworld's management better and learn more about the company. He may set up a joint venture with Toyworld if he has confidence in them and considers them to be a suitable partner. This is Mr Chung and Mr Wong's first visit to your company, and to your country.

Toyworld Senior Managers
Chief Executive
|
Managing Director
|
Finance Director — Marketing Director — Warehouse Manager

Personnel Manager   Chief Accountant   Sales Manager   Public Relations Manager   Advertising Manager   Transport and Distribution Manager

Chief Buyer

Administrative staff: 82; Warehouse workers: 20

Task

You are members of the planning committee for Mr Chung's visit. Read the documents. Then, plan a draft programme in small groups. After that, compare your ideas with the rest of the class and produce the final programme.

To...	Manager, Public Relations
From...	Chief Executive
Subject:	Mr Lee Chung's visit Date: 2 June

Mr Lee Chung and Mr John Wong will arrive at 9.10 a.m. on Monday 20 June and leave on Thursday 23 June.

When you prepare the draft programme, please schedule a meeting (morning or afternoon) during which we can discuss our business plans with Mr Chung and Mr Wong. Also, make sure that our visitors have opportunities to meet our staff and gain a complete understanding of our business.

The visitors will expect to have some basic information about Toyworld and to be offered activities which give them an understanding of the company. Please also arrange some social and cultural activities during their stay.

Above all, we do not want to make any cultural mistakes during the visit. We want Mr Chung and Mr Wong to leave with an excellent impression of our company and the way we treat foreign visitors.

To help you plan the visit, please could you attend the talk by Catherine Eng (an expert on Chinese business culture).

Key questions for the planning committee

1 Where will the visitors stay?

2 Who will meet them? What transport will be used?

3 What arrangements should be made for meals?

4 When will the business meeting take place?

5 What topics would be suitable for discussion at meals?

6 How will the visitors be entertained? Trips? Special events?

7 What gifts would be suitable? When and how should they be given?

8 Should there be local press and television coverage?

9 Is it necessary to provide an interpreter?

10 Any other ideas to develop a good relationship?

Listening

🎧 7.8 Listen to the talk given by Catherine Eng. Make notes on her key points.

Writing

As Marketing Director at Toyworld, send an e-mail to Mr Chung with details of the programme for his visit. The tone of the e-mail should be friendly and show that you and your colleagues are looking forward to meeting him soon.

➡ *Writing file page 133*

1 Brands

Vocabulary

Complete the sentences with expressions from the box.

value for money	luxurious	timeless	well-made
top of the range	durable	inexpensive	cool
reliable	stylish	fashionable	sexy

A product that

1 does not wear out is ....

2 is attractive and has style is ....

3 is cheap is ....

4 does not break down is ....

5 remains beautiful and does not become old-fashioned is ....

6 is modern and desirable is .... : a word used especially by young people.

7 is attractive in an exciting, glamorous way is ....

8 gives you a lot of features and is good quality in relation to its price offers ....

9 is manufactured well and assembled to a high standard is ....

10 is the best model in a range, or in relation to competitors' product ranges, is ....

11 is popular for a short period of time is ....

12 is very expensive, comfortable and beautiful is ....

Present simple and present continuous

The director of a supermarket chain is talking. Complete what he says, using the present simple or present continuous form of the verbs in brackets.

We usually .... [1] (open) about ten new stores every year, but this year we .... [2] (only build) five. This summer the weather is terrible and customers .... [3] (not buy) a lot of summer clothes. Normally we .... [4] (sell) a lot of shorts, T-shirts and so on when the weather is hot. Usually, I .... [5] (go to see) one of our stores every week. But this is a difficult period and currently I .... [6] (visit) three stores a week. It's not every day that we .... [7] (get) the chance to buy a chain of stores abroad, but currently we .... [8] (negotiating) to acquire a French chain. I .... [9] (not like) golf but, because of the French negotiations, I .... [10] (play) a lot of golf at the moment. The real decisions are made on the golf course! I .... [11] (read) a lot of books about leaders from history. At the moment, I .... [12] (enjoy) a very good book about Napoleon.

2 Travel

Vocabulary

Complete the text with the correct British English alternatives.

My last overseas business trip was a pleasure from start to finish. I got to the airport in record time – there was no traffic on the .... [1]. The car .... [2] was almost empty, and I parked very easily. I had an .... [3] class ticket, but they upgraded it to first class! My .... [4] was quite big and heavy, but they didn't make me check it in. When we arrived the .... [5] station was closed and there were no taxis, but I saw from the .... [6] that there was a bus leaving for the .... [7] immediately. The bus dropped me right in front of my hotel. I checked in and took the express .... [8] to my room on the 30th floor. What a view!

1 a) freeway	**b)** motorway	**c)** waterway	**d)** runway
2 a) pound	**b)** pool	**c)** park	**d)** port
3 a) economy	**b)** economic	**c)** economist	**d)** economics
4 a) handbag	**b)** hand luggage	**c)** carry in luggage	**d)** carry on luggage
5 a) subway	**b)** underpass	**c)** underground	**d)** underway
6 a) schedule	**b)** timetable	**c)** timeplan	**d)** timesheet
7 a) city centre	**b)** downtown area	**c)** hometown	**d)** city focus
8 a) elevator	**b)** riser	**c)** upper	**d)** lift

Writing

You organised the conference at the Modern Hotel for your conference but it did not go well, for the reasons given below. Write a letter (150 to 200 words) to the manager of the hotel complaining about the problems you had and asking for a discount on the bill. Suggest a figure for this discount.

- Restaurant – slow service (give an example)
- Conference facilities – equipment out of order (give a percentage)
- Swimming pool – closed some days (give number of days)
- Satellite TV – only French-language channels available
- Disabled facilities – some facilities not accessible (one of your delegates was in a wheelchair)
- Smoking – many guests (not your delegates) smoked in non-smoking areas

3 Organisation

Vocabulary

Match each noun in column 1 to two of the nouns in column 2 to make word partnerships.

1	business	**a)** leaders	**b)** park	**c)** work
2	management	**a)** game	**b)** car	**c)** level
3	sales	**a)** top	**b)** team	**c)** target
4	labour	**a)** relations	**b)** -intensive	**c)** manager
5	company	**a)** car	**b)** crown	**c)** culture
6	trade	**a)** union	**b)** talks	**c)** boss
7	consumer	**a)** people	**b)** power	**c)** products
8	research	**a)** firm	**b)** products	**c)** results
9	information	**a)** flow	**b)** computer	**c)** age
10	computer	**a)** crash	**b)** screen	**c)** fingerboard

Reading

Look at the case study on pages 28 and 29. In the end Auric Bank chose Resource PLC. A year later, a manager at Auric Bank writes a letter to them.

In most of the lines 1 to 5 there is one extra word that does not fit. One or two of the lines, however, are correct. If a line is correct, put a tick in the space next to that line. If there is an extra word in the line, write that word in the space.

Trevor Samuels
Resource PLC
700 New Church Street
8001 Cape Town
South Africa

27 July 200_

Dear Mr Samuels

I'm writing to congratulate you on the service you have done provided in the last year.   1 ....
Our survey shows that customers are more satisfied than before. 90 percent of them say that   2 ....
your agents answer on the phone promptly and have all the information that they need to deal   3 ....
with of their calls efficiently. 92 percent say that your agents are polite and friendly and easy   4 ....
to understand. Please to see the enclosed report for more of the survey findings – all very positive!   5 ....
Looking forward to continuing cooperation between our two organisations!

Yours sincerely

Leila Lombard

Leila Lombard

Writing

Your company chose one of the other organisations on page 29. A year later, the contract with them is not going well. Write a letter (80 to 100 words) to the organisation, ending the contract and giving the reasons for this.

4 Change

Past simple and present perfect

Complete the text with the past simple or present perfect forms of the verbs in brackets.

This year the Lamda agency .... 1 (have) catastrophic results. The past six months especially .... 2 (be) the worst period in its history. The founder, John Lamda, ... 3 (open) the agency's first office in 1968 in Madison Avenue with his brother Mark. John .... 4 (deal) with the clients and Mark .... 5 (work) on the creative side. The number of employees .... 6 (increase) to 5,000 ten years ago, working in 25 offices worldwide. John Lamda takes up the story: 'One day Mark and I .... 7 (have) a big argument about a client and he .... 8 (leave) the agency. He .... 9 (take) a lot of clients with him. We .... 10 (not speak) to each other since.'

The Lamda agency .... 11 (go) downhill ever since. Employee numbers .... 12 (fall) to around 50 today. Over the last ten years, John .... 13 (close) all the offices except the one in New York.

As John Lamda freely admitted when I spoke to him yesterday: 'Mark's new agency .... 14 (do) very well over the last ten years. He .... 15 (run) some brilliant campaigns. He's doing so well. I .... 16 (regret) our argument ever since that terrible day ten years ago!'

Describing change

Match the two parts of these sentences.

1 The company has created eight 'service regions' to de-
2 Train services have been up-
3 Of 8 million unemployed adults, 5 million lack the basic skills to be re-
4 Smith Software is having to down-
5 The technology division will also become a separate business and is re-
6 The European Union is trying to de-
7 The products were redesigned and re-

a) graded with the installation of new electrical systems on tracks and stations.
b) launched, but they still didn't sell.
c) centralise management and improve customer services.
d) locating from Washington DC to Chicago.
e) trained for hi-tech jobs.
f) size, and will cut programming and sales jobs worldwide by about 13 percent.
g) regulate the European airline market, but a lot of uncompetitive airlines remain.

5 Money

Financial terms

Complete the description with expressions from the box.

recession	share price	debt	stock market	investment
forecast	bankruptcy	dividend	revenues	

It has been a disappointing year for Smithson, and our .... [1] for the next six months is that things will get even worse. In the UK, Smithson made a loss of £50 million on .... [2] of £1 billion and because of a continuing .... [3] in the Asian economy and slow economic growth in Europe, profits from abroad, where Smithson has most of its activities, have also continued to fall.

Reflecting this performance, which was much worse than expected, the .... [4] fell 30 percent to 16.1 p on the London .... [5] yesterday. Of course, there is no question of a .... [6] this year, and shareholders are becoming increasingly angry. Smithson plans to reduce its .... [7] in plant and equipment over the coming two years as part of its effort to return to profitability. In any case, Smithson would be unable to borrow more in order to invest: the company has increased its .... [8] by 90 percent over the last three years, and may soon be unable to make repayments – the lenders are becoming very nervous. If things go on as they are, there is a real risk that Smithson will face .... [9] before long.

Trends

Complete the graph using the information on page 66.

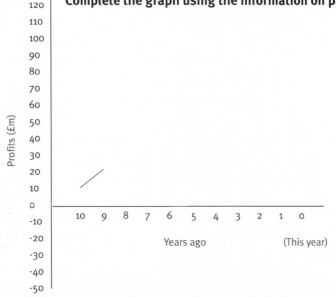

Ten years ago, Smithson made a profit of £10 million. Its products were in great demand and, over the next three years, its profits rose to £35 million. Profits then levelled off for two years, remaining at the same level. There was a slight drop in the following year to £33 million, before profits started rocketing again. They tripled to reach £100 million two years ago. It was then that Smithson's troubles started. Profits plummeted to only £7 million last year, and this year Smithson made its first ever loss, of £50 million.

6 Advertising

Vocabulary

Complete the table.

	Verb	Noun
1	exhibit	exhibition, exhibitor
2	launch	....
3	persuade	....
4	....	promotion
5	....	publicity
6	research	....
7	....	run
8	sponsor	....
9	target	....

Articles

Look at the case study on page 52. Focus got the contract for the campaign for sports cars. This e-mail is from the Marketing Manager at the client company to the Campaign Director at the agency.

In most of the lines 1 to 5 there is one extra word that does not fit. One or two of the lines, however, are correct. If a line is correct, put a tick in the space next to that line. If there is an extra word in the line, write that word in the space.

To...	anne.fontaine@focus.fr
From...	henry.porter@zgcars.com

Subject: Advertising campaign   Date: Oct 2, 2005

Anne,
A quick message to say that our campaign has started very well. The idea of putting ads into ¹ ....
business magazines read by a men in their 50s was excellent. A lot of our customers are ² ....
nostalgic for ZG models of the forty years ago, and now they have the money to buy one! We ³ ....
now need to look more closely at the potential market among younger men. This is some one ⁴ ....
of many points we should discuss at our first review meeting a next week, I think. ⁵ ....

Regards
Henry

Writing

Focus also got the contracts for the perfume and the restaurant chain. Write an e-mail (90 to 100 words) from the marketing manager at ONE of these two companies to Anne Fontaine, discussing the initial results of the campaign (good or bad), giving reasons for this success or failure.

7 Cultures

Modals of advice, obligation and necessity

Look at this advice for businesspeople about moving from the UK to another country. Choose the correct alternative from the brackets.

1 Visitors (*must / don't have to*) register with the police within one week of arriving. Anyone who does not can be fined $1,000.

2 It is very difficult to find somewhere to live. You will probably (*must / have to*) live in a hotel for the first few weeks while you find somewhere.

3 UK citizens (*mustn't / don't have to*) register at the British Consulate but doing so will help the consul to assist you if you get into trouble.

4 You (*shouldn't / must*) carry your passport with you at all times. The police carry out frequent spot checks.

5 Visitors and residents (*don't have to / mustn't*) go near military installations, especially when carrying a camera. You (*mustn't / should*) photograph military aircraft or warships.

6 You (*must / don't have to*) be very careful when driving. The roads are extremely dangerous.

7 Street crime is very rare, but you (*should / shouldn't*) be aware at all times of what is going on around you.

8 You (*should / shouldn't*) learn some common expressions in the local language. Very few people outside the capital speak English.

Writing

You move to the country mentioned in the previous exercise. You are Marketing Manager for a consumer goods company. A colleague in your home country is going to join you to work with you in the same country. Write an e-mail (about 250 words) to them to give advice about the cultural dos and taboos in the areas of:

- timing
- greetings and polite conversation
- business cards
- smoking
- gifts
- entertaining at home and out

UNIT 8 | Employment

OVERVIEW ▼

☐ **Vocabulary**
The recruitment process

☐ **Reading**
Retaining good staff

☐ **Listening**
Headhunting

☐ **Language review**
Indirect questions and statements

☐ **Skills**
Managing meetings

☐ **Case study**
Slim Gyms

> No matter how successful you are, your business and its future are in the hands of the people you hire.
>
> Akio Morita (1921–1999), Japanese business executive

Starting up

A In your opinion, which factors below are important for getting a job? Choose the five most important. Is there anything missing from the list?

appearance	hobbies	experience	sex
intelligence	marital status	personality	qualifications
references	age	astrological sign	handwriting
blood group	sickness record	family background	
contacts and connections			

B Think about jobs you've had and interviews you've attended. Ask each other about your best or worst:

1 a) job   b) boss   c) colleague

2 a) interview experience   b) interview question   c) interview answer

C Discuss these statements.

1 At work appearance is more important than performance.

2 You should keep your private life totally separate from your work.

3 People don't change much during their working lives.

4 It is best to work for as few companies as possible.

5 Everybody should retire at 50.

Vocabulary
The recruitment process

A Match the verbs 1 to 6 to the nouns a) to f) to make word partnerships.

1	to train	**a)**	a vacancy / post
2	to shortlist	**b)**	an interview panel
3	to advertise	**c)**	the candidates
4	to assemble	**d)**	references
5	to make	**e)**	new staff
6	to check	**f)**	a job offer

Now decide on a possible order for the events above from the employer's point of view.

For example: *1 to advertise a vacancy*

B 8.1 Listen to a consultant talking about the recruitment process to check your answers.

C Complete the text using words or phrases from the box.

> curriculum vitae (CV) / résumé   probationary period   interview
>
> application form   psychometric test   covering letter

These days many applicants submit their .... ¹ speculatively to companies they would like to work for. In other words, they do not apply for an advertised job but hope the employer will be interested enough to keep their CV on file and contact them when they have a vacancy. When replying to an advertisement, candidates often fill in a / an .... ² and write a / an .... ³. The employer will then invite the best candidates to attend a / an .... ⁴ . Sometimes candidates will take a / an .... ⁵ before the interview to assess their mental ability and reasoning skills. These days it is normal for successful candidates to have to work a / an .... ⁶ in a company. This is usually three or six months; after that they are offered a permanent post.

D Which of these words would you use to describe yourself in a work or study situation? Use a good dictionary to help you. Add any other useful words.

- motivated
- confident
- reliable
- proud
- dedicated
- loyal
- determined
- charismatic
- honest
- adaptable
- resourceful
- meticulous

E Compare your answers with a partner. Which of the qualities in Exercise D do you think are the most important to be successful in a job?

 *Vocabulary file pages 171 and 172*

Reading
Retaining good staff

A Discuss these questions before you read the article.

1 The article talks about people who are high performers. What does this phrase mean? What sort of people are they?

2 What do you think motivates high performers to stay with the same company?

B Read the article and answer these questions.

1 What qualities of high performers are mentioned in the article?

2 What are the problems of losing high performers?

3 Which motivating factors are mentioned in the article?

Motivating high-calibre staff

By Michael Douglas

An organisation's capacity to identify, attract and retain high-quality, high-performing people who can develop winning strategies has become decisive in ensuring competitive advantage.

High performers are easier to define than to find. They are people with apparently limitless energy and enthusiasm, qualities that shine through even on their bad days. They are full of ideas and get things done quickly and effectively. They inspire others not just by pep talks but also through the sheer force of their example. Such people can push their organisations to greater and greater heights.

The problem is that people of this quality are very attractive to rival companies and are likely to be headhunted. The financial impact of such people leaving is great and includes the costs of expensive training and lost productivity and inspiration.

However, not all high performers are stolen, some are lost. High performers generally leave because organisations do not know how to keep them. Too many employers are blind or indifferent to the agenda of would be high performers, especially those who are young.

Organisations should consider how such people are likely to regard important motivating factors.

Money remains an important motivator but organisations should not imagine that it is the only one that matters. In practice, high performers tend to take for granted that they will get a good financial package. They seek motivation from other sources.

Empowerment is a particularly important motivating force for new talent. A high performer will seek to feel that he or she 'owns' a project in a creative sense. Wise

employers offer this opportunity.

The challenge of the job is another essential motivator for high performers. Such people easily become demotivated if they sense that their organisation has little or no real sense of where it is going.

A platform for self-development should be provided. High performers are very keen to develop their skills and their curriculum vitae. Offering time for regeneration is another crucial way for organisations to retain high performers. Work needs to be varied and time should be available for

creative thinking and mastering new skills. The provision of a coach or mentor signals that the organisation has a commitment to fast-tracking an individual's development.

Individuals do well in an environment where they can depend on good administrative support. They will not want to feel that the success they are winning for the organisation is lost because of the inefficiency of others or by weaknesses in support areas.

Above all, high performers – especially if they are young – want to feel that the organisation they work for regards them as special. If they find that it is not interested in them as people but only as high-performing commodities, it will hardly be surprising if their loyalty is minimal. On the other hand, if an organisation does invest in its people, it is much more likely to win loyalty from them and to create a community of talent and high performance that will worry competitors.

From the *Financial Times*

FINANCIAL TIMES
World business newspaper.

C Use these words or phrases from the article to answer the questions below.

pep talk	mentor	CV
fast-tracking	headhunting	financial package

Which word or phrase:

1 is British English for the American English *résumé*? ....

2 refers to stealing employees from companies? ....

3 do you often find in job advertisements referring to money and benefits? ....

4 refers to an older, more experienced person who helps you? ....

5 usually leads to quick promotion? ....

6 means a short chat to motivate staff? ....

D What are the advantages and disadvantages of:

1 headhunting?

2 having a mentor system?

3 fast-tracking certain employees?

4 frequent pep talks?

Listening
Headhunting

▲ Dr Simon Kingston

A 🎧 8.2 **Dr Simon Kingston works for the international executive search consultants Heidrick and Struggles. Listen to the first part of the interview and complete the chart below.**

Methods for identifying candidates

```
...................... 1
in newspapers or
...................... 2

Asking for
...................... 3
from the organisation

Own original
...................... 4

From our
............... 5

From talking
to ...............
............... 6

From beginning
to ............ 7
the business
............... 8

Cross-............ 9
```

B 🎧 8.2 **Simon mentions three different types of experts which his company usually speaks to at the beginning of an executive search. Who are they?**

C 🎧 8.3 **Listen to the second part of the interview and complete the summary below.**

One common theme in the careers of a lot of successful people is an .... 1 of the individual's own .... 2. This allows them to .... 3 the sort of organisations in which they will work. It also allows them to .... 4 but appropriately to opportunities that are unplanned that present themselves.

D Which qualities does Lord Browne at BP demonstrate, according to Simon?

Language review
Indirect questions and statements

- **We often use indirect questions and statements to sound more polite, for example when asking for personal or sensitive information.**

  Could you tell me what your salary is?
  Would you mind telling me how old you are?
  I'm not sure when the interview finishes.

- Indirect questions have the same word order as direct statements.

  She left the job. (direct statement)
  Could you tell me why she left the job?

- We can use the following expressions to introduce indirect questions and statements.

  I wonder / I can't remember / I have no idea / I'd like to know / I am not sure …
  when the post will be advertised.

- For yes / no questions we use if or whether. We can also use if or whether in statements.

  Will he apply for the job? (direct question)
  *I wonder **whether** he'll apply for the job.*

 page 153

A **In which of these questions and statements is the word order correct? Rewrite the incorrect ones.**

1 Could you tell me what your strengths are?
2 I'd like to know what would your colleagues say about you.
3 Could you tell me how have you changed in the last five years?
4 Do you happen to know what salary I will start on?
5 I am not sure where want I to be in five years' time.

B **Put the words in the right order to form indirect questions or statements.**

1 do know where you the room interview is?
2 I ask you old are you how could?
3 I wonder you if could me tell what time is it?
4 I'd like why to know we you should hire.
5 do you mind I ask if your weaknesses are what?
6 could I you ask why left you your last job?

C **You are interviewing someone for a job. How would you *politely* find out the following information?**

1 Their age
2 Their current salary
3 Their reasons for leaving their last job
4 Their weaknesses

D **Role play this job interview. Use direct and indirect questions.**

Interviewees
Choose a job you would like to have in a company you would like to work for. Tell your partner what the position is.

Interviewers
Possible areas to cover include:
- strengths
- interests
- experience
- weaknesses
- achievements
- skills

Skills
Managing meetings

A Why are some meetings successful and others unsuccessful?

B Match the definitions 1 to 12 to the words and phrases a) to l).

1	the person in charge of the meeting	**a)** action points
2	the people at the meeting	**b)** chairperson
3	to go to a meeting	**c)** propose
4	a list of topics to be discussed	**d)** attend
5	one topic on the list	**e)** to send your apologies
6	the last topic on the list	**f)** item
7	to make a suggestion formally	**g)** vote
8	to support a formal suggestion	**h)** any other business (AOB)
9	a method of making a decision	**i)** participants
10	an official record of what was said and/or decided	**j)** second
		k) minutes
11	to say that you cannot go to a meeting	**l)** agenda
12	what needs to be done after the meeting, and by whom	

C 🎧 8.4 **A group of managers are discussing whether to offer an employee a full-time contract. Listen and tick the expressions in the Useful language box that you hear.**

Useful language

Starting
OK, let's get down to business.
Right, can we start, please?

Setting objectives
The purpose of this meeting is …
The aims of this meeting are …

Asking for reactions
How do you feel about …?
What do you think?

Dealing with interruptions
Could you let him finish, please?
Could you just hang on a moment, please?

Keeping to the point
I'm not sure that's relevant.
Perhaps we could get back to the point.

Speeding up
I think we should move on now.
Can we come back to that?

Slowing down
Hold on, we need to look at this in more detail.
I think we should discuss this a bit more.

Summarising
OK, let's go over what we've agreed.
Right, to sum up then …

D You are managers of a retail fashion chain called Space. You are holding your regular management meeting. Use the Managing Director's notes below as an agenda for your discussions. A different person should chair each item.

1 DRESS CODE
Following complaints from customers, we need to discuss ideas for a dress code for all employees, as well as guidelines on personal appearance.

2 POLICY FOR SMOKERS
Non-smoking staff complain that staff who smoke take frequent 'cigarette breaks' outside the store. Should smokers work extra time to make up for the time lost?

3 COMMISSION PAYMENTS
At present, commission is based on quarterly sales at each store and is divided equally between all staff. Now, our Sales Director wants each person to receive commission according to their individual sales.

4 END-OF-YEAR BONUS
Staff receive sales vouchers as an end-of-year bonus. The vouchers give discounts on a range of goods at major department stores. Some managers are proposing to issue no sales vouchers this year. Instead, staff will be invited to an end-of-year party.

5 STAFF TURNOVER
Staff tend to be young so employee turnover is high. As a result, training costs have increased dramatically. What can be done to keep staff longer?

Slim Gyms

Background

SLIM GYMS owns and operates six health and leisure clubs in Manhattan. The clubs appeals mainly to people aged 20–40. All the clubs have a gymnasium, with the latest equipment, an aerobics studio, a swimming pool, sun decks, a café, bar and clubroom. Three of the clubs are located in areas where large numbers of Spanish, Chinese and Italians live.

In recent months, Slim Gyms' profits have fallen sharply. Many members have not renewed their memberships and the club has been unable to attract a sufficient number of new members. Slim Gyms recently advertised for a General Manager. His/Her main task is to boost sales at the clubs and increase profits.

SLIM GYMS

General Manager

Required for our chain of Health and Leisure Clubs

- Salary negotiable
- Excellent benefits package

88 Harvey Place
11– C
New York
NY 10003–1324

The job

- Developing a customer-oriented culture in the organization of the clubs
- Increasing the revenue and profits of the company of the six clubs in Manhattan
- Exploiting new business opportunities
- Liaising with and motivating our team of managers and their staff
- Contributing to marketing plans and strategies

The person

- Dynamic, enthusiastic, flexible
- A strong interest in health and fitness
- A good track record in previous jobs
- The ability to work with people from different cultural backgrounds
- Outstanding communication skills
- A flair for new ideas and sound organizational skills

Task

You are directors of Slim Gyms. Study the file cards on the four short-listed candidates on the opposite page. Hold a meeting to discuss the strengths and weaknesses of each person. Try to agree on who seems to be the best candidate for the job.

Then listen to the interview extracts with each of the candidates and come to a final decision on who should get the job: ∩ 8.5 Guido Passerelli, ∩ 8.6 Martine Lemaire, ∩ 8.7 David Chen, ∩ 8.8 Gloria Daniels.

Writing

Write a letter offering employment to the successful candidate.

 Writing file page 132

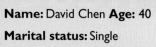

Name: Guido Passerelli **Age:** 52

Marital status: Married, with three children

Education: Bronx High School

Experience: Former American football player. Ran a small business for several years finding locations for film companies. Recently organised stunts* for a major film company.

Outstanding achievement: 'I was 5th in the New York marathon when I was aged 34.'

Skills: Fluent Italian and Spanish. Speaks English fairly well, but with an Italian accent and is sometimes hesitant.

Personality/appearance: Tall, handsome, tanned. Very self-confident. Wore a designer jacket and expensive designer tie at the interview.

Comments: Many interesting ideas for improving Slim Gym's profits. For example, thinks members should get a 50% discount off their subscription fee if they introduce a friend. Wants Slim Gyms to aim at all age groups. Believes his organising ability is his best quality. Expressed his points of view forcefully, sometimes arguing heatedly with the interviewer.

* actions in a film that are dangerous. They are usually performed by a stunt man or woman instead of by an actor.

Name: Gloria Daniels

Age: 36

Marital status: Married, with two children

Education: Diploma in Sports Management (Massey University, New Zealand)

Experience: Worked for three years for a chain of fitness centres. Joined Johnson Associates, an organisation promoting top sports personalities. Has travelled all over the world for the last ten years negotiating contracts with sportspeople.

Outstanding achievement: 'I negotiated a successful deal with Hank Robbins, the famous baseball player. We promote him exclusively.'

Skills: Has an elementary knowledge of Spanish and Italian. Was good at all sports when younger. Considered becoming a professional tennis player.

Personality/appearance: Wore a very expensive dress at the interview. Film star looks. Charismatic, over-confident (?) 'I like to win at everything I do, and usually I succeed. That's why I'm so good at my present job.'

Comments: Thinks Slim Gyms should raise more money by offering shares to wealthy individuals. In her opinion, Slim Gyms should immediately hire a firm of management consultants to review all its activities. In the interview, she seemed to be very competitive. Would she be a good team player?

Name: David Chen **Age:** 40

Marital status: Single

Education: Master's degree in Business Administration (Hong Kong University); Diploma in Physical Education (New University of Hawaii)

Experience: Several jobs in various companies before joining a large university as Sports Administrator. Has organised many sports events for the university.

Outstanding achievement: 'I have a black belt in karate.'

Skills: Numerate, extensive knowledge of computer programs. Fluent Chinese and English, some Italian.

Personality/appearance: Dressed in a formal dark suit but looked relaxed. Quiet, determined, polite and diplomatic. Asked many questions during the interview. Was rather shy if he didn't know the answer to a question.

Comments: Believes Slim Gyms should increase its services, for example, offer classes in salsa dancing, open a small boutique at each club selling sports equipment, etc. It should immediately cut costs by 10% in all areas of its business. Thinks his honesty is his best asset. Has an interest in all Eastern contact sports: judo, karate, aikido, etc.

Name: Martine Lemaire

Age: 32

Marital status: Divorced, with two children

Education: Degree in biology (Sorbonne, France); Master's degree in Dietetics (Yale University, US)

Experience: Worked for five years as a dietician in a hospital. Had a year off work when her health broke down because of stress. Joined a company selling health and skin-care products. For the last three years has been Assistant Sales Manager.

Outstanding achievement: 'I am proud of raising a family successfully while working full-time.'

Skills: Fluent French, good Spanish. Speaks and writes English fluently.

Personality/appearance: Well-dressed in fashionable clothes. Dynamic and ambitious. Sometimes assertive during the interview: 'Nothing will stop me achieving my goals.'

Comments: Her main idea for increasing profits: spend a lot of money on multi-media advertising and offer big discounts to new members. Believes her strongest quality is her creativity. In her leisure time, she runs a weekly aerobics class and also manages a local baseball team at the weekend.

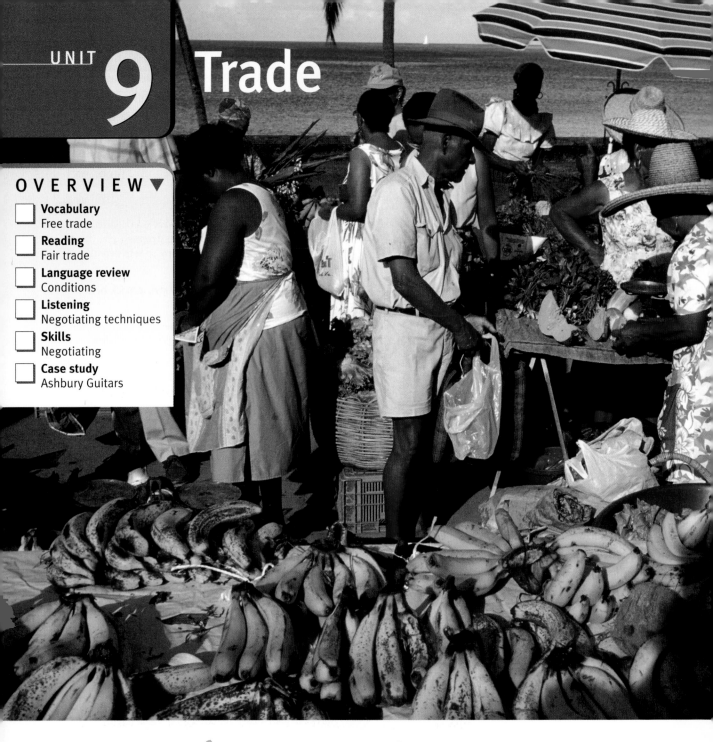

UNIT 9 Trade

OVERVIEW ▼

Vocabulary
Free trade

Reading
Fair trade

Language review
Conditions

Listening
Negotiating techniques

Skills
Negotiating

Case study
Ashbury Guitars

> ❝ *The merchant has no country.* ❞
>
> Thomas Jefferson (1743–1826), Principal author of the *Declaration of Independence*

Starting up

A Think of some of the things you own (for example, shoes, TV, car). Which are imported? Where were they made?

B Name some global companies. What kind of business are they?

C What is globalisation?

D Discuss these statements. Do you agree or disagree?

1 Globalisation damages local goods, services and cultures.

2 Globalisation increases competition among companies.

3 Globalisation raises people's living standards.

4 Globalisation improves international communication and understanding.

Vocabulary
Free trade

A 🎧 **9.1 Listen to the first part of a radio interview with Ian McPherson, an expert on international trade. Complete the definition of free trade he gives.**

It's a situation in which goods come into and out of a country without any
...*controls*.... ¹ or .... ². Countries which truly believe in free trade try to
.... ³ their trade, that's to say, they take away .... ⁴ to trade. They
have open .... ⁵ and few controls of goods at .... ⁶.

B 🎧 **9.2 Listen to the second part of the radio interview. Note down five things which stop people trading freely. Explain briefly the meaning of each one. For example:** *1 Tariffs. These are taxes on imported goods.*

C 🎧 **9.3 Listen to the third part of the radio interview and do the exercises.**

1 When there is a policy of deregulation:
   a) companies compete freely.
   b) there are a lot of government controls.
   c) companies must follow regulations.

2 According to Ian McPherson, what is the greatest benefit of free trade? Choose the best answer.
   a) more choice of products   **d)** higher salaries
   b) better-made products   **e)** a wider choice of jobs
   c) more expensive products

3 Complete this sentence.
   Some countries do not practise free trade because they wish to:
   • fight against .... ¹ competition, for example, dumping;
   • protect their .... ² industries, because they are important to the economy;
   • be less .... ³ on foreign imports, because their economies need developing.

4 What trend in international trade does Ian McPherson mention? Why does he think the trend is a good one?

D **Discuss these questions.**

1 To what extent do you have free trade in your country?
2 Should certain industries in your country be protected? If so, which ones?
3 Is free trade always a good thing, in your opinion?

E **Use the words and phrases in the box to complete the table. Use a good dictionary to help you.**

> ~~barriers~~   ~~open borders~~   free port   developing industries   dumping   tariffs
> strategic industries   restrictions   quotas   laisser-faire   liberalise   customs
> deregulation   subsidise   regulations

Open markets (Trade without restrictions on the movement of goods)	Protected markets (Trade with restrictions on the movement of goods, for example, import taxes)
open borders	*barriers*

F **Match these sentence halves.**

1 We're trying to break into
2 You should carry out
3 If you would like to place
4 If you can't meet
5 They've quoted
6 Let us know if you want us to arrange
7 It's essential to comply with

a) all regulations if you want the delivery to go through without problems.
b) the delivery date, let us know as soon as possible.
c) insurance cover for the shipment.
d) a market survey before you make a major investment.
e) the Japanese market.
f) an order, press one now.
g) us a very good price for the consignment.

G **Find verb + noun partnerships in the sentences above. For example,** *to break into a market.* **Which of them is normally done by:**

1 the supplier?   2 the buyer?   3 both the supplier and the buyer?

Reading

Fair trade

A **Before you read the article, answer these questions.**

1 Which countries traditionally export: **a)** bananas? **b)** coffee? **c)** sugar?
2 What typical problems do these exporters face when selling abroad?

B **Read the article and answer these questions.**

1 What does the article say about:
   a) Denise Sutherland?
   b) Juan Valverde Sanchez?
   c) Nicaraguan farmers?
   d) Sainsbury's, Starbucks and Carrefour?
   e) The World Trade Organisation (WTO)?

2 What do these numbers from the article refer to?

a) $500m	**b)** 400	**c)** 500,000	**d)** 36	**e)** 25

3 Why are Denise and Juan having problems selling their products?
4 What are the benefits to local producers of fair trade?
5 How did fair trade begin?

C **Choose the word a), b) or c) that is the odd one out in each group and matches the definitions.**

1 state of continuing to live or exist	**a)** ruin	**b)** bankruptcy	**c)** survival
2 slowly bringing to an end	**a)** phase out	**b)** lead	**c)** dominate
3 to make sure people know about a new product	**a)** prohibit	**b)** ban	**c)** promote
4 an official limit on the quantity of goods	**a)** tariff	**b)** quota	**c)** subsidy
5 people or companies that make or grow goods, food, materials	**a)** consumers	**b)** clients	**c)** producers
6 all the people who buy a particular product or use a particular service	**a)** product	**b)** niche	**c)** commodity
7 very successful	**a)** falling	**b)** declining	**c)** booming
8 the situation of being poor	**a)** prosperity	**b)** poverty	**c)** wealth

UK develops taste for fair trade

The UK has a taste for guilt-free food – sales are growing by 100% a year.

Along with tens of thousands of other banana growers in the Windward Islands, Denise Sutherland faces ruin. The World Trade Organisation (WTO) has forced the European Union to phase out its old quota system that guaranteed West Indian growers market access, and there's no way she can match the prices of the giant US corporations that dominate the market for the world's favourite fruit.

In Costa Rica, Juan Valverde Sanchez, a sugar cane grower who sells to a local farmers' association, is unsure if he and his colleagues will survive another year. Most of the world's sugar producers cannot break into the European or US markets because of high tariffs and the heavy subsidies that western farmers enjoy.

But there is now hope for Denise and Juan – they are selling some or all of their produce to the growing 'fair trade' market that protects them from depressed world commodity markets and the price wars between giant multinationals.

For its supporters, fair trade is an example of how world trade can and should be run to tackle poverty. Producers are all small scale and must be part of a cooperative or democratically-run association of workers who observe high social and environmental standards.

Their groups deal directly with first-world companies that pay well over the world market price. They also get an added premium, which goes directly to the group of farmers to be shared out in any way they choose.

The price difference can be as much as 100% and can save a farmer from bankruptcy or mean a family has the money to send their children to school.

At the other end of the chain, the first-world consumer pays about a penny extra for a cup of coffee or teaspoon of sugar, or a few pence more for a banana.

Fair-trade food is booming. What started as a way for Dutch consumers to support Nicaraguan farmers in the 60s has grown into a $500m a year global niche market with more than 400 northern companies now importing fruit, coffee, tea, bananas, nuts, orange juice and other foods.

Around 500,000 small-scale farmers and their families are thought to be benefiting in 36 of the world's poorest countries, and the latest figures suggest it is worth $40m extra to producers. Meanwhile, demand for other 'fairly traded' but unlabelled non-food goods, such as handicrafts and textiles, is also growing.

Fair trade food sales are growing by more than 25% a year internationally and almost 100% a year in Britain, now the largest market after Switzerland. This market is one of the most remarkable consumer success stories of the past decade, promoted quietly in Britain, and now attracting multinationals such as Sainsbury's, Starbucks and Carrefour.

It is ironic, though, that fair trade, which was designed to reduce the injustices of the world trading system, could itself become a victim of the WTO. Technically, it could be banned because WTO rules prohibit 'differentiation' between products on the basis of their means of production.

In the meantime, fair trade shows that charity is not needed to lift people out of poverty and that social and environmental standards can be put into trade.

From *The Guardian*

D What do the remaining two words in questions 1 to 8 in Exercise C have in common? Use a good dictionary to help you.

E Discuss these questions.

1 Do you buy fair trade goods? Why? Why not?

2 What local producers in your country could benefit from the growth of fair trade?

3 'We should not support fair trade because it subsidises small, inefficient producers.' Do you agree with this statement?

Language review
Conditions

We use the first conditional when we think the expected outcome of a situation is very likely.

*If you **give** us a 10% discount, we**'ll place** a firm order of 500 cases.* (This is a promise.)
*If you **don't deliver** on time, we **won't order** from you again.* (This is a threat.)
***Will** you give us a discount **if** we **double** our order?*

We use the second conditional when the outcome is less certain or is imaginary.

*If you **gave** us a 5% discount, we **would place** a much bigger order.*
*If they **didn't have** a guaranteed market, their business **wouldn't** survive.*
*What discount **would** you **offer** us **if** we **decided** to go to another supplier?*

 page 154

A Choose the correct verbs from the brackets to complete these sentences.

1 If you (*give us* /*'ll give us*) a discount of 10%, we (*'ll place* /*place*) a firm order.

2 (*Will you deliver* /*Do you deliver*) by the end of the month if we (*pay* /*'ll pay*) the transport costs?

3 If you (*will lower* /*lower*) your price by 5%, we (*buy* /*'ll buy*) at least 5,000 units.

4 (*Would* /*Does*) it help you if we (*sent* /*are sending*) the goods by air?

5 If you (*aren't improving* /*don't improve*) your delivery times, we (*'ll have* /*had*) to find a new supplier.

6 If we (*will join* /*joined*) an association of producers, we (*would get* /*will get*) a better price for our coffee.

B 9.4 Bella Ford, a buyer for Allgoods supermarket chain, is negotiating with Ranjit de Silva, Sales Director for a fair trade organisation in Sri Lanka. Listen and complete their conversation.

Bella   If I .... ¹ 5,000 boxes of tea, what discount will you offer us?

Ranjit   On 5,000, nothing. But if you buy 10,000 boxes, then .... ² offer you 10%.

Bella   OK, I'll think about that. And tell me, if we placed a very large order, say 15,000 boxes, ... ³ to despatch immediately?

Ranjit   We can normally guarantee to despatch a large order within two weeks. But if you .... ⁴ at a peak time, like just before Christmas, it will be impossible to deliver that quickly.

Bella   I take it your price includes insurance?

Ranjit   Actually, no. Usually, you'd be responsible for that. But if the order .... ⁵ really large, that would be negotiable, I'm sure.

Bella   What about payment?

Ranjit   To be honest we'd prefer cash on delivery as this is our first contact with you. If you .... ⁶ a regular customer, ... ⁷ you 30 days' credit, maybe even a little more.

Bella   That's alright. I quite understand.

Ranjit   Look, how about having some lunch now, and continuing later this afternoon? Then we could meet for an evening meal.

Bella   Yes, let's continue after lunch. If I had more time, ... ⁸ to have dinner with you, but unfortunately my flight leaves at seven tonight.

C Look at each conditional sentence in the dialogue in Exercise B. Decide if the events are a) very likely or b) less certain or imaginary.

Listening
Negotiating techniques

A 🎧 **9.5** Kevin Warren, Executive Vice President of Coca-Cola (UK), is talking about negotiating. Listen to the first part of the interview. What does Kevin say that the letters L-I-M stand for?

L .... I .... M ....

B In the negotiation that Kevin describes, what was his L-I-M?

C In the second part of the interview, Kevin gives three negotiating tips. Can you think of any tips for negotiating?

D 🎧 **9.6** Listen to the second part of the interview and complete these extracts.

a) And I guess the first one is to .... [1] who the ....
.... [2] is. So that's the first tip, make sure you know who
.... [3].

b) And in their enthusiasm, they ....
.... [4], rather than .... [5]. What they haven't done is
.... [6] the buyer's need.

c) ... once you've made the sale, ... [7]. I think it's very
important: ....[8], reinforce the buyer's
decision – everybody likes to feel they've made a good decision – and then
.... [9].

E Look at the audio script on pages 164 and 165 and find phrases which mean:

1 typical mistakes
2 to state your purpose directly without delay
3 a business contact over a period of time
4 causing no difficulty or trouble

▲ Kevin Warren

Skills
Negotiating

A Work in pairs. Try to sell something you have on you (watch, bracelet, etc.) or a household object, to your partner.

B Discuss these questions.

1 Were you pleased with the outcome of the negotiation in Exercise A?
2 What strategy or tactics did your partner use to achieve their objective?

C In his book *The Art of Winning*, Harry Mills says that most negotiations have seven stages. These are listed below, but are in the wrong order. Put the stages in order. What word do the initial letters of the stages spell?

- **Tie up loose ends**
  Confirm what has been agreed.
  Summarise the details on paper.

- **Explore each other's needs**
  Build rapport. State your opening position. Learn the other side's position.

- **Ready yourself**
  Prepare your objectives, concessions and strategy. Gather information about the other side.

- **Probe with proposals**
  Make suggestions and find areas of agreement.

- **Close the deal**
  Bring the negotiation to a clear and satisfactory end.

- **Signal for movement**
  Signal that you are prepared to move from your original position. Respond to signals from the other side.

- **Exchange concessions**
  Give the other side something in return for something you need or want.

D 🎧 **9.7 Listen to a negotiation between two buyers for a department store and a supplier of T-shirts, Eastern Fabrics, which is based in Hong Kong. Match each extract from the dialogue to one of the stages in Harry Mills' list.**

Extract **1**   **a)** Probe with proposals

Extract **2**   **b)** Close the deal

Extract **3**   **c)** Signal for movement

Extract **4**   **d)** Ready yourself

Extract **5**   **e)** Tie up loose ends

Extract **6**   **f)** Exchange concessions

Extract **7**   **g)** Explore each other's needs

E **Study the Useful language box below. Then role play these negotiations. Try to get a good outcome in each situation.**

Student A is a supplier.
Student B is a buyer.
Supplier: You want to increase the list price of your sports bag model PX7 by 10%. You also want to change your delivery times.
Buyer: You can only afford a 2% increase. You offer to buy a larger quantity of sports bags at a lower increase. You want the delivery times to stay the same. You also want to change the length of your contract with the supplier.

Student B is a company employee.
Student A is the employee's boss.
Employee: You think you should have a 10% salary increase.
Boss: You think the company can only afford a 2% increase.

Useful language

Starting positions
We'd like to reach a deal with you today.
Right, let's try to get 10% off their list prices.

Exploring positions
Can you tell me a little about ...?
What do you have in mind?

Making offers and concessions
If you order now, we'll give you a discount.
We'd be prepared to offer you a better price if you increased your order.
If necessary ...

Checking understanding
What do you mean?
Have I got this right?
If I understand you correctly ...
You mean, if we ordered ... would ...?
Are you saying ...

Refusing an offer
I'm not sure about that.
That's more than we usually offer ...
That would be difficult for us.

Accepting an offer
Sounds a good idea to me. As long as we ...
Good, we agree on price, quantity, discounts ...

Playing for time
I'd like to think about it.
I'll have to consult my colleagues about that.

Closing the deal
I think we've covered everything.
Great! We've got a deal.

Following up the deal
Let me know if there are any problems.
If there are any other points, I'll e-mail you.

Ashbury Guitars

Background

The Kim Guitar Company (KGC) in Seoul, South Korea, makes electric guitars for Japanese manufacturers and distributors in Europe and the US.

A major US distributor, Ashbury Guitars, has contacted KGC about marketing a range of guitars under its own brand name for the Californian market. Ashbury Guitars is a well-established company with an up-market image. It has had no previous dealings with KGC. Ashbury's owner, Richard Grant, plans to put three models on the market: the Ashbury SG1000 (the most expensive model), the SG500 and the SG200. The body of the guitars will have an experimental shape as well as advanced technical features.

It is now early January. KGC has agreed to manufacture the guitars for Ashbury, even though it is a very busy time of the year for them. The two companies have had some initial correspondence by e-mail and now a face-to-face meeting is required.

Several points of the contract need to be negotiated. KGC's owner, David Kim, has flown to San Francisco to meet Richard Grant. At the meeting, the Marketing Director of each company will be present. The purpose of the meeting is to make a deal acceptable to both sides, and which could be the basis for a long-term relationship.

CASE STUDY

Task

You are negotiating as either:
- The KGC team: David Kim and Marketing Director, turn to page 148.
- The Ashbury team: Richard Grant and Marketing Director, turn to page 143.

Read your information files. Identify your priorities and work out your strategy and tactics. Then negotiate so that you get the best deal for your company.

Writing

As the owner of either Ashbury Guitars or KGC, write an e-mail summarising the points agreed during the negotiation. Indicate any terms of the contract requiring discussion or clarification.

 Writing file page 133

UNIT 10 Quality

OVERVIEW ▼

☐ **Vocabulary**
Quality control and customer service

☐ **Reading**
Old-fashioned quality

☐ **Listening**
Quality management

☐ **Language review**
Gerunds and infinitives

☐ **Skills**
Telephone complaints

☐ **Case study**
Brookfield Airport

❝ Quality is remembered long after the price is forgotten. ❞
Gucci family slogan

Starting up

A Give examples of high-quality products or services. Explain your choices.

B Which of the words and phrases below best express your idea of quality?

reliable	value for money	long-lasting	traditional
well-known	expensive	hand-made	modern
genuine	made in (country)	well-designed	mass-produced

C Look at these sayings. What do they mean? Which of the ideas do you agree with?

1 'They don't make them like they used to.'
2 'Quality not quantity.'
3 'You get what you pay for.'
4 'Don't judge a book by its cover.'

Vocabulary

Quality control and customer service

A Use the words in the box to complete the flow chart.

identified	modified	failed	relaunched
durability	recalled	reliability	tested	~~launched~~

A DEFECTIVE PRODUCT

We ...*launched*...¹ the product two years ago.

We have a policy of zero defects so we were surprised when, shortly after the launch, we received complaints about the ....² and ....³ of this product.

Because of market feedback, we ....⁴ the product so that any faults could be investigated. At the same time, we withdrew it from sale.

After extensive tests, our engineers ....⁵ a fault.

As a result, they were able to correct the fault and we ....⁶ the product.

We ....⁷ the product under controlled conditions.

Finally, we ....⁸ the redesigned product in the market.

Unfortunately, it ....⁹ due to lack of consumer confidence caused by bad publicity.

B Complete the sentences below with words and phrases from the box. Use a good dictionary to help you.

consumer satisfaction questionnaire	compensation	monitoring
routine checks	guarantee	inspection
minimum standards	after-sales service	faults

Quality control

1 Quality control involves checking for .... before selling goods.

2 We are always .... the quality of our products.

3 The quality control department found several faults during one of their ....

4 We use a number of .... to measure quality.

5 During the .... a number of serious production flaws were found.

Customer service

6 We measure how happy our customers are with an annual ....

7 We ensure that the machines are well-maintained by offering ....

8 We provide our customers with a .... lasting 10 years.

9 If there is a faulty product, we usually offer customers ....

C Think of a product or service that you have complained about. Tell your partner what the problem was and whether it was solved.

Vocabulary file pages 170 and 176

85

Reading
Old-fashioned quality

A **Before you read the article, answer these questions.**

1 How can manufacturers guarantee product quality?

2 Which companies make the best domestic appliances (fridges, cookers, etc.)?

B **Read the article and match the headings to the correct paragraphs. Two of the headings have been done for you.**

a) Company strategy

b) Focus on detailed testing

c) High costs: increased reliability

d) Industry admiration for top quality

e) Innovation in working practices

f) Looking to the future

g) Manufacturing at home ensures quality

h) Loyalty for product that lasts

C **Match these people from the article to the summary of their views.**

1 Markus Miele   a) Miele is admired and respected by other manufacturers.

2 Nick Platt   b) Making one of the company's factories compete with other suppliers keeps them competitive.

3 Andrea Guerra   c) The company is able to keep its customers because there is confidence in its products.

D **Read the article again. Tick the factors below which have contributed to Miele's success.**

1 It has excellent quality control in its factories.

2 It changes its position in the market according to demand and fashions.

3 Its prices are very competitive.

4 It uses a lot of outside suppliers.

5 It spends more money than other manufacturers on creating new products.

6 It does a lot of testing.

7 It focuses on every detail of production.

8 Each component lasts a long time.

E **Match words or phrases from the article to these definitions.**

1 the most important company of its type in the world (noun, paragraph 1)

2 measures of quality by which the processes of producing goods in factories are judged (noun, paragraph 1)

3 to sell products more cheaply (verb, paragraph 1)

4 providing all the things that are needed without help from outside (adjective, paragraph 2)

5 employing another company to do work for you (verb, paragraph 2)

6 a high price for something special (noun, paragraph 4)

F **Discuss these questions.**

1 Can companies outsource and still maintain quality?

2 Can companies do everything in-house and remain competitive?

3 What methods or systems can companies use to maintain quality in:
   a) food production?   b) hotels?   c) airlines?   d) banking?

Miele focuses on old-fashioned quality

By Peter Marsh

1 *Company strategy*

At a time when life has rarely been tougher for manufacturers in the developed world, Miele's strategy for survival is to break almost all the rules. The German company, a global leader in high-quality domestic appliances such as washing machines and vacuum cleaners, is renowned for its high manufacturing standards and its refusal to move down-market and compete on price.

2 ....

Miele bases nearly all its manufacturing in high-cost Germany and is self-sufficient to a high degree. Rather than outsource to low-cost suppliers, it makes 4 million electric motors a year (enough for all its products) in its own plant near Cologne. Keeping the manufacturing base in the company's own plant is, Miele believes, essential to maintaining its quality standards. Sales last year were €2.2billion (£1.5billion).

3 ....

The approach is respected by Miele's industry peers. Andrea Guerra, Chief Executive of Merloni, the Italian white goods maker, regards it as the icon of quality in the industry – 'with a fantastic position at the top end'.

4 ....

The company sells appliances ranging from dishwashers to coffee machines, at a price premium of up to 70 percent over their competitors' products. It spends 12 percent of its revenue on product development – far more than the industry norm. Miele's attention to detail is legendary. Ovens are tested using machines that open and shut their doors 60,000 times to simulate the use they will have in their owners' kitchens.

5 ....

The company also believes it can make its German plants more competitive by changes in working practices. According to Markus Miele, co-owner of the company, 'We have a plant near Gütersloh that makes 50 percent of all the plastic parts we need. But we make this plant compete with outside contractors to see who gets the work for specific jobs. We make sure that the Miele plant charges prices no greater than the other bidders. This is one way we encourage our factories to make improvements and innovations in their production processes.'

6 ....

Even though Miele's manufacturing costs are higher than those of its competitors, the company says these are justified by its ability to produce appliances that – despite their high prices – people want to buy. Roughly 50 percent of Miele's manufacturing costs come from components it makes itself compared with about 30 percent for equivalent companies. But, the company says, most Miele appliances will work for 20 years, which is longer than comparable products. This, it says, is linked to the reliability of individual parts.

7 *Looking to the future*

The policy pays off, says Mr Miele. 'My father [who was in overall charge of Miele until 2002] once had a letter from an old lady in Eastern Germany. She said she didn't have much money but she was willing to pay 50 percent more for a Miele washing machine because she knew it would last for the rest of her life.' Nick Platt, a home appliance specialist at the GfK market research company, says such feelings are not uncommon. 'The company has built up a tremendous loyalty among consumers who know that the brand stands for quality,' he says.

8 ....

Miele faces a tough few years as it strives not just to keep ahead of competitors at the top end of the white goods market but also to interest new generations of increasingly cost-conscious consumers in buying machines that – in terms of kitchens – are the equivalent of luxury Swiss watches.

From the *Financial Times*

FINANCIAL TIMES
World business newspaper.

▲ Mike Ashton

Listening
Quality management

A 🎧 **10.1 Mike Ashton is Senior Vice President of Hilton Hotels International. The hotel employs 75,000 people in 65 countries. Listen to the first part of the interview. Complete the definition of quality.**

I believe the best way to define quality is to look very closely at customers' .... and then to look at the .... of a business to .... or .... those expectations, consistently.

B 🎧 **10.2 Listen to the second part of the interview. Which of the following does the hotel use to measure quality improvements?**

a) contacting guests **b)** inspecting rooms daily **c)** contacting team members

d) studying operational standards **e)** comparing check out times **f)** making unexpected visits

C 🎧 **10.3 Listen to the third part of the interview. According to Mike Ashton, why is investment in quality important?**

Language review
Gerunds and infinitives

- **We sometimes use one verb after another verb. Often the second verb is in the infinitive form.** *We can't afford to lower our standards. Should we refuse to pay them because the quality is so poor?*
- **But sometimes the second verb must be in the gerund form. This depends on the *first verb*. (See page 154 for a list of verbs that are usually followed by the gerund.)**
  My job involves maintaining production standards.
- **Some verbs can be followed by the gerund form or the infinitive form without a big change in meaning.**
  I started checking their order. / I started to check their order.
- **With other verbs, however, the meaning changes.**
  We stopped to check the machinery. (We stopped what we were doing in order to check the machinery.)
  We stopped checking the machinery. (We stopped our habit of checking the machinery.)
  page 154

A **In these sentences two of the verbs are possible and one is incorrect. Tick the two correct verbs.**

1 He .... to review our quality procedures.
   a) promised   **b)** delayed   **c)** wanted

2 I .... improving reliability.
   a) undertook   **b)** suggested   **c)** recommended

3 I .... to meet the Quality Director.
   a) decided   **b)** didn't mind   **c)** arranged

4 She .... to check the large order.
   a) refused   **b)** put off   **c)** failed

5 We .... to invest in new machinery.
   a) consider   **b)** hope   **c)** plan

B **Match these sentence halves.**

1 The board recommends	**a)** to make mistakes with this big order.
2 The factory can't afford	**b)** to turn around the company's reputation in the coming year.
3 The Research and Development department should consider	**c)** producing the faulty product.
4 The new Chief Executive promised	**d)** outsourcing some of the company's functions.
5 The factory stopped	**e)** to accept our apology for the fault.
6 The customer refused	**f)** changing its policy on product testing.

C **Choose the most appropriate form of the verb from the brackets to complete these sentences.**

1 He stopped (*working /to work*) on the project after three months because of ill-health.

2 She was driving in a hurry but she stopped (*answering /to answer*) her mobile phone.

3 Did you remember (*calling /to call*) the customer yesterday?

4 I can't remember (*offering /to offer*) you a replacement.

5 The sales assistant forgot (*giving /to give*) the customer a discount.

6 The customer forgot (*completing / to complete*) the five-year guarantee form.

Skills
Telephone complaints

A 🎧 **10.4 Listen to a customer making a complaint. Answer these questions.**

1 What is the customer's complaint?
2 What solution does the customer service representative suggest?
3 What solution does the customer want?
4 How does the call end?

B 🎧 **10.4 Listen again and complete the extracts from the dialogue.**

Customer services	I'm sorry to hear that. What .... ¹ to be the .... ²?
Customer services	Could you give me .... , ³ please?
Customer services	Can you bring it in? Then we can .... ⁴ the matter.
Customer services	I'm afraid it's .... ⁵ to replace items.
Customer	Well, that's not really .... ⁶.
Customer services	All right then. Bring the machine in and we'll see what .... ⁷ for you.

C **One of you is the Production Manager for a power tools manufacturer. The other is a supplier of components. Role play the following telephone call. Use phrases from the Useful language box below.**

Production Manager
Ring your supplier to complain about some electric motors (order No. PV205) which have a number of defects (don't fit, not up to usual standard, etc.).

Supplier
• Deal tactfully with the complaint. • Show understanding. • Get the facts. • Promise action.

Useful language

COMPLAINING

Making the complaint
I'm ringing to complain about ...
I'm sorry, but I'm not satisfied with ...
Unfortunately, there's a problem with ...

Explaining the problem
The CD player doesn't work.
There seems to be a problem with ...
We haven't received the ...

Insisting
It really isn't good enough.
I'd like to know why ...

Threatening
If you don't replace the product, I'll complain to the manager.
If you can't deliver on time, we'll have to contact other suppliers.

DEALING WITH COMPLAINTS

Showing understanding
Oh dear! Sorry to hear that.
Mmm, I see what you mean.
I'm sorry about the problem/delay.

Getting the facts
Could you give me some details, please?
What happened exactly?
What's the problem exactly?

Making excuses / denying responsibility
It's not our policy to replace items.
It's not our fault that it hasn't arrived.
I'm afraid that's not quite right.

Promising action
OK, I'll look into it right away.
I'll check the details and get back to you.

 Vocabulary file page 176

CASE STUDY

Brookfield Airport

Background

Built in the mid-1960s, Brookfield Airport, in the English Midlands, is operated by the Midland Airport Authority (MAA). In recent years, the number of passengers it handles has greatly increased because it has become a base for several budget airlines offering cheap flights to European destinations.

There is an excellent rail link from major cities in the UK to a station under the terminal building. Car parking is limited.

The terminal building, an award-winning modernist design, is now 'listed' and has a protected status. This means the structure cannot be altered in any way.

There is strong local opposition to extending the terminal or building a new runway. To cope with the increased passenger numbers, one suggestion is to schedule flights at any time of the day or night.

The rapid growth in business has brought problems. A recent survey showed that passengers had many complaints about the quality of the service at the airport.

MAA must therefore decide how to deal with the complaints and consider what action to take. There are some things MAA cannot change. The airport is always very busy at peak times.

Task

You are members of the Customer Relations Department.
1 Work in small groups. Consider the complaints and decide which:
   a) are the most important.
   b) require immediate action and which can be delayed.
   c) are more likely to be the responsibility of the airlines.
   d) are more likely to be the responsibility of the Airport Authority.
2 Meet as one group and share your ideas. Decide on an action plan.

Statistics

Total number of passengers using the terminal (per year)

five years ago 1.8 million	three years ago 2.6 million	last year 4.8 million

Results of a passenger survey

The results of a recent passenger survey have revealed several areas of complaint.

Passengers completed a questionnaire, ranking various services and facilities. The figures refer to the percentage of passengers answering the questionnaire.

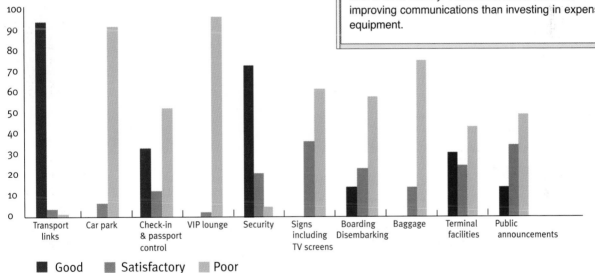

Good   Satisfactory   Poor

Listening

10.5 Listen to the passenger complaints recorded by the customer services department. Match the complaints with some of the categories in the survey.

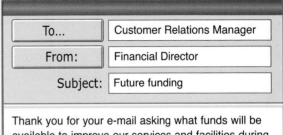

To...	Customer Relations Manager
From:	Financial Director
Subject:	Future funding

Thank you for your e-mail asking what funds will be available to improve our services and facilities during the coming year.

Because of rising costs, the funds available for improvements are limited. The Managing Director feels strongly that you should look for solutions that do not cost a lot of money. You should focus more on improving communications than investing in expensive equipment.

Writing

Write a short report for the Managing Director of Midland Airport Authority giving an action plan for the coming year to improve the services at the airport.

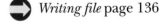

Writing file page 136

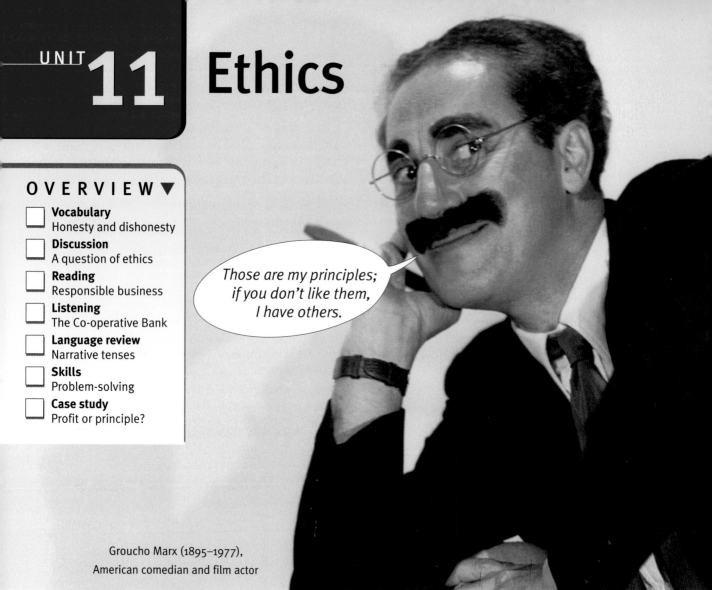

UNIT 11 Ethics

OVERVIEW ▼

☐ **Vocabulary**
Honesty and dishonesty

☐ **Discussion**
A question of ethics

☐ **Reading**
Responsible business

☐ **Listening**
The Co-operative Bank

☐ **Language review**
Narrative tenses

☐ **Skills**
Problem-solving

☐ **Case study**
Profit or principle?

Those are my principles; if you don't like them, I have others.

Groucho Marx (1895–1977),
American comedian and film actor

Starting up

A Discuss these questions.

1 What is the purpose of a business, in your opinion? Is it just to make money?

2 What do you understand by these phrases?

a) business ethics   **b)** a code of good practice   **c)** a mission statement

3 Should mission statements include statements about ethics?

B Are some jobs more ethical than others? How ethical do you think these professions are?

accountant	civil servant	lawyer	police officer
banker	estate agent	nurse	teacher
car sales executive	journalist	dentist	taxi driver

C Discuss this list of unethical activities. In your opinion, which are the worst? Are any common in your country?

1 Avoiding paying tax

2 Claiming extra expenses

3 Using work facilities for private purposes (for example, personal phone calls)

4 Accepting praise for someone else's ideas or work

5 Selling a defective product (for example, a second-hand car)

6 Using your influence to get jobs for relatives (nepotism)

7 Ringing in sick when you are not ill

8 Taking extended lunch breaks

9 Giving good references to people you want to get rid of

10 Employing people without the correct paperwork

Vocabulary
Honesty and dishonesty

A The sets of words and phrases below are related either to honesty or to dishonesty. Which word is different from the others in each set? Use a good dictionary to help you.

1 trustworthy	law-abiding	~~corrupt~~
2 a slush fund	a sweetener	compensation
3 insider trading	industrial espionage	disclosure
4 a whistleblower	a fraudster	a con artist
5 a bribe	a bonus	a commission
6 fraud	secrecy	integrity
7 a confidentiality agreement	a cover up	a whitewash

B Complete these sentences with words and phrases from the sets above. Choose from the first set to complete sentence 1, from the second set to complete sentence 2, and so on.

1 Our company does nothing illegal. We are very *law-abiding* .

2 We've got .... which is used in countries where it is difficult to do business without offering bribes.

3 Their car looked so much like our new model. We suspect ....

4 They fired him because he was .... He informed the press that the company was using under-age workers in the factory.

5 He denied accepting .... when he gave the contract to the most expensive supplier.

6 I admire our chairman. He's a man of his word and is greatly respected for his ....

7 Many companies ask new employees to sign .... to avoid future litigation problems.

Discussion
A question of ethics

A Work in groups. What should you do in each of these situations?

1 The best-qualified person for the post of Sales Manager is female. However, your customers would prefer a man. If you appoint a woman you will probably lose some sales.

2 Your company has a new advertising campaign which stresses its honesty, fairness and ethical business behaviour. It has factories in several countries where wages are very low. At present it is paying workers the local market rate.

3 A colleague working in a hospital has been making mistakes at work recently. This is because she has a serious illness. You are her friend and the only person at work who knows this. She has asked you to keep it a secret.

B Discuss these questions.

1 Why is corruption more common in some countries than in others?

2 What are the consequences of corruption in your opinion?

Reading
Responsible business

A Discuss these questions.

1 Do you think companies are responsible for
   a) people being too fat?
   b) children accessing pornography on the Internet?
   c) musicians not being paid because of illegal downloading of their music?

2 What examples can you give of businesses behaving badly?

B Read the article and answer these questions.

1 What ethical issues do these industries face?
   a) the food industry   e) the financial sector
   b) mobile phone operators   f) oil and mining groups
   c) record companies   g) footwear and clothing brands
   d) computer and telecommunications companies

2 Which areas of business do not give enough information about social and environmental matters?

3 What examples are given of companies taking positive steps?

No hiding place for the irresponsible business

By Alison Maitland

The food industry is blamed for obesity. Mobile phone operators are challenged to protect teenagers from online pornography. Record companies are attacked when they sue music-lovers for sharing illegal files on the Internet.

Big business is being asked to explain its approach to a growing number of social, ethical and environmental concerns.

'We're facing the greatest demand for our assistance that we've seen in our nine-year history,' says Bob Dunn, Chief Executive of Business for Social Responsibility (BSR), a US non-profit advisory organisation whose annual membership includes many top multinationals.

Microsoft, Lucent and United Technologies have joined BSR this year, as well as Altria, a more obvious target for pressure groups and litigation, as the parent company of both Kraft Foods and Philip Morris.

Industries that until now had avoided the spotlight are finding attention is now focusing on them. Campaigners are beginning to show interest in working conditions in factories in the developing world that make equipment for computer and telecommunications companies.

The financial sector has come under pressure over lending to controversial projects in the developing world. In June, a group of leading banks, including Citigroup, Barclays and ABN Amro, promised to avoid giving loans for socially or environmentally questionable projects.

Oil and mining groups have come under strong pressure this year from a coalition of investors, activists and the UK government to make public their payments to developing countries in an effort to fight corruption.

Some of the world's biggest footwear and clothing brands, including Levi Strauss, Nike and Reebok, have meanwhile taken voluntary measures through the US Fair Labor Association to increase the transparency of their supply chain. They published on the Internet the first independent audits of their supplier factories, along with the steps taken to improve often terrible labour standards.

Companies usually take action when they face a real or potential threat to their reputation, as when Kraft announced in July it would cut fat and sugar in its food, limit portion sizes and stop marketing in schools. A lawsuit against Kraft over fatty acids was rapidly withdrawn after it said it would address the issue.

A few companies are, however, taking a lead because they believe it will give them a competitive edge. Mr Dunn says the search for competitive advantage is one factor creating interest in corporate responsibility among companies in countries such as Russia, Poland, Turkey and South Africa.

In the UK, the trend is also reflected in the sharp rise in social and environmental reporting over the past two years. More than half the FTSE250 companies now produce annual reports, according to Directions, a study published this month by SalterBaxter and Context, two well-known UK consultancies.

Some sectors remain secretive, including hotels and leisure, and software and computer services. But they form a decreasing minority as investor interest, regulation and peer pressure combine to force greater disclosure.

When the first non-financial reports came out more than a decade ago, they focused on the environment. Now 100 of the FTSE250 cover environmental, social and ethical issues. Forty of the fifty largest European companies also produce reports. In the US, however, only 22 of the S&P top 50 reported, the study found. But how much can companies be expected to achieve on their own? What is the role of government? Can consumers have it all, demanding such high standards of companies while refusing to change their lifestyle?

From the *Financial Times*

FINANCIAL TIMES
World business newspaper.

C Which of the following groups of companies have the largest percentage of reports covering environmental, social and ethical issues?

a) FTSE250 (British)

b) US Standard and Poor's Top 50 (American)

c) 50 largest companies (European)

D Why are companies in countries such as Russia, Poland and Turkey becoming more interested in corporate responsibility?

E Check you know the meanings of the following words from the article. Use a good dictionary to help you. Then use the words to complete the text below.

controversial	corruption	transparency	threats
responsibility	regulation	peer pressure	

Companies in the oil and mining sector have been taking the issue of corporate .... ¹ much more seriously recently. They are worried about .... ² to their reputations due to rumours of .... ³ and bribery. Government .... ⁴ and .... ⁵ from other companies has resulted in more .... ⁶ in the industry and less secrecy. The aviation industry has also received attention. Senior managers have been criticised for .... ⁷ decisions regarding payments to secure contracts.

F Discuss the question.

What can **a)** consumers, **b)** shareholders and **c)** employees do to try to change the behaviour of businesses that are behaving unethically?

Listening
The Co-operative Bank

A 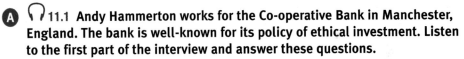 11.1 Andy Hammerton works for the Co-operative Bank in Manchester, England. The bank is well-known for its policy of ethical investment. Listen to the first part of the interview and answer these questions.

1 How was the bank's ethical policy developed?

2 How does the bank check that its policy is in touch with customers' views?

3 What example does Andy give of a business the bank will not invest in?

4 What kinds of businesses does the bank like?

B 11.2 Listen to the second part of the interview. Are the following statements true or false, according to Andy?

1 Business activity does not necessarily affect the environment and society.

2 It is easy to see how the financial services sector can affect society.

3 The bank has been actively involved in the following areas:

a) landmine removal   **b)** human rights   **c)** fair trade

▲ Andy Hammerton

C 11.3 Listen to the next part of the interview and complete these extracts.

1 The only truly successful businesses will be those that achieve a .... between their own interests and those of society and ....

2 Our position has enabled us to ...., develop our brand and have a .... on the bank's bottom line.

3 Higher trust creates .... First, because customers trust you, they are less likely to .... in the first place. Second, if you do make a mistake, they are more likely to ....

Language review
Narrative tenses

A **The sentences below describe stages in an unsuccessful product launch. Put them in a logical order.**

a) The newspapers asked questions.

b) We recalled the product.

c) The company lost a lot of money.

d) We launched the product.

e) The R & D department tested the product.

f) The number of complaints doubled.

g) People started to complain.

h) The product sold well.

B 🎧 **11.4** **Now listen to this conversation and check your answers.**

C **Answer these questions about the product launch.**

1 What was the product?

2 What was the problem?

We can use different tenses to narrate a story.

Past simple   *The newspapers **heard** about it.*
Past continuous *It **was going** really well.*
Past perfect   *We**'d tested** it for over six months, and there**'d been** no bad reaction to it.*
Present perfect *Since then, we**'ve kept** away from skin-care products.*

Which tense is normally used for:

1 setting the scene and providing background information?

2 events which happen before the story begins?

3 events in the story?

4 saying what the present results of the story are? ➡ page 155

D 🎧 **11.4** **Listen to the conversation again. Follow the audio script on page 166. Note down examples of each of these tenses:**

a) past simple   **c)** past perfect

b) past continuous   **d)** present perfect

E **Complete this text about a pharmaceutical company with the correct tenses.**

We like to think we are an ethical company, but we .... ¹ (have) a problem last year when we .... ² (launch) our new product.

Let me give you the background to the problem. The new product .... ³ (sell) very well and we .... ⁴ (get) good feedback, and sales .... ⁵ (increase) month by month. Everyone was happy.

Then it all .... ⁶ (go) wrong. In August we .... ⁷ (start) to get complaints from some doctors about one of our salesmen. They .... ⁸ (complain) about the methods that the salesman .... ⁹ (use) to persuade them to endorse the product. He ....¹⁰ (offer) them expensive gifts and .... ¹¹ (take) them to expensive restaurants. The doctors .... ¹² (feel) under pressure to promote the product.

By the end of the year we .... ¹³ (receive) over 30 complaints about that particular salesman. In December articles .... ¹⁴ (start) to appear in the press about our unethical sales methods. In the end we .... ¹⁵ (fire) the salesman. As a result of this, we .... ¹⁶ (recently issue) guidelines to all sales staff about appropriate gifts.

F Tell a story about any of these ideas.

1 A significant news event you remember well.

2 An ethical problem you know about.

3 A memorable event in your life (good or bad).

4 An unusual or memorable experience while you were travelling abroad.

5 Your first or last day in a job or organisation.

Skills
Problem-solving

A 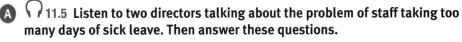 11.5 Listen to two directors talking about the problem of staff taking too many days of sick leave. Then answer these questions.

1 What are the first three solutions proposed by one of the directors to solve the problem of absenteeism?

2 What do the directors finally decide to do?

B Match the comments below to the correct headings in the Useful language box.

1 Let's discuss the advantages and disadvantages.

2 My solution, then, is to ...

3 We have a number of options.

4 Let's look at this a different way.

5 Let's think about the consequences of ...

6 It might be worth considering ...

7 What we've got to do now is ...

Useful language

a) Stating options
There are several ways we could deal with this.

b) Balancing arguments
Let's look at the pros and cons.
On the one hand ... On the other hand ...

c) Changing your approach
Let's look at this from another angle.

d) Considering less obvious options
We could try ...

e) Discussing possible effects
If we do this, then ...

f) Making a decision
The best way forward is to ...

g) Stating future action
The next thing to do is ...

C 11.5 Listen again. Tick the expressions from the Useful language box that you hear.

D Role play this situation.

> You are senior managers at a hi-fi manufacturer. Your company is losing market share. You strongly suspect your main rival is using unfair methods to promote its products.
>
> For example, you are almost sure that your rival has been:
> a) making cash payments to main dealers;
> b) offering expensive gifts to important customers.
>
> Hold a meeting to consider how to solve the problem.

CASE STUDY

Background

Nikos Takakis is the CEO of Livewire, an Australian manufacturer of electrical appliances. During the last three years, his General Manager, Carl Thomson, has turned Livewire round from being a loss-making company into a highly-profitable organisation with an exciting range of new products. Both men want the company to grow as fast as possible.

Problems

Recently a number of problems have arisen involving Carl Thomson.

- About three months ago, Bob Dexter, a senior manager, spoke to Nikos Takakis in the staff restaurant and gave him some worrying information about Carl.
- 🎧 **11.6** Listen to their conversation and note down what they say.
- A few weeks later, Nikos Takakis found out by chance that Carl had advised a friend to buy shares in Livewire just before it announced some excellent annual results (profits had risen by almost 40%). Livewire's share price rocketed and the friend made a quick profit.
- Last week, Joan Knight, Livewire's Marketing Director, sent Nikos an e-mail about an electrically operated can opener, code-named DC01, which Livewire is about to launch.

To...	Nikos Takakis
From...	Joan Knight
Subject:	DC01

I read a report in Business Weekly about new products. Rochester Electronics have put a new can opener on the market. It's electronically operated and looks just like our DC01. Yesterday, I took a look at it in a local store. Its design is very similar to ours, with just a few modifications to make it look different. Their can opener will affect sales of our DC01. Do you think someone is leaking information to Rochester Electronics? Is this industrial espionage? Or have we just been unlucky? What action do you think we should take?

• This morning Nikos Takakis received the following e-mail from Valerie Harper, Personal Assistant to Carl Thomson. Valerie joined Livewire just over a year ago. In the beginning, she seemed to be an outstanding employee, but more recently she has been having difficulties working with Carl.

To...	Nikos Takakis
From...	Valerie Harper
Subject:	Complaint about Carl Thomson

I would like to make a formal complaint about Carl Thomson.

1 As you know, I became his PA about a year ago. In the beginning our business relationship was very good. However, he wanted to have a personal relationship with me as well. It seems he was lonely following his divorce. I told him I was not interested in such an arrangement.

2 After I refused him, he completely changed his attitude towards me. He gave me orders rather than polite instructions. He criticised me if I made the smallest mistake and never praised me for good work. He also expected me to do hours of unpaid overtime. I felt constantly under pressure.

3 Because I no longer enjoyed my work, I applied for a vacancy in Accounts. Even though I am well-qualified in this area, I was not short-listed for interview.

4 I believe my application was unsuccessful because Carl Thomson wrote an unfavourable report on my work. He seems to have no integrity.

5 If I do not get a promotion in Livewire very soon, I will have to leave the company.

Please let me know what you will do to improve my situation.

Task

You are members of Livewire's board of directors.
1 Hold a meeting to discuss what action to take on the following issues:
    a) Carl's relationship with Monica Kaminsky, Design Manager for a rival company.
    b) his advice to a friend to buy shares in Livewire.
    c) the possible leak of information concerning the can opener.
    d) Valerie Harper's e-mail.
2 🎧 11.7 After finishing your meeting, listen to a conversation between Carl Thomson and Monica Kaminsky and make notes. Does it affect your decisions about any of the issues above?

Writing

Write a letter to Carl Thomson informing him of any action you are going to take concerning him, together with your reasons.

 Writing file page 132

UNIT 12 Leadership

OVERVIEW ▼

- [ ] **Vocabulary**
  Adjectives of character
- [ ] **Listening**
  Leadership qualities
- [ ] **Reading**
  The founder of Ikea
- [ ] **Language review**
  Relative clauses
- [ ] **Skills**
  Decision-making
- [ ] **Case study**
  Orbit Records

‘ *We all work together as a team. And that means you do everything I say.* ’
Michael Caine, British film actor (in the film *The Italian Job*)

Starting up

A **Discuss these questions.**

1 Which modern or historical leaders do you most admire? Which do you admire the least? Why?

2 What makes a great leader? Write down a list of characteristics. Compare your list with other groups.

3 Are there differences between men and women as leaders? Why have most great leaders been men?

4 Are people who were leaders at school more likely to be leaders later in life?

5 What makes a bad leader? Draw up a profile of factors.

6 What is the difference between a *manager* and a *leader*?

B **In groups, think of someone in a powerful position. List three positive qualities and three negative qualities about this person. Then compare your ideas.**

Vocabulary
Adjectives of character

A Which of the adjectives below would you use to describe an ideal leader? Give reasons for your choice. What adjectives would you add?

decisive	informal	accessible	motivating
charismatic	passionate	thoughtful	impulsive
cautious	adventurous	flexible	opportunistic
aggressive	energetic	persuasive	open
magnetic	ruthless		

B Can you think of adjectives with opposite meanings to the ones above?
decisive – indecisive

C Read what some commentators think about leadership. Do you agree with their ideas?

> Leadership is not magnetic personality – that can just as well be a glib tongue. It is not 'making friends and influencing people' – that is flattery. Leadership is lifting a person's vision to higher things, the raising of a person's performance to a higher standard, the building of a personality beyond its normal limitations.
>
> *Peter F. Drucker, author and management theorist*

> A leader is best when people barely know he exists, not so good when people obey and acclaim him, worse when they despise him. ... But of a good leader who talks little when his work is done, his aim fulfilled, they will say, 'We did it ourselves'.
>
> *Anonymous*

> Good leaders make people feel that they're at the heart of things, not at the periphery. Everyone feels he or she makes a difference to the success of the organisation. When that happens, people feel centred and that gives their work meaning.
>
> *Warren Bennis, author and professor of business administration*

> If there is a trait that does characterise leaders it is opportunism. Leaders are people who seize opportunity and take risks. Leadership then seems to be a matter of personality and character.
>
> *John Viney, former Chairman of Heidrick and Struggles, top recruitment consultants*

Listening
Leadership qualities

▲ Max Landsberg

A 🎧 12.1 Max Landsberg is a partner at Heidrick and Struggles, the international executive search consultants. Listen to the first part of an interview. What three qualities do leaders of large companies usually have?

B 🎧 12.2 Listen to the second part of the interview. Max talks about the ways that leaders can develop their skills.

1 Match the following percentages – 70%, 20%, 10% – with the development activity.

   a) training   b) coaching   c) on the job

2 What, according to Max, is the main way that companies develop leaders?

C 🎧 12.3 Listen to the third part of the interview. Max talks about three leaders that have influenced or impressed him. Make notes on what he says about each one.

Nelson Mandela   Winston Churchill   Bernie Ellis

Reading
The founder of Ikea

A The following article is about Ingvar Kamprad, the founder of Ikea, the home furnishings retail giant. Which of the following do you expect Ingvar to do or to be?

- drive an old car
- travel first class
- be dyslexic
- be formal
- be careful with money
- dress smartly
- love detail
- make short-term decisions

B Read the article to check your answers to Exercise A.

The bolt that holds the Ikea empire together

By Christopher Brown Humes

Ingvar Kamprad is no ordinary multi-billionaire. The founder of the Ikea furniture empire travels economy class, drives a 10-year-old Volvo and buys his fruit and vegetables in the afternoons, when prices are often cheaper. Ask him about the luxuries in his life and he says: 'From time to time, I like to buy a nice shirt and cravat and eat Swedish caviar'.

Mr Kamprad is one of Europe's greatest post-war entrepreneurs. What began as a mail-order business in 1943 has grown into an international retailing phenomenon across 31 countries, with 70,000 employees.

Sales have risen every single year. The Ikea catalogue is the world's biggest annual print run – an incredible 110m copies a year. And Mr Kamprad has grown extraordinarily rich. He is worth $13.4bn (£8.7bn) and is the 17th richest person in the world, according to Forbes, the US magazine.

The concept behind Ikea's amazing success is unbelievably simple: make affordable, well-designed furniture available to the masses. And then there is Mr Kamprad himself – charismatic, humble, private. It is his ideas and values that are at the core of Ikea's philosophy.

Best known for his extremely modest lifestyle, he washes plastic cups to recycle them. He has just left his long-standing Swedish barber because he found one in Switzerland, where he lives, who charges only SFr14 (£6) for a cut. 'That's a reasonable amount,' he chuckles.

All Ikea executives are aware of the value of cost-consciousness. They are strongly discouraged from travelling first or business class. 'There is no better form of leadership than setting a good example. I could never accept that I should travel first class while my colleagues sit in tourist class,' Mr Kamprad says.

As he walks around the group's stores, he expresses the feeling of 'togetherness' physically, clasping and hugging his employees. This is very uncharacteristic of Sweden. 'Call me Ingvar,' he says to staff. The informality and lack of hierarchy are emphasised by his dress style, with an open-necked shirt preferred to a tie.

Mr Kamprad has had both personal and business battles. He has fought against dyslexia and illness.

One of Mr Kamprad's characteristics is his obsessive attention to detail. When he visits his stores, he talks not only to the managers but also to the floor staff and customers. A recent visit to six of the group's Swedish stores has produced '100 details to discuss', he says.

By his own reckoning, his greatest strength is choosing the right people to run his businesses.

He is determined that the group will not go public, because short-term shareholder demands conflict with long-term planning. 'I hate short-termist decisions. If you want to take long-lasting decisions, it's very difficult to be on the stock exchange. When entering the Russian market, we had to decide to lose money for 10 years.'

Mr Kamprad has been slowly withdrawing from the business since 1986, when he stepped down as group president. He maintains that he is still 'too much involved and in too many details', although he admits to a distinct reluctance to withdraw altogether.

The question is: can there be an eternal Ikea without Mr Kamprad? Does the group depend too much on its founder? Will the empire continue, as control of Ikea gradually moves to Mr Kamprad's three sons?

From *the Financial Times*

FINANCIAL TIMES
World business newspaper.

C What winning formula is behind Ikea's success?

D Read the article again and make notes about Mr Kamprad under these headings.

Wealth	Personality	Lifestyle	Leadership style

E Find words or phrases in the article that match these definitions.

a) an awareness of the price of things ....

b) the feeling you have when you are part of a group of people who have a close
relationship with each other ....

c) a relaxed and friendly situation without too many rules of correct
behaviour ....

d) the lack of a system in an organisation where a group of people have power
or control ....

e) an extremely strong focus on every small fact or piece of information
....

F Discuss these questions.

1 What, in your opinion, are the strengths and weaknesses of Ingvar
Kamprad?

2 Would you like to work for him?

3 When is the correct time for a leader or founder to leave his or her
company?

Language review
Relative clauses

Defining clauses provide essential information about the subject or object of a sentence. Without this information the sentence often does not make sense or has a different meaning.

- *Who* or *that* are used for people.
  *People **who** are in leadership roles often have to act alone.*

- *Which* or *that* are used for things.
  *It is his ideas and values **that** are at the core of Ikea's philosophy.*

Non-defining clauses provide *extra* information about the subject or object of a sentence. The sentence still makes sense without this information.

- *Who* (not *that*) is used for people.
  *Ingvar Kamprad, **who** is the 17th richest person in the world, drives an old Volvo.*

- *Which* (not *that*) is used for things.
  *Ikea, **which** recently entered the Russian market, remains a private company.*

➡ page 155

A Complete the sentences in the job advertisement below with *who* or *which*.

Qtxt

Managing Director
c. €270,000 plus expatriate package, Europe-based

Qtxt is a leading European mobile technology services provider ....¹ enables clients to provide high-quality mobile marketing and mobile content solutions. Founded in 1993, Qtxt is a fast-growing company .... ² is looking for a first-class leader .... ³ can meet the challenge of international growth. We are seeking a highly motivated candidate .... ⁴ must be fluent in three European languages. We need a Managing Director .... ⁵ will rise to the challenge and .... ⁶ will provide strong strategic leadership. The successful candidate will lead a winning team .... ⁷ achieved record sales last year.

In the first instance and in complete confidence, please write with CV to Marie Foussat at: M.Richaud, 19 rue de Trevise, Paris 75009, France.

B Use the relative pronouns below to complete these quotations.

| who | which | that | where |

1 'The job for big companies, the challenge .... we all face as bureaucrats, is to create an environment .... people can reach their dreams.' *Jack Welch (US business leader)*

2 'He .... has never learned to obey cannot be a good commander.' *Aristotle (Greek philosopher)*

3 'A leader shapes and shares a vision, ... gives point to the work of others.' *Charles Handy (British writer)*

4 'A leader should be humble. A leader should be able to communicate with his people. A leader is someone .... walks out in front of his people, but he doesn't get too far out in front, to where he can't hear their footsteps.' *Tommy Lasorda (US sports personality)*

5 'A leader is someone .... knows what they want to achieve and can communicate that.' *Margaret Thatcher (British politician)*

C In the article below the relative pronouns are missing. Add the pronouns to the text, where appropriate.

Leader turns Porsche around

By Uta Harnischfeger and Wendelin Wiedeking

Wendelin Wiedeking, is the head of Porsche, drives a red Porsche 9114S cabriolet. He smokes thick Cohiba cigars 5 and likes to discuss golf, sports cars and organic farming. Mr Wiedeking, has won many German 'manager of the year' awards, will need all his 10 leadership skills to pull Porsche through its latest difficulties. He is admired for putting up a fight against the Frankfurt stock exchange 15 operator, Deutsche Börse, expelled Porsche after Mr Wiedeking refused to publish quarterly reports. He laughs when he recalls Porsche's 1994 20 capital issue, sold out in a few hours after Deutsche Bank had refused to underwrite the deal. His favourite stories centre on his home-grown potatoes, he harvests 25 with a bright red 1960s vintage Porsche tractor, a wedding present from his wife. Mr Wiedeking, is credited with saving Porsche from bankruptcy in the early 1990s, has 30 turned the legendary sports car into a coveted brand and has made Porsche the world's most profitable car maker.

From *the Financial Times*

FINANCIAL TIMES
World business newspaper.

Skills

Decision-making

A Discuss these questions.

1 How important are rational and emotional factors when making decisions about the following?

| a present for someone | a new company logo | a partner |
| a holiday destination | a new product to develop | someone for a job |

2 Think of an important decision that you have made. How did you decide?

3 Do you think men and women have different ways of making decisions?

4 Who makes the big decisions in your household?

B Which ideas below do you agree with? Which do you disagree with? Why?

1 Before making a decision it is advisable to:
   a) write down the pros and cons.
   b) take a long time.
   c) have a sleep or a rest.
   d) consult a horoscope.
   e) consult as many people as possible.
2 If a choice has cost you a lot of time and money, stick to it.
3 Rely on the past to help you make a decision.
4 Reduce all decisions to a question of money.
5 Be totally democratic in group decision-making.

C 🎧 12.4 Listen to the management of a retail group discussing the problem of their store in Paris. Tick the expressions in the Useful language box that you hear.

Useful language

Asking for the facts
Can you bring us up to date?
Can you give us the background?
Where do we stand with ...?

Making a suggestion
We should sell out as soon as possible.
Why don't we sell out?

Disagreeing
I don't agree with that at all.
I totally disagree.

Identifying needs
We've got to get more information.
We need more information about where we're going wrong.

Agreeing
You're absolutely right.
I totally agree with you.

Expressing doubt
I am worried about the store's location.
I'm not sure about that.

Making a decision
The solution, then, is to keep the store going.
I think, on balance, we feel we should keep the store going.

Stating future action
So, the next thing to do is ...
What we've got to do now is ...

D 🎧 12.5 Listen to a marketing consultant presenting her report to the management of a retail group. Complete these extracts.

1 I .... you review your product ranges as soon as possible.
2 What .... is more knowledge of the youth market.
3 I think .... a top executive to run that part of the business.
4 I'm .... with the furniture department.
5 I just .... it will ever make much money for you.
6 I also have .... about your stationery department.
7 The answer .... is to do something quickly.
8 So, this is .... now. In my opinion reduce your range of products, cut out the loss makers.

E Choose a section in the Useful language box for each of the missing words and phrases 1 to 8.

F Role play this situation. You are board members of a manufacturing firm. As your company is making a loss, you must cut costs. Hold a meeting to decide which one of these options to follow.

- Cut factory workers' wages by 10%
- Pay no end-of-year bonuses
- Make 50 employees redundant
- Reduce everyone's salary by 8%

CASE STUDY

ORBIT
RECORDS

Background

Orbit Records was founded in London 20 years ago, and now has 12 large stores in the UK and five in Germany. The company grew quickly because it had a successful marketing strategy. The stores offer a wide range of CDs which they sell at reasonable prices. Their record stores carry over 80,000 titles – about three times more than their main competitors.

About five years ago, Orbit stores diversified into selling computer games, DVDs, videos, T-shirts, adventure holidays, concert tickets, books and comics. Not all the new areas of business were profitable and, as a result, the company's profits fell sharply.

A change of leadership

After the founder of Orbit Records died, a new Chief Executive, Sheldon Drake, took over. However he failed because he had no clear vision of where the company was going. Also he did not communicate well with employees, who started to lose confidence in the business. They began to worry about losing their jobs and their morale suffered.

Three months ago Sheldon Drake resigned and his place was taken by someone from outside the company.

Task of the new CEO

One of the new CEO's main tasks was to motivate staff and raise morale, so that staff would be more productive. The HR Department sent questionnaires to all employees below senior management level. The results are summarised in the chart on the next page.

STAFF ATTITUDES (%)	Yes	No	Don't know
1 Do you feel you participate fully in decision-making?	12	70	18
2 Do you feel valued by the company?	48	46	6
3 Do you understand the company's objectives and overall strategy?	16	20	64
4 Do you have enough contact with senior management?	18	50	32
5 Do you have enough opportunities to express your ideas or make suggestions?	42	26	30
6 Are you paid adequately?	48	45	7
7 Do you think you will be working for this company in five years' time?	25	14	61
8 Do you have enough opportunities to meet each other socially?	55	42	3

Task

1 Work in small groups. Discuss the results of the survey. What are the most important findings?
2 Think of six practical ideas for motivating staff, improving morale and increasing loyalty. Note them down.
3 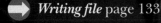 12.6 Listen and make notes on the CEO's ideas on these issues.
4 Choose the six best ideas from the CEO's list and your own list, giving reasons for your choices.
5 As one group, try to agree on the six best ideas for further action.

Writing

You are the manager of an Orbit Records store. Write a persuasive e-mail to the agent of a famous recording star inviting them to visit your store. Explain why you want the star to come to the store and what you expect them to do if they accept your invitation. Offer a suitable fee for the visit.

➡ *Writing file* page 133

OVERVIEW ▼

☐ **Vocabulary**
Describing innovations

☐ **Reading**
Innovation at Procter
and Gamble

☐ **Language review**
Passives

☐ **Listening**
Presentation techniques

☐ **Skills**
Presenting

☐ **Case study**
Style is everything

> *Innovation! One cannot be forever innovating. I want to create classics.*
>
> Coco Chanel (1883–1971), French fashion designer

Starting up

What are the most important innovations for you in your daily life? Think about the following areas.

- communication
- transport
- home entertainment
- food
- other

What innovations would you most like to see in the areas above?

Vocabulary
Describing innovations

A The nouns below are often used when talking about innovation. Check that you know the meanings of the words and phrases in the box and complete the extract from the talk below.

> drawing board   prototype   brainwave   patent   concept
> ~~discovery~~   setback   R & D (research and development)
> breakthrough   pioneers

The idea of a lone inventor who makes a ...*discovery*...¹ or has a sudden clever idea or .... ² is maybe a little out of date today. While these types of .... ³ do still exist, these days companies often have large .... ⁴ departments – teams of people who are constantly innovating and perfecting designs. Perhaps they begin with a .... ⁵ and then build a .... , ⁶ or working model. Sometimes during testing there is a .... ⁷ when it becomes clear the design has a fault. At this point maybe it is time to start again or go back to the .... ⁸. More work is done and there is a .... ⁹ – a solution is found. The product can be retested and then, hopefully, manufactured. The company will apply for a .... ¹⁰ for the design so that others cannot copy it and steal the idea.

B 🎧 13.1 Listen and check your answers to Exercise A.

C The adjectives below can be used to describe inventions or new ideas. Which have a positive meaning? Which have a negative meaning? Write + or – next to each one.

> brilliant   beneficial   silly   life-saving
> pointless   ridiculous   time-saving   annoying
> wasteful   life-changing   practical   money-saving
> revolutionary   space-saving   ground-breaking

D Look at the following list of twentieth-century innovations. In your opinion, which is:
- the most important?
- the most controversial?
- the most useful?
- the most unpopular?

Use words from Exercise C to describe the innovations. What other innovations would you add to the list?

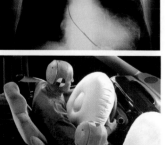

1900	the escalator
1901	the vacuum cleaner
1923	the traffic signal
1950	the heart pacemaker
1956	TV remote control
1973	cars with airbags
1974	the Post-it note
1979	personal stereo
1986	laptop computer
1987	disposable contact lenses
1994	GM (genetically-modified) tomatoes
1997	Dolly the sheep (The first mammal cloned from an adult cell.)

Reading
Innovation at Procter and Gamble

A Do you know which of the following products Procter and Gamble manufactures?

- cars
- shampoo
- washing powder
- furniture
- toothpaste
- anti-ageing cream

B Read the first three paragraphs of the article and answer these questions.

1 How is Procter and Gamble better than its competitors in terms of innovation?

2 How has Procter and Gamble benefited from organic growth?

3 Which companies are having problems innovating?

4 Which of these statements is true?

   a) Over 66 percent of senior executives think innovation is very important.

   b) More than 50 percent of senior executives are pleased with the return on their investment in innovation.

C Read the rest of the article. Choose the correct heading for steps 1 to 6 of Lafley's model for innovation from the list below.

- One-on-one consumer research
- Reach outside for ideas
- Stop testing so much
- Give designers more power
- Know what not to do
- Get employees to exchange ideas

Inside Procter and Gamble's innovation machine

By Patricia Sellers

A. G. Lafley, the CEO of Procter and Gamble, has brought a lot of creativity and rigor to P&G's innovation process. During the past 2 years, P&G has raised its new-product hit
5 rate (the percentage of new entries that deliver a return above the cost of capital) from 70% to 90%. That's terrific in an industry where half of new products fail within 12 months, according to market
10 research firm Information Resources. 'In the 18 years that I've followed Procter,' says Deutsche Bank analyst Andrew Shore, 'I have never seen the company this good'.

Organic growth – meaning growth from core
15 businesses, excluding gains from acquisitions – is at the root of P&G's transformation. According to Lafley, organic growth strengthens a company's ability to innovate.

20 Coke, Kraft and Unilever are just a few of the giants that are struggling to innovate and build the brands they already have. According to a recent Boston Consulting Group survey of senior executives, more than two-thirds
25 say innovation is a priority, but 57% are dissatisfied with the returns on their innovation investments.

Lafley has a model for innovating in a big company:
1 *One-on-one consumer research*
30 Jim Stengel, Procter's Chief Marketing Officer, has cut his reliance on focus groups – the conventional method for studying consumers. 'You don't really learn anything insightful,' he says, contending that P&G and
35 its rivals have already met consumers' obvious needs and that today's opportunities lie in meeting needs that consumers may not articulate. So he has urged the marketers to spend lots of time with consumers in their
40 homes, watching the ways they wear their clothes, clean their floors, and asking them about their habits and frustrations.

2 ....
Procter and Gamble has 7,500 R & D people located in nine countries. In order to collect
45 feedback over this vast area, the company encourages employees (both scientists and marketers) to post problems on an internal website. Lafley evaluates the ideas that have been shared between employees. Each year
50 he presents his findings in half-day 'innovation reviews' for each business unit.

3 ....
Lafley says that his goal is to get half of P&G's invention from external sources, up from 20% four years ago and about 35%
55 today. 'Inventors are evenly distributed in the population, and we're as likely to find invention in a garage as in our labs,' he explains.

4 ....
It's not the P&G way to put out a product
60 without test-marketing it. But consumer testing takes time – a luxury that P&G executives increasingly don't have. Says Susan Arnold, P&G's beauty queen: 'We don't have time to cross all the T's and dot all
65 the I's. This business is trend-based and fashion-based. You have to be intuitive.' By cutting down on test-marketing (but not, mind you, on science), P & G has reduced product launch time from laboratory to roll-out from
70 three years to eighteen months company-wide.

5 ....
Lafley believes that P&G needs to market not just the product itself but the consumer's experience of the product – how it looks,
75 smells and feels. Three years ago he added a head of design at P&G, a company veteran named Claudia Kotchka, who reports directly to him. Her designers used to labour in anonymity on logos and packaging. But they
80 are now deeply involved in all aspects of product development. For Olay Regenerist, they helped with the formulation and the fragrance too.

6 ....
In an attempt to encourage growth, some
85 companies offer fat bonuses for innovation or hire stars from outside. Lafley hasn't done either of those things. He doesn't need to revamp pay schemes, he says, noting that managers who fail to share ideas simply do
90 not get promoted. He does motivate the rank and file by giving out modest rewards, such as giving 50 stock options, for creative ideas and by celebrating innovators on P&G's internal website.

From *Fortune Magazine*

D **Find words or phrases in the article which mean the following:**

1 recruitment of an experienced person

2 additional payments for innovation

3 customer habits

4 the company's intranet

5 laboratories

6 shorter time for introducing products

Language review
Passives

- We make passive verb forms with the verb *to be* + the past participle.
  *The World Wide Web **was invented** by Tim Berners-Lee.*
- We often choose a passive structure when we are not interested in who performs an action or it is not necessary to know.
  *The Millennium Technology Prize **was awarded** to Tim Berners-Lee.*
- If we want to mention who performs the action, we can use *by*:
  *Tim Berners-Lee **was named** as one of the top 20 thinkers of the twentieth century **by** Time magazine.*
- We often use a passive structure to be impersonal or formal (for example, in notices, announcements or reports):
  *It **has been agreed** that the prototype **will be tested** next month.* page 156

▲ Tim Berners-Lee, 'Father of the Web'

A **Look at these sentences from an article on the inventor of the World Wide Web. Which use passives?**

1 The inventor of the World Wide Web, Tim Berners-Lee, has won a prestigious award.

2 The 'Father of the Web' was named as the first winner of the Millennium Technology Prize.

3 The British scientist was knighted for his pioneering work in 2003.

4 In the early 1990s, his computer code was called 'the World Wide Web'.

5 The Web has enhanced many people's ability to obtain information central to their lives.

6 Just under 80 people from 22 countries were nominated for the prize.

7 The Millennium Technology Prize was set up by the Finnish Technology Award Foundation.

8 Sir Tim is now based at the Massachusetts Institute of Technology in Boston.

9 He founded the World Wide Web Consortium at MIT in 1994.

10 He was born in London in 1955.

B **The sentences below describe stages in the launch of a new drug. Use the verbs in the box to complete the sentences. Then put the stages in a more logical order.**

develop	test	publish	test	grant
train	approve	carry out	apply for	

a) The drug .... on animals.

b) The drug .... in the labs.

c) Market research ....

d) The drug .... on humans.

e) The trials .... by the Ethics committee.

f) A licence ....

g) The results of the trials ....

h) Approval .... by the authorities.

i) The drug representatives ....

C Use the notes below to describe stages in the launch of a new car. Include passive and active structures. Use words like *first*, *next*, *then* and *finally*.

1 designer – choose
2 design – produce
3 model – build
4 modifications – make R & D department and engineers
5 design – modify
6 prototype – build
7 new engine – use – or existing engine develop – can be very costly

8 new model – test – special roads
9 deal with problems – costly if problems serious
10 journalists – invite – test-drive model
11 reviews – write – by journalists – major newspapers and car magazines
12 model – display – famous motor exhibition – Geneva or London Motor Show

Listening
Presentation techniques

A 🎧 13.2 Listen to Eve Jones, an expert on presentations, and answer these questions.

1 What does Eve say you need to do to prepare for a presentation?
2 What can you do at the beginning of a presentation to attract people's attention?
3 What is a typical structure of a presentation?

B 🎧 13.3 Listen to the second part of Eve's talk and complete the sentences below.

1 Most people are .... before a presentation.
2 Many people .... the opening and that helps them calm their nerves.
3 Keep good .... with your audience, even when using equipment.
4 It is important to develop a .... with your audience to create a good atmosphere.
5 .... can be useful to emphasise important points.
6 Avoid .... in case your audience doesn't understand it.

Skills
Presenting

A Comment on the following statements. In your opinion are they:
a) essential   b) helpful   c) unhelpful for a successful presentation?

1 Tell a joke at the beginning to relax the atmosphere.
2 Speak more slowly than you normally do.
3 Smile a lot.
4 Involve the audience.
5 Invite questions during the presentation.
6 Always keep to your plan.
7 Move around during your presentation.
8 Use gestures to emphasise important points.
9 Read out your presentation from a script.
10 Stand up when giving your presentation.

B What other useful techniques do you know for giving a presentation?

C 🎧 13.4 Listen to a presentation addressed to a company's sales team about the launch of their new chocolate bar. Tick the expressions in the Useful language box that you hear.

Useful language

Introducing yourself
Good morning, everyone.
Hello everyone, welcome to ...

Structuring the presentation
I'm going to divide my talk into four parts.
First, I'll give you ... . After that, ... Finally, ...

Inviting questions
If you have any questions, don't hesitate to ask.
I'll be glad to answer any questions (at the end of my talk).

Giving background information
I'll give you some background.
Let's start with the background.

Referring to the audience's knowledge
As you know, ...
As you are aware, ...

Changing the topic
Right, let's move on to ...
OK, I'll now look at ...

Referring to visuals
If you look at the graph ...
Could I draw your attention to the chart?

Concluding
To sum up, ...
To summarise, ...

Ending
Thanks very much. Any questions?
Well, that's all I have to say.
Thank you for listening.

D Prepare a short presentation of three to five minutes. Choose one of the situations below.

Topic	Audience	Suggestions	
A country you have visited on holiday or done business in	A group of people who will shortly be working there	• way of life • transport • accommodation • food and drink • standard of living	• customs and traditions • weather • language • people • entertainment
Your company's main competitors	The board of directors of your company	• identifying the competition • their strengths and weaknesses • how powerful they are in the market	
Your job	A group of high school students at a careers evening	• responsibilities and tasks • the future • perks and special advantages, e.g. foreign travel • qualifications • career structure	

E Now make your presentations in groups. After each presentation rate the following aspects of the presentation from 1 to 5 (1 = unacceptable, 2 = fair, 3 = average, 4 = good, 5 = excellent).

	1	2	3	4	5
The presentation was interesting.					
The presentation was clear.					
The presentation's beginning made an impact.					
The presentation had a logical structure.					
The presentation had a summary or conclusion.					
TOTAL: 25					

Style is everything

Background

The International Clothing Association (ICA) represents clothing manufacturers and retailers. Its main aim is to promote innovative new products in the clothing industry. Each year, the ICA awards prizes to companies with outstanding new ideas. Companies send a detailed product description and a marketing plan, and the four best products are selected. These companies then present their products to a panel of judges. The presentations are televised and the event is broadcast worldwide.

ICA guidelines to competitors

1 The purpose of the competition is to encourage innovation in the clothing industry.

2 Any product with innovative features may be entered.

3 Product concepts should be creative and have excellent sales potential.

4 It will be an advantage if a company's management team presents their product effectively and show that they are a good team.

5 Judges will award extra points for companies which use unusual materials in the manufacture of their clothes. Originality and imagination will be particularly valued by the judges

Guidelines for presenters

1 Introduce your team. Outline the structure of your presentation.

2 Describe the product design, features and consumer benefits.

3 Describe the product's target market.

4 Mention other competing products.

5 Present your strategy for the new product. For example:
  - branding, packaging, other product features (guarantee, etc.)
  - pricing strategy
  - distribution (What sales outlets will be used?)
  - promotion (What advertising, product launch and sales promotion?)

6 Describe any ideas for television or radio commercials.

New materials

The clothing industry shows great interest in new materials as these extracts from fashion magazines show.

Innovative designs at ICA awards

There was huge excitement and tension before Vivienne Lordan, President of the International Clothing Association, announced the winner and runner-up of the competition.

When the result was announced, cheers and applause greeted the popular winner. Ludmilla Petrova from Russia won first prize. Smiling, often in tears, she accepted the prize and thanked the judges for the award. After congratulating the other competitors on the quality of their work, she said that she hoped many people all over the world would enjoy the products her company had created.

▲ *Newsline* magazine article on last year's competition

s and Belts

a girl carry in her handbag? Well, just
thing these days and more besides.
these days get away with a 'smallish'
ying a briefcase as well. You never know
ou will need before you get back to your
ce / hotel.

leather bags are always in style – this
k out for textured leathers and mock
The more tailored the bag, the more

here is more to handbag design than the
Adventurous designers are creating bags
s of new materials: modern bags in
slick space-age plastics and printed fabrics;
al bags in soft pretty fabrics, embroidery
ls.

Clothes That Change Colour

All too often, you eagerly open a clothes catalogue and find something you'd like to wear – but it's in a colour you hate. A new thread, developed for the military, will make this kind of disappointment a thing of the past.

At Massachusetts Institute of Technology, Professor Joel Fink has developed an innovative process to combine plastic and glass. The result: a new fibre that can reflect all the light that hits it, from any direction. The new thread will be used to make military uniforms. However, it could enjoy a major commercial future in fashion.

Clothing could be made from the fibre and equipped with a tiny battery pack. When you want to change your suit or dress from, say, black to red, you flick a switch and your clothes change colour.

Some experts think that the fibre is 'incredibly revolutionary'. The fashion industry 'might start by using the thread in accessories, to change the colour of a bag or a hat or a scarf. For men I can see it used to make jackets and even shoes.'

ny is competing for the ICA's top
lieve that you have an outstanding
ncept.
ur product presentation and
to the rest of the group. Answer
ons they may have.
are not making a presentation,
member of the judging panel.
o should get the top prize. (You
te for your own product concept.)

Writing

Write a press release about this year's competition for the ICA website.

 Writing file page 132.

Competition

Competition brings out the best in products and the worst in people.

David Sarnoff (1891–1971), American businessman

OVERVIEW ▼

☐ **Vocabulary**
Competition idioms

☐ **Reading**
Losing competitive edge

☐ **Listening**
Staying competitive

☐ **Language review**
Modals of probability

☐ **Skills**
Negotiating

☐ **Case study**
Beverley Watches

A Before doing the quiz below, do you think you are:

a) very competitive?

b) fairly competitive?

c) not at all competitive?

B Answer the questions in the quiz. Then turn to page 145 to find out your score. Compare your score with a partner.

How competitive are you?

1 **Which of the following statements do you agree with?**
a) Winning is everything.
b) It's not the winning that counts, it's the taking part.
c) We are in this world to help each other.

2 **Which of the following would satisfy you?**
a) Earning more than anyone else you know.
b) Earning more than most of your friends.
c) Earning enough to have a comfortable life.

3 **You have just won €50,000 and need to buy a new car. Do you:**
a) spend €12,000 on a reliable car that will get you from A to B?
b) spend €26,000 on a middle-range car?
c) spend the entire €50,000 on a flashy top-of-the-range car that will impress all your friends?

4 **If a colleague did something very successful, would you feel:**
a) pleased for them?
b) pleased for them, but a bit jealous?
c) very jealous and unhappy?

5 **If you lose at something, do you:**
a) forget about it immediately?
b) think about it for a while?
c) never forget?

6 **How do you feel when you win? Do you:**
a) boast about it and tell everyone?
b) feel good, but keep it to yourself?
c) feel sorry for the person who lost?

7 **What do you want for your children? Do you want them:**
a) to be happy?
b) to achieve more than you did?
c) to be the best at everything?

8 **You are at the traffic lights next to another car. The lights change to 'go'. Do you:**
a) let the other car go first?
b) move away slowly, without being aware of the other car?
c) try to be the first away?

9 **You are waiting to check in at a crowded airline counter. There does not seem to be a system of queuing. Would you:**
a) push your way to the front?
b) insist loudly that a fair system is adopted?
c) keep quiet and wait?

10 **How do you feel about doing this quiz? Do you want to:**
a) show you are the most competitive person in the group?
b) show you are the least competitive person in the group?
c) find out something about yourself?

Vocabulary
Competition idioms

A There are many idioms from sport used in business, particularly when talking about competition. Use the nouns from the box to complete these idioms.

| game | ~~field~~ | ball | seat | horse | goalposts | race | neck |

1 a level playing ....*field*....
2 in the driving ....
3 to be neck and ....
4 flogging a dead ....
5 move the ....
6 keep your eye on the ....
7 ahead of the ....
8 a one horse ....

B Which of the idioms in Exercise A refer to:

a) a situation of fair competition? *1*
b) being in front of the competition?
c) being at the same level as the competition?
d) being the only competitor?
e) wasting your time on a hopeless situation?
f) staying focused?
g) a change in the rules?
h) being in control?

C Complete the following with the most suitable idiom from Exercise A. Remember to choose the correct verb form where necessary.

1 It's not a level .*playing field*. any more. As a small company it is difficult for us to compete with the big multinationals.
2 They are so far ahead of their competitors in terms of new products that it has become .... It will be years before they face any serious competition.
3 We have left all our competitors behind. We spend a lot of money on R & D so we can stay ....
4 The government have changed all the rules for exporters. They have .... , so we will have to rethink our international operation.
5 It's a waste of time continuing with the project. It will never work. We are ....
6 With our market dominance in the US, we are really ....
7 We have exactly the same market share as our nearest rival. We .... in terms of our profits so far this year, too.
8 We really need to concentrate on what our competitors are doing. In today's market you need to .... at all times.

D Discuss these questions.

1 Have you ever felt you were *flogging a dead horse*
   a) at work? b) in your private life?
2 Which companies are *ahead of the game* in your industry or the industry you would like to work in?
3 How do you feel when
   a) someone *moves the goalposts*?
   b) you are *in the driving seat*?

Reading
Losing competitive edge

A Discuss these questions. Then read the article.

1 Who are the main competitors of the following companies?

Coca-Cola Nike Levi Strauss Nokia Evian

2 What actions can a company take to compete against its rivals?

3 Suggest five words or phrases which you associate with Nokia.

Nokia and the insistent ringing of competition

By John Gapper

In 1983, Nike enjoyed dominance of its industry, with a market share of more than 35 percent, having crushed Adidas, its original rival. But a tiny competitor was about to knock it sideways: Reebok.

A similar situation exists today with Nokia and Samsung. Although the Finnish company's share of the global market for mobile handsets is similar to Nike's in athletic shoes 21 years ago, its South Korean competitor has momentum. Samsung's camera phones, with twisting flip-up screens that allow users to take, send and display photos quickly and easily, are hot; Nokia's are not.

Samsung's market capitalisation exceeded that of Nokia last week as this fact became evident in the companies' first-quarter results. Even more annoying for Nokia is the transfer of something intangible, yet highly valuable: market leadership. The high end of the market – phones that retail for $300 or more in the US – is no longer Nokia's. Samsung makes the expensive camera phone that a young consumer wants to have.

Nokia seems to realise how potentially serious its situation is, but two obstacles stand in the way of Nokia regaining authority. One (product design) should be solvable, given the company's heritage. The other (that Samsung is South Korean) will be harder to tackle, as other western companies are likely to find as well.

Design should be Nokia's strength, since it originally overtook Motorola by turning handsets into handsome and desirable consumer goods, rather than bland technological objects. Yet in its recent models, Nokia appears to have forgotten the first rule of modernist design – that form follows function. Instead, it has placed most emphasis on making its handsets colourful and zappy, with snap-on covers.

Samsung's approach to digital communication has more substance. Its twisting flip-up screen is a neat way of making the most of camera technology. The screen can even be folded outwards, so friends' photos appear when they call.

There is no obvious reason why Nokia should not regain its lead in design. But Samsung has another advantage, which is more difficult for any European rival to counter: the willingness of young South Koreans to pay high prices for new electronic devices. In terms of access to broad-band and telecommunications infrastructure, Samsung happens to be sitting in one of the world's most wired – and wireless – markets.

Nokia had a similar advantage in Finland in the

1990s and exploited it to establish a strong presence round the world, including in Asia. But Europe has trailed Asia in high-speed mobile services. South Korea has more than 5m subscribers to third-generation services. That has helped Samsung to develop better designs for camera handsets at home before applying the lessons in Europe and the US.

One thing Samsung learnt – and Nokia did not – was to make its camera handsets small. Masamichi Udagawa, co-founder of Antenna Design in New York, says he was 'shocked' when he saw one of Nokia's first camera phones in Tokyo; companies such as Panasonic and Sharp were already making much smaller models for Japan. 'It was a nice design, with a sliding lid, but its sheer size made it unacceptable,' he says.

For consumer companies in Europe and US, Nokia's experience points to a broader challenge. Nike has remained innovative by developing a range of premium-priced shoes in the US and then selling them around the world.

Samsung has shown that companies in Asian economies can use their own domestic markets to develop global products. Of course, Japanese companies, including Sony and Toyota, have done that for several decades, blending design and technology in ways unmatched by western companies. But countries such as South Korea have a demographic advantage over Japan and Europe – a plentiful supply of young people. As south-east Asian economies develop, those consumers will become increasingly valuable.

From the *Financial Times*

FINANCIAL TIMES
World business newspaper.

B Now answer these questions.

1 What changes have taken place regarding:

a) the value of Nokia?   **b)** Nokia's position in the market?

2 Why is Nokia no longer the leader in the mobile phone market?

3 What is preventing Nokia from regaining its position in the market?

4 Why is Samsung competing successfully against Nokia?

5 Why was Nokia's first camera phone unsuitable for the Japanese market?

6 According to the writer, what advantage will South Korea have over Japanese and European companies in the future?

C The following verbs related to competition all appear in the article.

> crush   match   exceed   regain   dominate   overtake   rival

Which of the words in the box suggest the idea of:

1 being in a strong position? (2 verbs)
2 equality? (2 verbs)
3 moving in front of?
4 recovery?
5 doing better than?

D Select the best alternative in each example below.

1 Our sales results (*rivalled* / *exceeded*) all our expectations.
2 After buying their largest competitor they totally (*dominated* / *exceeded*) the market.
3 Our factory (*rivals* / *regains*) many of our competitors.
4 After only three years, US sales (*crushed* / *overtook*) sales in Europe.
5 Following the bankruptcy of our main competitor we (*overtook* / *regained*) our position as market leader.
6 They can (*match* / *dominate*) us on price but not on quality.
7 We are going to (*regain* / *crush*) the competition with our new handset.

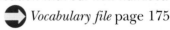 *Vocabulary file* page 175

Listening
Staying competitive

A ⌒ 14.1 **Ian Barber is Marketing Manager with Barclaycard, the credit card business. Listen to the first part of the interview and decide whether the following statements are true or false.**

1 Barclaycard launched in 1976.
2 There were no competitors for ten or twelve years.
3 Today there are almost a thousand other credit card providers.
4 In the UK, Barclaycard is more widely recognised than its competitors.
5 Barclaycard's price strategy is to always be the cheapest.
6 Keeping customers happy is important, but it doesn't affect competitiveness.

B ⌒ 14.2 **Listen to the second part and answer these questions.**

1 Which three types of borrowing other than using a credit card does Ian Barber describe?
2 Under the current Barclaycard offer, how long can you borrow money for at zero percent?
3 How does the 'cashback' scheme work?
4 What two benefits for the customer has competition brought?

▲ Ian Barber

C ⌒ 14.3 **Listen to the third part and complete this summary.**

Generally speaking, people borrow for one of three reasons. They borrow to ....[1]: a car or holiday, something like that. They borrow to............ ....[2] – so they put all their debts in one place and they have to make just one monthly payment.

Or they borrow .... [3], simply to spread the cost of their monthly spending in a more manageable way.

Competition is really about providing our customers with .... [4] and .... [5].

Language review
Modals of probability

Modals of certainty, probability, possibility

We use different modals to say that an event or situation is *certain*, *probable* or *possible*.

1 *will / won't*
   We often use *will / won't* with an adverb to show how certain we are that something will or will not happen.
   Prices for airline tickets **will certainly** *rise next year.*
   They **probably / definitely / certainly won't** *cut their prices again.*

2 We use *should, ought to, be likely to* when we think something will probably happen.
   Our sales **are likely to** *improve next quarter.*
   When we expect something will not happen, we use *shouldn't, ought not to, be unlikely to.*
   That **shouldn't** *be a problem.*

3 We use *may, could, may not, might not* when there is only a *possibility* that something will or will not happen.
   The situation **may** *improve in the longer term.*

4 We use *must* or *can't* to make a logical deduction.
   They **must** *be tired after such a long flight.*
   They **can't** *be in financial difficulty – their profits are up.*

 page 156

A Look at these sentences. Decide if they are *certain*, *probable*, *possible* or *not possible*. The first sentence is given as an example.

1 Easyjet are likely to lower their prices. *probable*
2 The airline might outsource its catering to reduce costs.
3 Easyjet should have much higher sales next quarter.
4 It shouldn't be difficult to book a flight at this time.
5 Some airlines are sure to lower their prices to increase their market share.
6 The price of aircraft fuel certainly won't fall in the short run.
7 Some airlines definitely won't lower their prices because their revenue is falling.
8 This airline might not go bankrupt if the government supports it financially.
9 There ought not to be a problem obtaining landing rights at this airport.
10 We may get a reservation if we are very lucky.

B Underline the correct word in each sentence.

1 The competition is increasing. We (*might / should*) have to lower our prices.
2 There are several flights each day to Paris. There (*mustn't / shouldn't*) be a problem getting tickets.
3 Our plane's been delayed. There (*may not / shouldn't*) be anyone at the airport to meet us.
4 Their new product has had many technical problems. They (*must / can't*) be very disappointed.
5 The weather conditions are good. We (*should / must*) arrive on time for our meeting.
6 That (*can't / mustn't*) be Peter, he's in New York at the moment.
7 We (*may not / ought not to*) launch the product in July because many sales reps are on holiday.
8 Next Friday is possible. I (*must / might*) be available early in the evening.

Skills
Negotiating

A 🎧 **14.4 Listen to a cycle manufacturer discussing an agreement with a new agent. Then answer these questions.**

1 Which of these points did the two sides agree on during the negotiation?

   a) the type of relationship they wish to have

   b) who sets prices

   c) payment of commission

   d) who pays for advertising and promotion

2 Why does the agent want the contract to be longer than two years?

B **Match the phrases on the left with the more diplomatic phrases on the right.**

1 We must talk about price first.	**a)** Your price seems rather high.
2 There's no way we can give you any credit.	**b)** Unfortunately, I can't lower my price.
	c) Could you possibly give me a discount?
3 I want a discount.	**d)** I'm afraid we can't give you any credit.
4 I won't lower my price.	**e)** I think we should talk about price first.
5 Can you alter the specifications?	**f)** I wonder if you could alter the
6 Your price is far too high.	specifications.

C 🎧 **14.5 Listen to these extracts from the negotiation. Complete the sentences below. Decide whether the speakers are being diplomatic (D) or not diplomatic (ND).**

1 A non-exclusive contract .... for us, too.

2 No, that's .... for us.

3 We know the market conditions .... than you.

4 I .... a rate of 15% on all the revenue you obtain.

5 Fifteen percent is too low. We .... 20%.

6 We .... with this.

7 How much ....?

8 We .... about the commission later.

9 .... , with a new distributor we prefer a shorter period.

10 It .... at least three years.

D **Role play the negotiation below between a shop owner and a chocolate manufacturer. Be diplomatic.**

Shop owner

- You want to order 50 boxes of deluxe chocolates at the quoted price.
- You want a 20% discount.
- You want 30 days' credit.
- You want delivery in two weeks.

Chocolate manufacturer

- You get a bonus if the order is over 100 boxes.
- You don't give a discount for orders of less than 100 boxes.
- You want payment on delivery.
- You can deliver in three weeks.

Useful language

Diplomatically giving bad news
I'm sorry, we weren't able to agree on this.
I'm afraid your price is rather high.

Using speculative language
It would probably arrive late.
It could be a problem.
It may be difficult to deliver.
We might not be able to do that.

Using a past form to express disappointment
We were hoping for ...
We were expecting ...

Beverley Watches

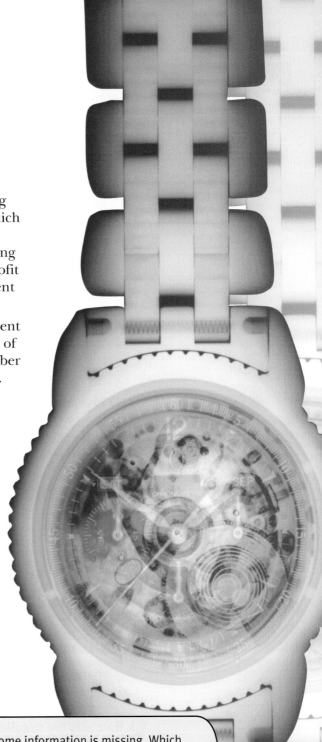

Background

Beverley Watches, located in Los Angeles, California, owns a chain of stores selling jewellery and fashion watches. Its best-selling products are high-quality ladies' watches which are innovative and offer a variety of 'face' colours. The company is increasingly sourcing its products from Asian countries and its profit margin on such products is usually 80 percent to 100 percent.

The date is October 1. The buying department wishes to purchase 5,000 ladies' watches, all of which must arrive in Los Angeles by November 15, in time for the Christmas buying season. The company believes it can definitely sell 3,000 watches but the remaining 2,000 will depend on demand – which is uncertain. Because Beverley Watches has cash-flow problems, it wishes to pay for the goods as late as possible.

The target consumer is price-conscious, but will pay more if the watches have original designs. Members of the buying department are now in Asia looking for a reliable supplier with whom they can build a long-lasting relationship. They have contacted three companies who could supply the watches.

Task

1 Read the information about each supplier. Some information is missing. Which supplier looks the most attractive at this stage? What problems, if any, could there be with each supplier?

2 Work in groups of three buyers and three suppliers.
- Buyer 1: turn to page 148.
- Buyer 2: turn to page 143.
- Buyer 3: turn to page 142.
- Supplier 1: turn to page 145.
- Supplier 2: turn to page 146.
- Supplier 3: turn to page 141.
Read your role cards.

3 Each buyer meets *one* of the suppliers. Find out the missing information concerning delivery, discount, returned goods and guarantee. Negotiate to get good terms for your company.

4 Buyers meet together and discuss the negotiation. Decide together which supplier to use. Suppliers meet together and discuss how you feel about the negotiation. What are you happy or unhappy about? What would you do differently?

5 Buyers: announce your decision and, diplomatically, explain why you rejected the suppliers you did.
Suppliers: say how you would negotiate differently next time.

Supplier 1: Chung Ka (Hong Kong)

Quantity	1,000 in stock; 4,000 available in Hong Kong by November 1
Product features	Very slim and light; 3 colours; mechanism made in the company's factory in China
Unit cost	US $48
Delivery	No information
Payment	50% deposit when order placed; remainder payable when the goods are shipped
Discount	No information
Returned goods	No information
Guarantee	No information

Supplier 2: Soong Jewellery (Malaysia)

Quantity	3,000 in stock; 2,000 available in Malaysia by November 1
Product features	2 classic designs; 4 colours; mechanism made in Japan
Unit cost	US $55
Delivery	No information
Payment	Pay when the goods are sent; no deposit
Discount	No information
Returned goods	No information
Guarantee	No information

Supplier 3: Timeline Watches (South Korea)

Quantity	5,000 in stock
Product features	8 colours; multiple functions; mechanism made in Switzerland
Unit cost	US $60
Delivery	No information
Payment	20% deposit when order placed
Discount	No information
Returned goods	No information
Guarantee	No information

Writing

Write an e-mail to the person you are negotiating with confirming the details of your negotiation and any outstanding points to be decided on.

 Writing file page 133

8 Employment

Vocabulary

A Complete the table.

Adjective	Noun
1 motivated	motivation
2	dedication
3	honesty
4 charismatic	....
5	pride
6 confident	....
7 loyal	....
8	adaptability
9 reliable	....
10 determined	....

B Now match the nouns to their meanings.

1 Someone with .... wants to succeed despite all obstacles and problems.

2 If you are ...., you do what you say you are going to do.

3 .... is when someone supports and acts in the interests of their organisation.

4 .... is when someone does not lie, cheat or steal.

5 Someone with .... believes that they have the ability to do things well.

6 If you have the quality of ...., you are able to choose the best way to approach different situations and problems, rather than always approaching them in the same way.

7 Someone with .... has a powerful natural ability to attract others.

8 .... is when someone wants to work and does not need to be told to or forced to.

9 If you have ...., you put a lot of effort into your work because you care about it and believe in it.

10 Someone with .... admires their own work and has respect for him- or herself.

Reading

Look at the case study on page 74 and 75. You decide to appoint Martine Lemaire to the job. Complete the letter using the correct alternatives.

Dear Ms Lemaire

It was a .... ¹ meeting you here at Slim Gyms last Thursday. We had a very interesting discussion. We have now .... ² your .... ³ and they were both very positive. I am therefore .... ⁴ to offer you the .... ⁵ of General Manager for our chain of Health and Leisure Clubs. We can offer a salary of $70,000 a year, plus the usual .... ⁶.

We would like you to commence work on September 1st. However, we have a special week of .... ⁷ for all our managers during the week of August 15th in Kansas City, and I think it would be helpful and useful if you could .... ⁸ this. It will help you to get to know the company and your future .... ⁹!

Please could you confirm that you wish to .... ¹⁰ this post, and also let me know if you can go to Kansas City for the course?

I look forward to hearing from you.

Yours sincerely

1 a) happiness	**b)** pleasure	**c)** fun	**d)** gladness
2 a) controlled	**b)** certified	**c)** tested	**d)** checked
3 a) refers	**b)** referees	**c)** references	**d)** referred
4 a) delighted	**b)** content	**c)** ecstatic	**d)** over the moon
5 a) location	**b)** situated	**c)** position	**d)** spot
6 a) benefactors	**b)** benefits	**c)** kindnesses	**d)** vantages
7 a) formation	**b)** training	**c)** educating	**d)** teaching
8 a) assist	**b)** attenuate	**c)** attend	**d)** locate
9 a) cooperatives	**b)** co-employees	**c)** colleges	**d)** colleagues
10 a) take off	**b)** take out	**c)** take up	**d)** take in

Writing

Now write a letter (80 to 100 words) to one of the applicants who failed to get the job. Include the following points:

• thank the applicant for coming to the interview

• all the candidates were very strong

• you regret that despite their skills and experience, you are not able to offer them the job

• you will keep the applicant's name on file and let them know about any future job openings

• thank the applicant for their interest in the job

9 Trade

Vocabulary

Replace the underlined parts of the sentences with appropriate forms of expressions from the box. (Not all of the expressions in the box are used.)

barriers	open borders	free port	developing industries
dumping	tariffs	a strategic industry	restrictions
quotas	laisser-faire	liberalise	Customs
	deregulation of	subsidies	regulations

1 In 2003, the US imposed <u>special taxes</u> on imported steel

2 Farmers who boast of their independence are the first to ask the government for <u>financial help</u>.

3 Car companies that want to export to South Korea complain about the <u>obstacles</u> that they face, for example <u>limits</u> on the numbers of cars that are allowed into the country.

4 Manufacturers sometimes complain that importers are <u>selling goods at less than they cost to make</u> so that they can build their market share.

5 France sees banking as <u>an industry that is especially important for the country</u>. The government will prevent any attempt by a foreign bank to take over a French bank.

6 The UK has decided to merge <u>the department responsible for collecting import taxes</u> with the Inland Revenue, the department responsible for collecting income tax.

7 Since the <u>reduction in the number of regulations governing</u> the US airline industry 30 years ago, a lot of airlines have been started and a lot have gone bankrupt.

Conditionals

Complete the sentences with the correct form of the verbs in brackets.

1 If you offer us a 15 percent discount .... (we / give) you an order for 50,000 bottles.

2 What discount .... (you / offer) us if we decided to spend ¤1 million a year with you?

3 If .... (we / improve) the payment terms, would you consider buying from us?

4 If we meet again next week, ... (you / change) your position?

5 We could negotiate a better price if .... (you / shorten) the delivery time.

6 .... (you be able) to deliver next week if we ordered 100,000 units today?

7 If you .... (not offer) such good terms, we wouldn't do business with you.

10 Quality

Gerunds

Tick the correct sentences and correct the rest.

1 Ajax Plc is considering buying one of its smaller rivals, Brotox.

2 Her personal assistant denied to make the mistake.

3 When you have finished to write the report, would it be possible to make these phone calls?

4 The work involves studying our markets for potential threats.

5 Don't put off to read that management book I gave you – there are some useful ideas in it.

6 The best preparation for your Japanese business trip is to practise to play golf.

7 The boss has promised to give us all a salary increase.

8 Invest in that company, and you risk to lose all your money.

9 The market leader failed to notice new developments in the market.

10 He recommended buying the most expensive product in the range.

Reading

Look again at the case study on page 90. Now look at the letter below received by the Customer Services Manager at Brookfield Airport before any of the changes were made.

In most of the lines 1 to 5 there is one extra word that does not fit. One or two of the lines, however, are correct. If a line is correct, put a tick in the space next to that line. If there is an extra word in the line, write that word in the space.

Customer Services Manager
Brookfield Airport
Brookfield B98 4FU

3 August 2005

Dear Sir or Madam

I am writing to complain in the strongest terms about the baggage reclaim facilities at   1 ....
Brookfield Airport. On a recent flight back from Barcelona, we has waited 35 minutes for   2 ....
our baggage to arrive after getting off the plane – a two minute walk. Why did it take off so   3 ....
long? Also, one of my suitcases was badly damaged up. This may have happened at   4 ....
Barcelona, but the airport there is very modern. I'm sure the damage was done in by the   5 ....
baggage handlers at Brookfield.

I look forward to receiving your reply.

Yours sincerely

Fiona Giddings

Fiona Giddings

Writing

You are the Customer Services Manager. Write a reply (130 to 150 words) to Fiona Giddings.

• Thank her for her letter.

• Apologise for the inconvenience.

• Then continue the letter depending on what you decided when you did the case study.

EITHER: If you decided to spend money on improving the baggage reclaim area and process, explain this and give an idea of when the facilities will improve.

OR: If you decide not to spend money on improving the baggage reclaim area and process, explain this. Say that you understand the problem, but the Airport's resources are limited.

• In either case, say if you will offer compensation of some kind for the damaged suitcase.

• End suitably.

11 Ethics

Vocabulary

Complete the sentences with the correct alternatives.

1 A high-level politician tells a friend in the police not to investigate the murder of his mistress, and not to reveal the murder to journalists. This is a .... (covering / cover-up).

2 Company A is negotiating an important contract with Company B. Company A says that it is not negotiating with any other company, but then Company B finds it is talking to Company C. There is now a complete lack of .... (truth / trust) between them.

3 A customs official refuses to let goods through at a sea port. The local import agent hands him $100 in a brown envelope and the goods are let through. The money is a .... (bribe / bribery) or a .... (sugaring / sweetener).

4 You receive an e-mail saying that you have won €1 million on a lottery you have never heard of. You can get this money only if you send a 'release fee' of €1000. This is .... (fraud / freedom).

5 A governing political party receives a donation from a millionaire about to be affected by government legislation. There should be full .... (closure / disclosure) of the donation, according to opposition members.

6 Someone is found photocopying plans for a company's new product after office hours. Selling plans to another company is known as industrial (espionage / relations).

Reading

Read this text. In each of the lines 1 to 8 there is one wrong word. Underline the wrong word and write the correct word in the space provided.

E-commerce is now entered a more stable, mature period after the boom and bust   1 ....
of a few years ago. On some websites, for example those that sell books, you seeing   2 ....
comments from other users, who becomes, in effect, the site's book reviewers. An ethical   3 ....
problem that emerges recently is that some of the reviewers of the books are not   4 ....
ordinary readers, but sometimes working for publishers. In some cases, the reviewers of the   5 ....
books are the authors themselves. Using a false name, one author has describing his own book   6 ....
as 'a work of genius'. The book site in question is said that it is putting stricter controls on   7 ....
the reviews on its site. It be checking that the names of reviewers are real by asking them for   8 ....
their credit card details.

12 Leadership

Vocabulary

Complete these statements about leadership qualities by using correct forms of the words in brackets.

1 Someone who is confident about what to do in different situations is .... (decide).

2 A leader who has a special quality that attracts people is .... (charisma).

3 Someone who acts to get what they want without worrying about hurting people displays .... (ruthless).

4 Leaders often complain that they suffer from .... (lonely): they do not have anyone to talk to or socialise with.

5 .... (impulse) people do things without thinking about the consequences.

6 Someone who is .... (obsession) thinks only about one or two things and nothing else.

7 If a leader is attractive and makes people want to be with them and follow them, they are .... (magnet).

8 .... (access) leaders are easy to meet and to talk to.

9 Someone may be criticised for being an .... (opportunity) when they act to gain an advantage in a particular situation.

10 If someone is able to change the way that other people think or behave, they are .... (persuade).

Reading

Look at the writing task at the end of the case study on page 107. Below is a possible letter.

In most of the lines 1 to 5 there is one extra word that does not fit. One or two of the lines, however, are correct. If a line is correct, put a tick in the space next to that line. If there is an extra word in the line, write that word in the space.

Brian Shearer
99 Notting Hill Square
London W2 9ZZ

28 May 2005

Dear Mr Shearer

Having recently taken over as Chief Executive at Orbit Records, it was
great meeting you – one of the key players in the UK record industry –
at the UK Music Awards last month.

As you may can know, we are organising a Jazz Month event at all of our UK stores in   1 ....
October. As the agent for some leading jazz musicians, we would like you to participate   2 ....
in this event by inviting you off to our Oxford Street store. It would be great if you could give a 3 ....
presentation about subject your work. This would give you the chance to promote some of   4 ....
your musicians by playing up extracts from their recordings.   5 ....

We would, of course, be willing to pay a suitable fee. I very much hope that you will be willing to participate in this event.

Looking forward to hearing from you.

Yours sincerely

Jason East

Jason East

Writing

Now write a reply from Brian Shearer (60 to 100 words).
Either:

accept the invitation. Ask about the fee and possible dates. Thank Jason East and end suitably.

Or:

decline the invitation. Give a reason. Thank Jason East and end suitably.

13 Innovation

Reading

Complete the text with the correct alternatives. (Not all the alternatives are real expressions.)

People think they have a clear idea of the process of inventing something. The inventor has a .... ¹. A .... ² is developed. There are difficulties and .... ³ : at some point someone shouts 'Back to the .... ⁴ !' Eventually there is a .... ⁵ and the problems are ironed out. A product is launched and its inventor is hailed as a .... ⁶ and .... ⁷ pioneer. He or she .... ⁸ the idea and becomes rich. Or the pioneer is overtaken by others who manage to commercialise the idea more successfully.

But the process of invention is not as straightforward as it seems. Take the steam engine. It was not .... ⁹ by James Watt – his contribution was to make key improvements to the original design. It was not initially used to power locomotives, but to pump water out of coal mines. The .... ¹⁰ for fax machines and photocopiers existed for many years before these inventions were .... ¹¹ in large numbers. Inventions are not always adopted as quickly as we imagine, or for the .... ¹² that they were originally intended for.

1	a) wavebrain	b) brainwave	c) idea	d) ideal
2	a) fore-type	b) pre-type	c) front-type	d) prototype
3	a) back-sets	b) setbacks	c) let-downs	d) outlets
4	a) floorboard	b) draw board	c) drawing board	d) hardboard
5	a) break-off	b) break-out	c) break-in	d) breakthrough
6	a) gate-crashing	b) grate-falling	c) ground-breaking	d) floor-smashing
7	a) revolting	b) revolving	c) revving	d) revolutionary
8	a) patents	b) pastes	c) patients	d) parents
9	a) innovated	b) invented	c) inverted	d) involved
10	a) technicities	b) techniques	c) technicians	d) technologies
11	a) adapted	b) added	c) admitted	d) adopted
12	a) utilities	b) uses	c) utilisations	d) usefulness

Passive

Use the correct forms of the verbs in brackets to complete the sentences about early mobile phones. Then put the stages in a logical order. The first is a) and the last is i).

a) There was an early mobile phone system that was .... (introduce) in the UK in the 1980s.

b) A few years later, 'proper' mobile technology was .... (launch).

c) All this meant that not enough subscribers were .... (recruit).

d) Another problem with the system was that calls could only be .... (make) , not .... (receive).

e) But it was severely .... (limit) in what it could do. You had to be within a few hundred metres of a base station – so you had to find one before you could make a call.

f) Calls could be .... (make) and .... (receive) anywhere.

g) It was .... (call) Rabbit.

h) These base stations were .... (show) by a rabbit symbol.

i) And now 3G technologies are being .... (offer), with a wide range of services including video. Rabbit seems a long time ago now!

14 Competition

Modals

In each of these sentences, one of the alternatives is not possible. Cross it out.

1 I am absolutely certain that oil (*are likely to / is going to / will*) run out by 2050.

2 Other potential energy sources are limited, so nuclear power (*must / will / couldn't*) be the answer.

3 Solar power is (*unlikely / impossible / unable*) to provide more than 20 percent of our energy needs.

4 Wind power (*will / is certain to / is probable*) provide only a small part of our energy needs in 2050.

5 The rising price of oil (*ought to / should / unable*) make other energy sources more attractive.

6 New forms of energy (*might / may / won't*) be found, but this is not very probable.

7 A miracle solution (*might / shouldn't to / is unlikely* to) appear magically.

Reading

Look at the case study on page 122. Chung Ka was chosen as the supplier.

Read this e-mail. In each of the numbered lines there is one wrong word. For each numbered line, underline the wrong word and write the correct word in the space provided.

Date...	October 7, 2005
From ...	Jimmy Chen
To...	cheryl.stephens@beverley.com
Subject:	Supplying watches

It was a pleasure to meeting you on Tuesday – I hope you had a good trip back to Los   1 ....
Angeles. Following our discuss, this is to confirm that we can deliver 1,000 watches now, with   2 ....
another 4,000 by the end of November. The unit cost will be $43 for a minimum command of   3 ....
5,000 units, with no further discounts. We would ask for a paying of 30 percent when you   4 ....
place your order, and the remainder when goods are ship. Unsold goods may be returned and   5 ....
the amount credited to your discount. We can extend our guarantee to 12 months.   6 ....
I hope you will find these conditions accepting. We would need confirmation this week in   7 ....
order to provide all the good by the end of November.   8 ....

Looking forward to hearing from you,

Best regards

Jimmy Chen

Writing file

Letters

FAR EASTERN AIRWAYS COMPANY LIMITED

Regent House, 5th Floor,
12/16 Haymarket, London W1V 5BX
Administration: 020 7285 9981
Reservations: 020 7564 0930
Fax: 020 7285 9984

15 February 2006

Mr Roberto Garcia
Universal Imports
28 Whitechapel Court
London E10 7NB

Dear Mr Garcia

Re: Roxanna Garbey

Roxanna Garbey has been accepted for a position as Passenger Service Agent with Far Eastern Airways at Gatwick Airport.

In order for Roxanna to work at Gatwick, she must have a special pass which would permit her to visit high security areas. She has given your name as a reference.

I would appreciate it if you could complete the enclosed form and return it to us as quickly as possible. She is due to start work with us on 15 March, but can only do so after we receive your reference.

Thank you for your cooperation. I enclose a stamped addressed envelope.

Yours sincerely

J. P. Dent

J. P. Dent
Personnel Manager

Press release

Press release

For:	Business editors, national press; motoring press
Release date:	26 October
Subject:	Revolutionary new car to be unveiled at Motor Show

After weeks of rumour and speculation, ITS will unveil their revolutionary new concept car at the Tokyo Motor Show on 3 November. The vehicle requires very small amounts of petrol and instead uses a combination of solar energy and hydrogen to power it. Massive public interest is expected in this vehicle of the future.

For more information, contact:
Sarah Wells, High Profile Communications
sarah@hpc-centre.com

E-mails

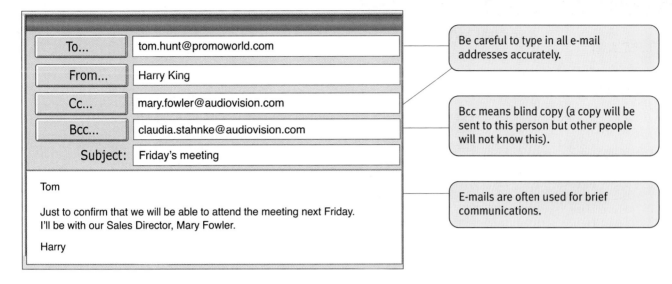

Be careful to type in all e-mail addresses accurately.

Bcc means blind copy (a copy will be sent to this person but other people will not know this).

E-mails are often used for brief communications.

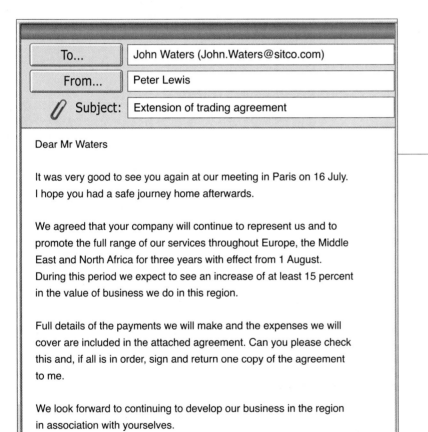

This style of e-mail is similar to a standard business letter. The ending can be the less formal *Best wishes* or *Best regards* or the more formal *Yours sincerely*, depending on how well the writer knows the recipient.

Faxes

FALCON HOTELS

FAX

TO   Alice Wong

Fax No   00 852 7514329

FROM   Zofia Nadstoga
              Reservations Dept. Falcon Hotels

Fax No   020 7945 2647

Date   5 July

No of pages (including this)   1

Dear Ms Wong

This is to confirm your booking for a single room
from 20 July to 27 July inclusive at a rate of
£150.00 per night (excluding Sales Tax).
As requested, we will hold your room until
midnight on the day of your arrival.
We look forward to meeting you shortly.

Yours sincerely

Zofia Nadstoga

Zofia Nadstoga

> Information transmitted by fax may be presented in various formats, for example in letter, memo or note form.

> Faxes may contain the following headings: To / From / Date / Subject / No. of pages / Fax numbers

> The style of a fax message may be formal, informal or neutral depending on the subject and recipient.

Agendas

> Always put the title, date, time and venue (place).

> Larger meetings and committee meetings may also include the following:
> a) Apologies for absence
> b) Matters arising from last meeting
> c) Correspondence
> d) Date of next meeting

> A.O.B. means *any other business*. This is for other relevant issues that were not included in the agenda.

Management meeting

AGENDA

Date: 1 March
Time: 14.00
Venue: Room 23M, Shaw House

1. Complaints about reception staff.

2. New brochure.

3. Price list for next year.

4. New product presentation.

5. A.O.B.

Action minutes

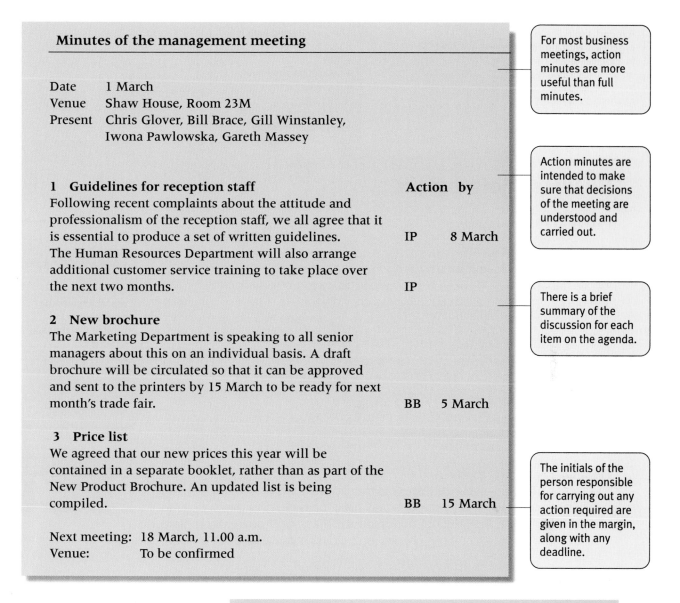

Minutes of the management meeting

Date	1 March
Venue	Shaw House, Room 23M
Present	Chris Glover, Bill Brace, Gill Winstanley, Iwona Pawlowska, Gareth Massey

1 Guidelines for reception staff **Action by**

Following recent complaints about the attitude and professionalism of the reception staff, we all agree that it is essential to produce a set of written guidelines. IP 8 March

The Human Resources Department will also arrange additional customer service training to take place over the next two months. IP

2 New brochure

The Marketing Department is speaking to all senior managers about this on an individual basis. A draft brochure will be circulated so that it can be approved and sent to the printers by 15 March to be ready for next month's trade fair. BB 5 March

3 Price list

We agreed that our new prices this year will be contained in a separate booklet, rather than as part of the New Product Brochure. An updated list is being compiled. BB 15 March

Next meeting: 18 March, 11.00 a.m.
Venue: To be confirmed

> For most business meetings, action minutes are more useful than full minutes.

> Action minutes are intended to make sure that decisions of the meeting are understood and carried out.

> There is a brief summary of the discussion for each item on the agenda.

> The initials of the person responsible for carrying out any action required are given in the margin, along with any deadline.

> An action plan focuses on key events and is usually based on a timetable. Sentences are short and verbs are usually imperatives (*complete*, *agree*, etc).

Action plan

We plan to launch the new range in November. The following stages are all critical to the success of the launch.

January

Complete test marketing and report back findings to Research and Development.

April

Agree final specifications with manufacturers.

Book advertising space with media agency.

May, June

Manufacturing.

July, August

Distribution of stock to key wholesalers.

September, October

Advertising campaign including media interviews and features.

November

Launch at Milan Trade Fair.

Reports

A report should be well organised with information in a logical order. There is no set layout for a report. It will depend on:
a) the type of report
b) the company style

The format used here is suitable for formal reports:
• title
• executive summary
• introduction
• findings
• conclusion
• recommendations

Business Software plc

Product report

Executive summary
We have been contacted by Lenz AG, a German manufacturer of mobile telephones, and asked about the possibility of a co-operation agreement. We would adapt our business software for use in their products. Tests show that their product is a very good one and popular with our target market.

Introduction
This report will look at:
• the hardware manufacturer and their equipment
• software that could be used on their mobile phones
• the advantages of working together
• recommendations for action

Findings
1 Lenz has been developing cheap, small-scale electronic devices for thirty-five years. In the last five years they have focussed on more expensive mobile phones for businesspeople. These have been very successful. One in four mobile phones for the business market is a Lenz.

2 Our new 'Executive Organiser' software has a lot of attractive features for the travelling businessperson (e.g. address book, e-mailware, voice recorder, street finder function, etc.)

3 Market research shows that there is a big interest in our products being used on machines apart from computers.

Conclusion
The two companies have products which fit well together.

Recommendation
We should have a meeting with representatives from Lenz as soon as possible to discuss a joint venture between our companies, with the aim of putting our software onto their mobile phones.

Tracy Cruickshank
Research and Development Director
19 October 200 -

The *executive summary* is a summary of the main points and conclusion of the report. It gives the reader a quick overview of the total situation.

The *introduction* shows the points that will be looked at.

The *findings* are the facts discovered.

The *conclusion* is what you think about the facts and how you interpret them.

Recommendations are practical suggestions to deal with the situation and ideas for making sure future activities run more easily.

Summary

When you summarise something, you express the most important facts or points about something in a short and clear form.

Writing a summary involves:
- selecting the most important ideas or facts from a text.
- rewriting those ideas/facts in a short, concise form, using your own language.
- producing a text which is shorter than the original – usually at least half the number of words.

Here is an example of an original text and a sample summary.

Hispanics are more influenced by advertising than other US consumers, suggesting that the growth of the Spanish-speaking population could prove beneficial to big corporate sponsors, according to two studies.

A Nielsen Media Research study released on Wednesday found that Spanish-language television viewers pay more attention to commercials and are more likely to base their purchasing decisions on advertisements than other US consumers. The report was issued after Euro RSCG, the marketing communication agency, released a study that showed Hispanics are more aware of brand names than other US consumers.

Taken together, the reports suggest that growing corporate interest in Hispanic marketing might involve factors that go beyond the mere size of the Spanish-speaking population. The US Hispanic population is estimated at about 39m.

The studies also suggest that Hispanic consumers offer big companies the chance to use the kinds of sales pitches that worked with US consumers in decades past, but which are now less popular with advertising-weary viewers.

Fifty-two per cent of Hispanics say they frequently get information for making purchase decisions from watching TV commercials in Spanish, compared with seven percent of non-Hispanics watching English-language television.

This summary is effective because:

- it contains the key ideas from the original text.
- the language used to express the key ideas is different from the original.
- the new text is much shorter in length.

The Spanish speaking population in the United States (about 39m) is an important group of consumers for large companies.

Recent research has found that Spanish TV viewers are very influenced by television commercials when they buy products, and they also know more about brands than other people in the United States.

Another finding of the research was that conventional methods of advertising appeal to Spanish-speaking people even though other viewers are tired of them. Some interesting statistics: 52% of Hispanics depend on TV commercials for information about what to buy, whereas only 7% of non-Hispanics do. (96 words)

Sometimes a summary can be expressed in a series of numbered short statements.

1 The Spanish speaking population in the United States is 39m. Research has been carried out into this group's buying habits. Spanish TV viewers are very influenced by television commercials when buying products.

2 They know more about brands than other consumers.

3 Spanish-speaking people respond to conventional methods of advertising, but other consumers do not.

4 52% of Hispanics use television commercials to help them choose products; Only 7% of non-Hispanics do so.

Notices

Notices are used to inform people about changes of plan, instructions or warnings.

A notice needs a clear heading.

Information must be presented in a clear, concise form.
The tone of notices is usually rather formal and impersonal.

It must have the name and position of the person who wrote it, and the date.

AURIC BANK

CUSTOMER NOTICE

This branch will be closed until 10.30 a.m. on Tuesday 7 November for staff training.

We apologise in advance for any inconvenience caused.

Antonia Valdes
Branch Manager
2 November

The social-cultural game

What do you say?	**1** You have forgotten the name of the person you are talking to. Find out their name politely.	**2** You are late for a meeting.
6 You are in an important business negotiation. The other person asks you if he/she can smoke.	**7** The waiter in a restaurant has just given you the bill. You are sure it is much too high.	**8** You are having dinner with a foreign colleague in their country. The food is unfamiliar to you and you do not know what to choose.
12 An important client invites you to the theatre. You cannot attend because you have already accepted another invitation.	**13** At a conference you meet someone you think you've met before.	**14** You have just spilled red wine on a client's dress.
18 Spell your name.	**19** Give your telephone number.	**20** In which country is chewing gum forbidden by law? a) Iran b) Iraq c) Indonesia d) Singapore
24 Give directions from your office to the closest station or airport.	**25** In which country is it illegal to drink anything alcoholic and drive? a) Sweden b) France c) the UK d) the US	**26** Recommend a restaurant to a client.
30 In which country is it common to go out to eat after 10 p.m.? a) the UK b) Sweden c) Japan d) Spain	**31** You arrive for an appointment with your bank manager. Introduce yourself to the person at the reception desk.	**32** You are visiting a company and you want to use their telephone.

How to play

1 Decide how many players per board (6 maximum)
2 Place counters on **WHAT DO YOU SAY?**. The first player to throw a six begins.
3 Take turns to throw the dice. When you land on a square, answer the relevant question.
4 If the other players do not accept what is said, the player must go back to the square he or she has just come from.
5 The winner is the player who reaches **FINISH!** first.

3
You are at a party. You want to get away from someone who will not stop talking.

4
You are offered some food that you hate.

5
You should not point the sole of your foot towards your hosts. Which area does this refer to?
a) Arab world b) West Indies
c) Scandinavia d) Australia

9
You are at a cocktail party and the host / hostess has just handed you a glass of champagne. You do not drink alcohol.

10
In which country would it be a grave insult to touch someone on the head?
a) Thailand b) Japan
c) Pakistan d) Iraq

11
You have been invited to your colleague's house for dinner. He/She telephones you to ask if there is anything you don't eat.

15
In which country is it quite likely that you will be asked to sing a song?
a) Italy b) Austria c) Japan
d) Germany

16
A visitor wants to buy some local souvenirs.

17
A visitor wants advice on how to spend an evening in your town.

21
Talk about today's weather.

22
You are on the phone. Describe yourself to someone you are going to meet at the airport, so they can recognise you.

23
You are at an international conference. Complain about your hotel room.

27
You are on a plane. Introduce yourself to the person sitting next to you.

28
Introduce your boss to a person visiting your organisation.

29
You are having a small dinner party. Introduce two of your friends to each other.

33
You see an attractive person at an international conference. Start up a conversation.

34
You meet a business contact at a railway station. Offer to carry some of his luggage for him.

Finish!

3 Organisation, Case study: Auric Bank, page 29

Student D
You want AB to use the firm in India, X-source India.

You think:
- many American firms cut costs by outsourcing to India.
- the employees will be very skilled – mostly university graduates.
- service will be fast and efficient.
- the contract will be cheap.

If AB chooses one of the other options, you do not feel:
- the cost savings will be sufficient
- AB will not be able to reduce the prices it charges its customers
- You feel running call centres is time-consuming and distracts the bank from developing its main business.

2 Travel, Case study: Work, rest and play, page 20

Stage 1: Manager, ICON Travel Service

The Account Manager for Corporate Travel will ask you some questions about the seminar and its participants. Use this information to answer his/her questions.

No of participants	20 (Male 12 / Female 8)
Requirements	Single rooms for all participants, conference room and 3 smaller seminar rooms
Arrival	Most will arrive on Friday afternoon, a few will come later
Departure	After 5 p.m. on Sunday evening
Type of hotel	A comfortable stylish hotel in an interesting area
	3- or 4-star hotel, if possible
Equipment required	Overhead projector, flip chart, PowerPoint, VCR
Meals required	Friday evening: dinner; Saturday and Sunday: breakfast, lunch, dinner
Special requirements	Two participants are vegetarian.
	Four do not drink alcohol.
	One participant uses a wheelchair.
	Six are smokers.
Meeting	Suggest a meeting next Wednesday

14 Competition, Case study: Beverley Watches, page 123

Supplier 3: you represent Timeline Watches
These are the terms you usually offer.
- Delivery: Normally 30 days by ship after receiving an order but there have been problems with deliveries recently. However, you now have a new shipping agent who should be more reliable.
- Discount: No discount on orders up to 5,000; 2% on orders over 5,000
- Returned goods: no returns except for faulty goods
- Guarantee: 5 years

1 Brands, Skills: Exercise D, page 11

Student A

In your opinion, Jonson has a problem with its brand image.
- People consider their clothes to be boring, old-fashioned, over-priced and unexciting. They used to think they were well-made, value for money, durable and reasonably priced.
- Nowadays, the store sells clothes aimed at different age groups – young, middle-aged and old.
- People do not enjoy visiting the store because it needs redecorating in brighter colours.
- Staff uniforms do not help the company's brand image.

You think Jonson should focus on one segment of the clothing market. You are not sure which segment would be best, so you want to spend a lot of money on market research.

3 Organisation, Case study: Auric Bank, page 29

Student A

You want AB to keep their call centres in-house, in the south of England.

You think AB staff in the call centres:
- can give customers a personal service.
- know the bank's products and services well.
- can build relations with customers.
- will show customers that AB is still an 'English' bank.

If AB chooses one of the other options, you feel:
- the unions will be against the move and cause trouble.
- the quality of service will not be as good.
- data protection could be a problem (personal details might not be 'secure').

7 Cultures, Reading: Article C: South Korea, page 57

Conversation

You may be asked personal questions about your age, salary, education, religion, and family life. If you don't want to answer, remain polite but try to politely avoid answering. In most cases, people ask in order to establish a rapport by finding common ground.

Gift-giving

Giving gifts is a common practice in the workplace, and the receiver is expected to give a gift in return. Good gifts for a first trip include office items with your company logo or something produced in your country. Your gift should be of good quality but modestly priced. When you plan to give a gift to several people within an organisation, be sure to give a gift of greater value to the senior person.

Entertainment

Drinking is an important part of doing business. It is common to be invited out in the evening to a restaurant/bar where there will be a lot of alcohol. Towards the end of an evening the most honoured person will be asked to sing solo. Make sure that you know one very simple song and do your best. Refusing to sing is considered bad manners.

Adapted from www.executive.com

2 Travel, Case Study: Work, rest and play, page 20

Stage 2: Manager, ICON Travel Service
You must rearrange your meeting with the Universal Airlines Account Manager. Here is your diary for the week.

	Morning	Afternoon
Monday	All-day meeting to discuss the department's budget	
Tuesday	Meeting & dental appointment	
Wednesday	All-day training session	
Thursday	Interviewing candidates until 4 p.m.	
Friday	Department meeting until 2.30 p.m.	

14 Competition, Case study: Beverley Watches, page 123

Buyer 3: you meet the supplier representing Timeline Watches.
Get details of the missing information.
Study the supplier's offer.
You want the following:
- face colours – at least five
- delivery by 15 November at the latest
- discount of at least 5% on all goods ordered
- to be able to return all unsold goods, with the amount credited to your account
- a guarantee for 1 year

14 Competition, Case study: Beverley Watches, page 123

Buyer 2: you meet the supplier representing Soong Jewellery.
Get details of the missing information.
Study the supplier's offer.
You want the following:
- face colours – at least five
- delivery by 15 November at the latest
- discount of at least 5% on all goods ordered
- to be able to return all unsold goods, with the amount credited to your account
- a guarantee for 1 year

9 Trade, Case study: Ashbury Guitars, page 83

Information file: Ashbury Guitars

Models	You want KGC to supply three models: Ashbury SG1000, SG500 and SG200. The SG1000 has some special additional features.
Quality	You want KGC to produce *all* the guitars in their own factory. If they use other manufacturers for part of the order, the quality of the guitars may not be very good.
Quantity	You want to place the following first order:

Model	Quantity
SG1000	400
SG500	1,200
SG200	200

You are sure that demand will be good for the SG1000. The cheaper guitars may sell well. However, there is strong competition in the lower price ranges.

Price	KGC have quoted these prices:

SG1000	US$ 920
SG500	US$ 550
SG200	US$ 440

All prices include transport costs to Pusan, Korea.

Payment	By bank transfer. You want to pay a deposit of 50% immediately, and the remaining 50% one month after receiving the goods.
Delivery	By 1 June. A later date will result in reduced sales. (Music festivals in California in May create demand.)
Discounts	Although this is a first order, you hope to negotiate a discount of at least 6% off the quoted price. If you place other orders in the future, you hope to have a discount of 8%.
Guarantee	At least three years.

1 Brands, Starting up: Exercise B, page 6

Brand name*	Industry	Brand value in 2003 ($billions)
1 Coca-Cola	Beverages	70.45
2 Microsoft	Technology	65.17
3 IBM	Technology	51.77
4 General Electric	Diversified	42.34
5 Intel	Technology	31.11
6 Nokia, Finland	Technology	29.44
7 Disney	Leisure	28.04
8 McDonald's	Food retail	24.70
9 Marlboro	Tobacco	22.18
10 Mercedes, Germany	Automobiles	21.37

* All US-owned unless stated.
Companies ranked according to:
Weight (market share)
Breadth (cross section of society reached)
Depth (brand loyalty)
Length (brand-stretching ability)

Source: *Interbrand Brand Consultant*

4 Change, Skills: Exercise C, page 35

Student B

Proposal 1

Your colleague made this proposal. You are against the proposal because, in your opinion:
- senior managers and sales staff will not be happy about the change. Some may leave the company.
- a 10% increase in salary does not compensate for losing a company car.

Ask your colleague to clarify these points.
- Will the company cancel the 10% increase after one year?
- Has any other company made a similar change?

Proposal 2

Your colleague has proposed these changes. You are against the changes because, in your opinion:
- a barrier is not necessary. Two receptionists sitting at a table could check the arrival and departure of staff.
- staff will often forget their identity cards. This will cause problems in their department.

5 Money, Skills: Exercise A, page 39

Yahoo has strengthened its European presence with the four hundred and seventy-five million euro acquisition (that's a five hundred and seventy-eight million dollar acquisition) of Kelkoo, the French-based on-line shopping service. The European on-line retail market is forecast to grow to one hundred and seven billion euros in the next three years. The Nikkei two two five Average climbed nought point seven percent to eleven thousand, three hundred and sixty-four point nine, nine while the Topix index rose one point two percent to one thousand, one hundred and forty five point nine five. Banking shares benefited most, with Mizuho jumping five point six percent to four hundred and thirty-seven thousand yen, SMFG rising four point seven percent to seven hundred and fifty two thousand yen, MTFG gaining seven point nine percent to close at one million and fifty thousand yen and UFJ up four point two percent to six hundred and forty-six thousand yen.

14 Competition, Starting up: page 116

Key

	a)	b)	c)
1	3	2	1
2	3	2	1
3	1	2	3
4	1	2	3
5	1	2	3
6	3	2	1
7	1	2	3
8	1	2	3
9	3	2	1
10	3	2	1

Over 26: You are extremely competitive. You have high standards and expect a lot from yourself and other people. You are probably an impatient person. You like to win at all times and get upset if you lose. You perform well under pressure and enjoy a challenge.

18–26: You are fairly competitive. You are competitive in areas that are important to you. You don't always have to be the best. You are pleased when other people are successful, such as members of your family or your colleagues. You don't believe that 'winning is everything'.

12–17: You are not very competitive. You believe it is more important to take part than to win. You enjoy working in a group rather than individually. You try to avoid pressure as much as possible.

11–10: You are not at all competitive. You are probably a good team player. You want to enjoy life and be as relaxed as possible. You don't like being the centre of attention. You try to avoid working under pressure or having to meet tight deadlines.

14 Competition, Case study: Beverley Watches, page 123

Supplier 1: you represent Chung Ka.
These are the terms you usually offer.
- Delivery: By sea; 1,000 available within 30 days of order; 4,000 by end of November. No delivery by air.
- Discount: 2% on the first 2,000. 5% on larger orders.
- Returned goods: unsold goods may be returned and the amount credited to the customer's account.
- Guarantee: 6 months.
  You cannot offer a longer guarantee as the watches are not very reliable.
- Face colours: you offer 3 colours; if more face colours are required, you increase the unit cost by 5%.

14 Competition, Case study: Beverley Watches, page 123

Supplier 2: you represent Soong Jewellery
These are the terms you usually offer.
- Delivery: By sea; 3,000 available within 30 days of order; 2,000 by the end of November. Goods can be sent by air, you add 5% to the unit cost.
- Discount: 3% on up to 5,000 units, 5% on larger orders
- Returned goods: no returns unless the goods are faulty
- Guarantee: 1 year
- Face colours: you offer 4 colours; if more are required, you increase the unit cost by 8%.

4 Change, Skills: Excercise C, page 35

Student A
Proposal 1:

You have proposed this change to the Board of Directors. You like the idea because:
- the salary increase will cost less than providing a new car every four years.
- The cost of maintaining cars is very high.

You may need to clarify certain points. This information could be useful.
- The company will not cancel the increase after one year.
- Several other companies in the industry are making the same change.
- The Board of Directors will make their decision on the proposal at the end of the month.

7 Cultures, Reading: Article D: Brazil, page 57

Conversation

Conversations tend to be fast and lively. You may sometimes be asked personal questions about your income, religion, and marital status. If you don't want to reveal this information, remain polite but give a vague reply.

Gift-giving

Giving a gift is not necessary during a first meeting. Instead, offer to buy lunch or dinner and use this opportunity to learn more about your guest's tastes. This way, later on when gifts are exchanged, you'll be able to give an appropriate gift. Do not give anything that is obviously expensive. Your generosity may cause embarrassment or be misinterpreted. Small electronic items are often appreciated. Good choices include scientific calculators, electronic address books and pocket CD players, etc.

Entertainment

Business entertaining is conducted over lunch or dinner. You are expected to arrive on time. It is business etiquette in Brazil to shake hands with everyone in your company, both upon arrival and upon departure. It's unusual to touch food with your fingers. Cut all foods, including fruit and sandwiches, with your knife.

Adapted from www.executive.com

3 Organisation, Case study: Auric Bank, page 29

Student B

You want AB to use Resource Plc, the South African firm.

You think:
- Resource Plc will manage the call centres efficiently.
- staff will be trained to sell the Bank's new products and services.
- Resource Plc is not the cheapest but it offers value for money.
- its staff have telephone voice training and are extremely professional.

If AB chooses one of the other options, you feel:
- reducing the hours of business at the in-house call centres is not a good idea.
- the Scottish and Indian companies have taken on too much business so there may be problems getting through.

1 Brands, Skills: Exercise D, page 11

Student B

In your opinion, the brand image of Jonson is excellent. People think that Jonson's products are high quality and durable. But they are aiming at too many segments of the market.
- They should focus on the 30–50-year-old segment of the clothing market.
- They should not compete in the 15–30-year-old segment and should reduce floor space for these products.
- They should use the additional space to sell more food.
- They need to spend more money on advertising and promoting their clothes.

2 Travel, Case study: Work, rest and play, page 20

Stage 1: Account Manager, Universal Airlines

When the manager of ICON's travel service calls you, find out the following information.
- Participants: how many male? female?
- Arrival and departure times
- What kind of hotel do they want?
- Any special equipment for the seminar?
- Meals: When? How many?
- Any special requirements? For example, do any participants smoke?
- Anything else?

Meeting   Agree to meet

9 Trade, Case study: Ashbury Guitars, page 83

Information file: KGC

Models	You can supply three models in the first year: Ashbury SG1000, SG500, and SG200. The SG1000 will be costly to produce because it has advanced technical features.
Quality	To reduce costs of production, you want 40% of the order to be manufactured by other Korean firms.
Quantity	You want Ashbury Guitars to place a first order of at least 2,000 guitars. You need a large order to cover the costs of setting up the production lines. Try to persuade Ashbury to buy a large number of the SG1000 model because your profit margin on this guitar is high.

List price (US$)	Estimated cost of production	Prices quoted to Ashbury
SG1000	510	920
SG500	340	550
SG200	290	475

Payment	By bank transfer, as soon as the goods have been dispatched.
Delivery	30 June . If an earlier delivery is required, production costs will increase by 10% because of overtime payments to workers. Before 30 June , the factory will be fulfilling orders for other customers.
Discounts	Your company policy is to offer new customers 3% off list price for a first order, and 5% for second and further orders.
Guarantee	You usually offer a guarantee of 5 years.

14 Competition, Case study: Beverley Watches, page 123

Buyer 1: you meet the supplier representing Chung Ka.
Get details of the missing information.
Study the supplier's offer.
You want the following:
- face colours – at least five
- delivery by 15 November at the latest
- discount of at least 5% on all goods ordered
- to be able to return all unsold goods, with the amount credited to your account
- a guarantee for 1 year

3 Organisation, Case study: Auric Bank, page 29

Student C
You want AB to use Orion Plc, the Scottish firm.
You think:
- the cost of the contract is very reasonable.
- there are many skilled workers in the area.
- the move will create a lot of jobs in the area (good public relations for AB).
- there will be good data protection.

If AB chooses one of the overseas options, you feel:
- personal information may not be secure.
- service will not be as good.
- employees will not know enough about AB's customers or its products.
- You do not think the cost saving suggested for the in-house call centres are sufficient.

2 Travel, Case study: Work, rest and play, page 20

Stage 2: Account Manager, Universal Airlines
You must try to arrange a suitable day and time for your meeting with IDP's travel service Manager. Here is your diary for the week.

	Morning	Afternoon
Monday	All-day visit to a conference centre	
Tuesday	Free	Appointment with your son's headmaster at 3 p.m.
Wednesday	Free after 10.30 .a.m	Free
Thursday	Entertaining foreign visitor all day (including the evening)	
Friday	Presentation to Board	Free after 3 p.m.

1 Brands, Skills: Exercise D, page 11

Student C

In your opinion, Jonson's problem is that it is selling the wrong clothes at the wrong price.
- It doesn't have enough top-selling products at low prices.
- The products are not stylish or colourful.
- The store is dull. It needs to be redecorated in bright colours.
- It needs to improve the display of the clothes.

You think Jonson should focus on the young segment of the market (the 15–30 age group). It should recruit a fashion expert with an international reputation – someone who knows what to buy and when to buy.

Grammar reference

1 Present simple and present continuous

Present simple

We use the present simple:

1 to give factual information, for example about company activities.
   *Unilever **makes** a wide variety of consumer goods.*
   ***Does** it **market** these goods globally?*
   *It **doesn't sell** in every sector.*

2 to talk about routine activities or habits.
   *I always **buy** the supermarket's own brand of detergent.*
   ***Do** you usually **pick up** groceries on the way home?*
   *He **doesn't choose** clothes with large designer labels.*

3 for actions and situations which are generally true.
   *Many consumers **prefer** well-known brands.*

4 for timetables and scheduled events.
   *We **launch** the new range on 15 January.*

Present continuous

We use the present continuous:

1 to talk about ongoing situations and projects.
   *We**'re developing** a completely new image for the brand.*
   ***Are** you still **working** with those designers?*
   *They **aren't saying** anything to the press this time.*

2 to describe temporary situations.
   *We**'re testing** a new logo at the moment.*
   ***Are** they **offering** a good discount during the launch period?*

3 to describe trends.
   *The number of people shopping online is **growing**.*

4 to talk about personal arrangements and plans.
   *I**'m meeting** Frau Scharping next week.*

2 Talking about the future

1 We use *going to* to talk about what we intend to do or what someone else has already decided to do.
   *I'm **going to** buy a new car.*
   *She's **going to** tell us about the ideas they've come up with for the ad campaign.*

   Both *going to* and *will* are used for predictions.
   *There's **going to** be a flight of capital from the West towards India and China.*
   *The Fortune Garment Company **will** continue to lose market share unless it solves its problems.*

2 We use *'ll* to make a spontaneous promise or offer to do something.
   *'I haven't got time to do this myself.' 'Don't worry. I**'ll** give you a hand.'*

3 We use the present continuous to talk about fixed plans or arrangements.
   *I**'m meeting** Mrs da Silva next week. She**'s arriving** on Wednesday.*

4 We use the present simple to talk about a schedule.
   *The flight **leaves** at 15.50 tomorrow.*

   In time clauses, we use the present simple to refer to future time. It is incorrect to use *will* in a time clause.
   *We won't start until everyone **gets** here.*
   *I'm going to go round the world when I **retire**.*
   *As soon as I **have** the results, I'll give you a ring.*
   *Come and see me before you **go**.*

3 Noun combinations

1 We use 's to express a relationship between a person or organisation and another person or thing.

Mr Blake's secretary   her husband's car
BA's employees   Volvo's reputation

The 's very often means that the relationship can be expressed using *have*.

*Mr Blake **has** a secretary.*
*Volvo **has** a reputation.*

2 When two nouns are used together, the first noun functions as an adjective and describes the second noun.

a business card   a job description
an office complex a travel agency

Sometimes three or more nouns occur together.

a company credit card (a credit card issued by a company)
a management training programme (a training programme designed for management)

3 Two nouns are joined by *of* when the ideas are more abstract.

*the cost **of** living*
*independence **of** mind*
*the joy **of** working and lifelong learning*

4 Some compound nouns are written as one word.

database   answerphone
letterhead   headquarters

5 When compound nouns are used with a number in expressions of measurement, the first noun is singular.

a six-lane motorway   a four-day week

4 Past simple and present perfect

Past simple

1 We use the past simple to refer to events that took place in the past.

*A pharmacist called John Pemberton **invented** Coca-Cola.*
*'**Did** you **go** to Berlin last week?' 'Yes, and I **met** Herr Gnuchtel.'*

2 We frequently use a time adverb to situate the event in finished past time.

*Rolls Royce went bust **in 1973**.*
***A few years ago**, the City Plaza hotel was a leader in its segment of the market.*
*Many people lost a lot of money on the Stock Exchange **during the 1990s**.*

3 We use the past simple in annual reports to describe the company's performance over the last year.

*Last year **was** a good year for our group.*
*Sales **rose** by more than 11% and we **made** substantial gains in market share in a number of countries.*

Present perfect

1 We use the present perfect to say that a finished past action is relevant now.

*They **have developed** a new brand of toothpaste.*
*The chairman **has** recently **resigned**.*

2 We use the present perfect when we are thinking of a period of time continuing up to the present.

*For over 50 years, Stirling Cars **has developed** classic sports cars.*
*Calvin Klein **has been** one of the leading fashion designers since the mid-1970s.*

3 We often use this tense to talk about our life experiences.

*She **has had** a number of interesting jobs.*
*He**'s worked** for a variety of firms.*

5 Trends

1 To describe changing circumstances we can use verbs of movement.

improve	*increase*	*recover*	*rise* (↗)
decline	*decrease*	*drop*	*fall* (↘)

A dramatic movement may be expressed by:

rocket	*soar*	(↗)
dive	*plummet*	(↘)

A slight movement can be indicated by:

edge up		(↗)
edge down	*dip*	(↘)

The amount of increase can also be indicated using these verbs:

halve	(/2)
double	(x2)
triple	(x3)
quadruple	(x4)
increase tenfold	(x10)

Or with a preposition:

*Our business grew **by** 15% last year.*
*Sales have increased **from** €5 million **to** €5.8 million.*

2 Changes which have not reached their end-point are expressed using *-ing*.

*Profits are fall**ing**.*
*Unemployment has been ris**ing**.*

If the change is complete we use a perfect tense.

*The Government **has privatised** the rail network.*
*Sales **have increased** and that has meant higher profits.*

6 Articles

The indefinite article: *a/an*

We use *a/an* in the following ways:

- before unspecified singular countable nouns.
  *She works in **an** office.*

- with the names of professions.
  *She's **an** executive and he's **a** manager.*

- in expressions of measurement.
  *We charge $500 **an** hour.*
  *It sells at €1.75 **a** litre.*

- before a noun to mean all things of the same type.
  ***A** loss leader is **an** article that a store sells at a low price to tempt customers to buy other goods.*

The definite article: *the*

We use *the*:

- when it is clear from the context what particular thing or place is meant.
  *I'll meet you in **the** reception area.*

- before a noun that we have mentioned before.
  *They had **a** villa in Cannes and **a** chalet in Innsbruck but they sold **the** villa.*

- before adjectives to specify a category of people or things.
  ***the** rich, **the** poor, **the** French, **the** unemployed, **the** World Wide Web*

Zero article: (Ø)

1 We do not put an article before mass nouns used in general statements.

(Ø) Money is the root of all (Ø) evil.

2 Usually there is no article before the names of places and people.

(Ø) Poland	*(Ø) Japan*	*(Ø) Dr Spock*
(Ø) President Clinton		

7 Modal verbs 1

Advice

1 We can use *should* and *shouldn't* to give or ask for advice.

You **should** *always learn something about a country before visiting it.*

Should *I invite our agents out to dinner after the meeting?*

- *Should* often follows the verbs *suggest* and *think*.

I think we **should** *find out more about them before signing the contract.*

2 For strong advice we can use *must* or *mustn't*.

They **must** *pay their bills on time in future.*
You **mustn't** *refuse if you're offered a small gift.*

Obligation / Necessity

1 We often use *must* when the obligation comes from the person speaking or writing.

We **must** *ask them to dinner when they're over here.*

2 We use *mustn't* to say that something is prohibited, it is not allowed.
You **mustn't** *smoke in here.*

3 We often use *have to* to show that the obligation comes from another person or institution, not the speaker.

You **have to** *renew your residence permit after three months.* (This is the law.)

Lack of obligation / Lack of necessity

We use *don't have to* when there is no need or obligation to do something.
You **don't have to** *wait for your order. You can collect it now.*

- Compare the uses of *must not* and *don't have to* here.

We **mustn't** *rush into a new partnership too quickly. We* **don't have to** *make a decision for at least six months.*

8 Indirect questions and statements

1 Indirect questions are often used to ask for possibly sensitive information politely.

Could you tell me *what your salary is?*
May I ask *why you want to leave your current post?*

2 We also use indirect questions and statements to sound generally more polite and less abrupt.

Do you know *why the e-mail system is down?*
I wonder *how long we should allow for the trip into town.*
I think *he doesn't want to be disturbed right now.*
She feels *it's not a good time to raise the issue.*

3 Indirect questions have the same word order as statements.

You want to work abroad. (statement)
Could you tell me *why you want to work abroad?*

4 We can use the following expressions to introduce indirect questions and statements.

I wonder / can't remember / have no idea / 'd like to know / 'm not sure when *the interview starts.*

5 For *yes / no* questions we use *if* or *whether*.

Will he apply for the job? (direct question)
I don't know **if** *he'll apply for the job.*
I wonder **whether** *he'll apply for the job.*

9 Conditions

First conditional

1 We use conditional sentences when discussing the terms of an agreement, making hypothetical proposals, bargaining and making concessions.

*If you order now we **will** give you a discount.*
*We **will** reduce the price by 10% **if** you give us a firm order in advance.*
*If we give you 90 days' credit instead of 60, **will** you give us the interest you would have paid?*

The use of *if* + *will* + base form of the verb suggests that the acceptance of the condition is the basis for a deal.

2 We use *unless* in conditional sentences to mean *if not*.

*We **won't** be able to start construction **unless** you train our personnel.*

3 *As long as* and *provided that* are also used to state conditions.

*We **will** sign the contract **as long as** you guarantee prices for the next eighteen months.*
*We can reach agreement on a joint venture **provided that** our firm has a representative on your board.*

Second conditional

If the proposal is more tentative and possibly less feasible we use past verb forms.

*If we **said** we were prepared to deliver in March **would** you make a firm order?*
*If you **agreed** to create more jobs we **might** think about a productivity deal.*
*If the Government **found** some extra money, **would** you be prepared to create a subsidiary in our country?*

10 Gerunds and infinitives

1 We sometimes use one verb after another verb. Often the second verb is in the infinitive form:

*We **are continuing to cut** our manufacturing costs.*
*Management **agreed to offer** generous redundancy terms to all staff affected.*

- The verbs below are often followed by the infinitive.

intend	attempt	promise	plan
mean	try	arrange	offer
want	pretend	hope	forget
seem	fail	wish	expect
claim	guarantee		

2 But sometimes the second verb must be in the *-ing* form (the gerund). This depends on the *first verb*.

*The decision **involves reducing** our heavy losses.*

- The verbs below are usually followed by the gerund.

admit	appreciate	contemplate
give up	involve	deny
enjoy	consider	carry on
mean	mind	justify
can't stand	don't mind	remember
resent	detest	recommend
risk	delay	miss
suggest	avoid	put off
look forward to		

3 Some verbs can be followed by the gerund or the infinitive form without a big change in meaning.

*She **started loading** the software. / She **started to load** the software.*

- Sometimes, however, the meaning changes.

*She **stopped to read** the manual. (She stopped what she was doing in order to read the manual.)*

*She **stopped reading** the manual. (She no longer bothered to read the manual.)*

11 Narrative tenses

1 The past simple is common when we describe a sequence of events or tell a story in chronological order about events that happened in the past.

   *On Monday 3 December 1984, a poisonous cloud of gas **escaped** from a pesticide plant in Bhopal, India. Eye witnesses **described** a cloud in the shape of a mushroom which **rose** above the plant and then descended over the town.*

2 We use the past perfect to situate an event that happened before another past event.

   *By the end of the week, 1,200 people **had died** and at least 10,000 **had been affected** very seriously.*

3 The present perfect is used to describe past events of current significance.

   *A major problem for doctors in Bhopal was lack of information on how to treat the chemical's effects. A pathologist said: 'Why **hasn't** Union Carbide **come forward** to tell us about the gas that **has leaked** and how to treat it. Is it not their moral duty? They **have not come** forward.'*

4 We use the past continuous to describe unfinished events which were in progress around a particular past time.

   *By Monday 10 December, the death toll had risen to 2,000 and American lawyers representing Indian families **were suing** Union Carbide for $12.5 billion in compensation. Meanwhile journalists **were asking** the company difficult questions about its safety procedures and the share price **was dropping** sharply as investors became worried about the billions of dollars of compensation that the company might have to pay.*

   (Adapted from Ian Marcousé, *Business Case Studies*, Longman 1990)

12 Relative clauses

1 We use *who* or *that* in a relative clause to identify people.

   *The people **who/that** we employ are very highly qualified.*
   As *people* is the object of the clause, the relative pronoun can be left out.
   The people we employ are very highly qualified.
   If the relative pronoun defines the subject of the sentence, it must be included.
   *A counterfeiter is a person **who** copies goods in order to trick people.*

2 We use *that* or *which* in a relative clause to identify things.

   *Have you read the report **that/which** I left on your desk?*
   If *that* or *which* identifies the object of the clause it can be left out.
   Have you read the report I left on your desk?
   If *that* or *which* defines the subject of the sentence, it must be included.
   *Organisations **that** are flexible can respond to change.*

3 Non-defining clauses provide extra information about the subject or object of a sentence. The extra information is separated by commas.

   *Philip Condit, **who was** chairman of Boeing, wanted the airline to become a global company.*
   Note that it is not possible to use *that*.
   *The Dorfmann hotel, **which** is situated 30 kms outside Vienna, charges US$ 1,400 per person.*
   Again, it is not possible to use *that* in a non-defining clause.

13 Passives

1 We use a passive structure when we are not interested in who carries out an action or it is not necessary to know.

*The company **was founded** in 1996.*
*Some changes **have been made**.*
*He **has been promoted** to the post of Sales Director.*
*A new low-alcohol lager **is being developed**.*

2 If we also want to mention who performs the action we can use a phrase beginning with *by*.

*The self-extinguishing cigarette was invented **by Kaj Jensen**.*
*The prototype is being checked **by the design team**.*

3 In a passive sentence, the grammatical subject receives the focus.

***You will be met** at the airport by a company driver.*
(*You* receives the focus of attention.)

Compare with:
***A company driver will meet** you at the airport.*

4 The passive is often used to describe processes and procedures.

*First of all an advertising agency **is contacted** and the aim of the campaign **is discussed**. Then a storyboard **is created** and, if acceptable, the TV commercial **is filmed** and **broadcast** at prime time.*

5 We also use the passive in a formal or impersonal style.

*It **was felt** that our design should be more innovative.*
*Company procedures **must be respected** at all times.*

14 Modal verbs 2

We use different modal verbs to say that an event or situation is certain, probable or possible.

1 We often use *will /won't* with an adverb to show how certain we are that something will or will not happen.

*Price-cutting in the car industry **will certainly** continue next year.*
*But we **probably** /**definitely** /**certainly won't** cut our prices again.*

2 We use *should, ought to, be likely to* when we think something will probably happen:

*Our profits **are likely to** improve next quarter.*

• When we expect something will *not* happen, we use *shouldn't, ought not to, be unlikely to*.

*That **shouldn't** be a problem.*
*The government's forecasts **are unlikely to** be wrong this time.*

3 We use *may, could, may not, might not* when there is only a *possibility* that something will or will not happen.

*The situation **may** improve in the longer term.*
*There **could** be a recession next year.*
*The new model's success **might not** be enough to save the company.*

4 We use *must* or *can't* to make a logical deduction.

*She **must** be exhausted after such a long delay.*
*They **can't** be serious. That's an impossible deadline to meet.*

Audio scripts

1 Brands

🎧 1.1 (I = Interviewer, R1 = Respondent 1, R2 = Respondent 2)

I   Do you buy brands?

R1 Yes I do. I am basically pro brands. If you buy a branded product it's a guarantee that the quality is fairly good and the product is reliable. Another reason is you attract a bit of attention if you buy something stylish, and branded products are usually stylish and have a good design. Let's face it, most people buy brands because they want to impress other people. They want to show that they have style and good taste.

I   Do you buy brands?

R2 No. I don't want to give free advertising to companies. I hate all the advertising hype around brands. And I don't want other people to think I'm trying to impress them with lots of logos. And I also get fed up seeing the same things wherever you go. If you buy a suit from a famous brand you'll see five people with the same suit that month. It's so boring. Another thing – am I buying the genuine product or an illegal copy? Basically I want value for money. I won't pay inflated prices for a name, a fancy logo and packaging. However, I do buy brands for my kids – especially sports goods and trainers – it's always Nike, Adidas or Reebok.

🎧 1.2 (I = Interviewer, SG = Sandra Greaves)

I   What are brands and why do we need them?

SG Well, brands are all about trust. You know what a brand is about, what it means, what it's going to deliver and you actually trust it to deliver time and time again. So in a world of endless choice, a brand can give you something to fix on – it's a kind of beacon in the darkness. So you know that Coca-Cola will taste exactly the same wherever you are in the world.

You can argue that we don't need brands, that we'd all be better off in a world where nothing is branded and we all wear blue overalls and buy oats out of sacks and have no choice over who we bank with or what TV channels we watch. And I think one thing about brands is they add a lot of colour and enjoyment and fun, as well as giving you the power to choose things.

🎧 1.3 (I = Interviewer, SG = Sandra Greaves)

I   And what's the secret of a really successful brand?

SG Really successful brands are ones that tap into an emotion and that way they can inspire fierce loyalty. So they're much more than just a product or a service – they're an attitude, and that's carried through in everything about the brand – from the communications to the culture of the organisation, to everything you see about the brand. So, Apple is a good example. It stands for a kind of anti-authoritarianism. It's against big corporations, though it is a big corporation itself, and Apple started out when computers were big and scary and quite off-putting. Apple invented the Mac and you turned it on and you got a smiley face, it was really easy to use and that's something that Apple has carried through right through till today, where people are in love with the i-Pod and the i-Mac and the i-Book.

🎧 1.4 (I = Interviewer, SG = Sandra Greaves)

I   Can you give an example of how you've helped a company with its branding?

S   Yes, our er… the classic example we have is Orange, the mobile phone service, and Orange really changed the way people felt about mobile phones. When everyone else was talking about technology, Orange talked about lifestyle and communication. It was originally going to be called Microtel and we worked with the parent company to get them away from all of that and create something entirely different. Something that was about optimism. 'The future's bright, the future's Orange' is the line that everyone remembers and it created a new world of communication – people became quite passionate about using Orange and it was highly successful financially.

🎧 1.5 (M = Marcia, A = Alain, V = Valerie, B = Barbara)

M OK, we all agree we want to increase our revenue by licensing our 'Luc Fontaine' product range. As you know, Susan Li, one of our contacts in Hong Kong, is very interested. Alain, how do you feel about this? Is she the right person for us?

A   Definitely. In my opinion, she's ideal. She's well-known in Asia, she's got an excellent reputation in the industry. She's got a modern factory and a large customer base; I'd say she's just what we're looking for.

M Right. Valerie, what do you think?

V   I agree because she's very good at marketing. I've met her several times. She'll work twenty-four hours a day to get a sale. Just the sort of person we want.

M Barbara, you're shaking your head. What's your opinion?

B   I'm afraid I can't agree. I don't think she's suitable at all. All her products sell at the lower end of the market. They're in the cheaper price ranges. But our Luc Fontaine range is exclusive. The male and female perfumes are for people who don't mind spending a lot of money to look good. They're not a good match for what she's selling.

M So what do you suggest then?

B   I think we should find someone else. I do have someone in mind. I met Hiroshi Takahashi recently. He's based in Nagoya. His health-care company is doing really well. He makes various skin products and sells them under well-known European labels. In my opinion, his company has a lot to offer. Why don't we meet him and see if he's interested?

🎧 1.6 (MM = Marketing Manager, SD = Sales Director)

MM Pietro, can I have a word with you? I've just been talking to Gina Delassi, Majestic's new Purchasing Manager. They're going to cancel their contract with us. They won't change their mind.

SD Why, what's the problem? That's fifty percent of our business: we can't afford to lose them. What reason did they give for cancelling?

MM You know that Café Velvet has just launched a new advertising campaign? Well, Majestic's Head Chef is endorsing it! They're introducing Café Velvet in all their hotels. Café Velvet is also talking to the supermarkets, apparently.

SD What can we do? Are you talking to other hotel chains? Any ideas on who we can get to endorse our product? We need to talk to the supermarkets about our new campaign.

MM Yes, our department has already brainstormed a shortlist of possible celebrity names. And we have drawn up an action plan to target supermarkets. We aim to put these plans before the board next week.

SD Good to see a sense of urgency. Don't forget to survey other hotel chains. We can't rely on one chain in the current situation.

2 Travel

🎧 2.1

Traveller 1

What I really don't like is the way airlines treat people on the plane. There are far too many seats on most planes, so there's not enough leg room, and I'm not even particularly tall! Also the poor-quality food and drink you get on airlines annoys me. It's all so processed and packaged, I just can't eat it. I prefer trains!

Traveller 2

I like flying, but I really don't enjoy being at airports. Things like long queues at check-in irritate me. Also when I have a lot of luggage and there are no baggage trolleys available, it's really inconvenient. What I find even more frustrating is when I finally do find a trolley and then find the departures board is full of flight delays and cancellations.

Traveller 3

I must be very unlucky because it seems I am always a victim of lost or delayed luggage. It usually turns up but never with an apology. I don't like the attitude of the airlines. They seem to treat passengers like just another piece of luggage to be moved around the world. They seem to forget that we are people. For example, they overbook seats and just expect people to be able to take the next flight if their flight is full. What I really hate though is jet-lag. It's a big problem for me, as I travel a lot to the Far East on business.

🎧 2.2

My last overseas business trip was a nightmare from start to finish. First of all there was a delay on the way to the airport as there was an accident on the freeway. When I got there the lower level of the airport parking lot was flooded. Next my carry-on baggage was too big and heavy so I had to check it in. When we arrived the subway was closed and there were no cabs at all. After a long time trying to read the schedule and waiting for forty minutes, we finally got a bus downtown and found the hotel, but the elevator wasn't working and our rooms were on the fifth floor.

🎧 2.3 (I = Interviewer; ST = Stephanie Taylor)

I What are the main priorities for business travellers today?

ST The first thing I'd say is the need for, for good organisation: for someone to organise everything for you. Erm…air tickets of course – transport to and from the airport… accommodation. It's really important to erm, to have, to have that support. And the second thing I'd say relates to the airline that you choose or the cost of the flights. I think it's important to balance cost concerns with the need for comfort for the business traveller. So, on a short haul flight into Europe, perhaps cost is, er, is the main factor – looking for a cheap ticket, erm – whereas travelling to a different continent, it's important to, to look more at the comfort factor: plenty of space and, and, sleep, the ability to sleep on the flight. So cost, comfort is important. And then thirdly, I think, for the business traveller, erm, it's a big advantage if you can be very patient, because, er, there are often delays, and also, erm, it's important to be able to work in the airport. It is sort of an extension of your office when you're travelling a lot. So, if you're in a business lounge, that's okay, but it's also important to be able to work in an economy class, general airport, I think. So it helps to be very patient.

I With new communications technology, do businesspeople need to travel so much?

ST Yes, I think they probably do, particularly… I think it's particularly important to establish good face-to-face relations with colleagues or with customers. Perhaps after the first meeting you can continue your relationship by telephone and by Internet. But I think, er, yes, from a PR perspective, and contact with customers, I think business travel will continue to be as important as it is now.

🎧 2.4 (I = Interviewer; ST = Stephanie Taylor)

I What are the best travel experiences you've had?

ST Ooh, lots, lots. Particularly, it's particularly good when you get a great hotel with beautiful towels and beautiful bathrooms and nice soft bed, erm, and good sports facilities. Things like that – that's always a luxury. Erm, and the Virgin, the Virgin lounge, I think. That's a good experience with all the high tech things. I like that.

I What are the worst?

ST Probably related to bad accommodation, but probably more, I think, to do with those things out of your control. Just to choose one example, it would be a flight back from the US which was delayed, and delayed, and delayed, and finally cancelled. And we all slept on the floor of the airport, with no information. And it was very hard on the floor.

🎧 2.5 (I = Interviewer; ST = Stephanie Taylor)

I What further developments do you see in business travel?

ST Hmm. Perhaps, particularly in the area of accommodation, I think hotels will need to improve their standards in general. There are some very good hotels already, but I think more hotels will provide facilities for businesspeople…perhaps some specific facilities for businesswomen.

🎧 2.6 (R = Receptionist, PK = Philippa Knight, MB = Maria Bonetti)

Conversation 1

R Good morning, CPT. How may I help you?

PK It's Philippa Knight here. Could you put me through to extension 281, please?

R Certainly. Putting you through.

MB Hello. Maria Bonetti speaking.

PK Hello Maria. It's Philippa Knight from The Fashion Group in New York.

MB Hi Philippa, how are things?

PK Fine thanks. I'm calling because I'll be in London next week and I'd like to make an appointment to see you. I want to tell you about our new collection.

MB Great. What day would suit you? I'm fairly free next week, I think.

PK How about Wednesday? In the afternoon? Could you make it then?

MB Let me look now. Let me check my diary. Oh yes, that'd be no problem at all. What about two o'clock? Is that OK?

PK Perfect. Thanks very much. It'll be great to see you again. We'll have plenty to talk about.

MB That's for sure. See you next week then.

PK Right. Bye.

MB Bye.

🎧 2.7 (R = receptionist, PK = Philippa Knight, MB = Maria Bonetti)

Conversation 2

R Good morning, CPT. How may I help you?

PK I'd like to speak to Maria Bonetti, extension 281, please.

R Thank you. Who's calling, please?

PK It's Philippa Knight, from The Fashion Group.

R Thank you. I'm putting you through. … Hello, I'm afraid she's engaged at the moment. Will you hold or can I take a message?

PK I'll leave a message, please. The thing is, I should be meeting Ms Bonetti at 2 p.m., but something's come up. My plane was delayed and I've got to reschedule my appointments. If possible, I'd like to meet her tomorrow. Preferably in the morning. Could she call me back here at the hotel, please?

R Certainly. What's the number, please?

PK It's 020 7585 3814. I'll be leaving the hotel soon, so if she can't call me back within, say, within the next quarter of an hour, I'll call her again this morning. Is that OK?

R Right. I've got that. I'll make sure she gets the message.

PK Thanks for your help. Goodbye.

R Goodbye.

3 Organisation

🎧 3.1

1 Stock levels have been low for two weeks now.

2 Can you e-mail these sales figures through to head office as soon as possible?

3 Hold on a minute, please, I'll transfer you to a supervisor.

4 We need to deliver this consignment on Friday.

5 The production line is operating at full capacity.

6 The Board of Directors have fixed the Annual General Meeting for Tuesday the second.

7 Why do we always have to check with the parent company before making decisions?

8 All our engineers are out working on repairs at the moment.

🎧 3.2 (I = Interviewer, RB = Richard Brown)

I How does Cognosis analyse the character of a business?

RB Understanding the character or personality of a business is important because it shapes and defines everything the organisation does and can do. So we use a combination of four approaches. First, we study the tone and style of the company's communications. Second, we interview the company's top executives in depth. Third, we conduct research, more broadly, across the company's staff and its customers. And finally, we'll analyse the company's internal documents. That provides insight into how the business talks to itself. And when we've got that sort of input we can classify a business as one of sixteen distinct character types. And these handle aspects of change, innovation and relating to customers in very different ways.

🎧 3.3 (I = Interviewer, RB = Richard Brown)

I Can you give an example of how a business changed its organisation and why?

RB Yeah. Many businesses try to change their organisation – their culture – and they do that to be better able to compete and grow. But it's a very hard thing to do. It's often easier to change a business's character by merging with or acquiring a competitor. A good example of this was the merger of Guinness and Grand Metropolitan in 1998. This created a twenty-three-billion-pound company, Diageo, the world leader in spirits. The top team achieved a very substantial change in culture by being very clear at the outset that it was creating a new and different culture from the two companies that merged. And they did that by laying out a very clear vision. They were very specific about how the new business would be run. They laid out clear values and ways of working for staff and they backed this up with a huge investment in staff training. This created a completely new culture which has been hugely successful.

🎧 3.4 (I = Interviewer, RB = Richard Brown)

I Are some types of business organisation always more successful than others?

RB Well, our research suggests that there are sixteen different types of organisational character, or culture. And no single type is consistently associated with business success or market leadership. Having said that, we do find that particularly successful companies tend to be similar in three ways. First, they're future-oriented: they have a very clear sense of where they are headed. Second, they're customer-driven: they invest huge time and energy in understanding and responding to their markets. And third, they are values-driven. By that I mean that people inside the organisation are very clear about the values that should guide their decisions and behaviours – the principles by which the business is run.

3.5 (L = Louise, M = Marcus)

Conversation 1

L Hello Marcus, nice to see you again.

M Hi Louise. How are you?

L Fine thanks. I haven't seen you for ages. We last met at the Frankfurt fair, didn't we? How's everything going?

M Pretty well at the moment. I'm still in the same department and I got promoted last year, so I'm now head of data processing. I'm in charge of about thirty people.

L Fantastic!

M How about you? Are you still in Accounts?

L Actually no. I changed my job last year. I'm in marketing now. I'm really enjoying it.

M That's good.

L Yes, but the big news is, Marcus, I got married last year.

M Really? That's great! Well, congratulations! Anyone I know?

3.6 (DL = Don Larsen, EK = Erika Koenig)

Conversation 2

DL Hi, my name's Don Larsen.

EK Pleased to meet you. I'm Erika Koenig.

DL Which part of the group do you work for?

EK I've just joined MCB. We provide financial services. How about you?

DL I work for Atsource Solutions.

EK I don't know much about Atsource Solutions. What sort of projects do you work on?

DL Well, we're basically an outsourcing business. We supply large companies with various services including payroll, IT services and human resources.

EK Is Atsource Solutions a new company?

DL No, we're well-established. The company was founded in 1978. It's organised into three divisions. We have over six thousand employees; we've got our headquarters in Frankfurt and offices in over twenty countries – we're pretty big.

3.7 (J = John, M = Miriam, H = Heinz)

Conversation 3

J Heinz, I'd like you to meet Miriam. She's on a work placement here, she'll be with us for the next three months.

M Nice to meet you, Heinz.

H It's a pleasure.

J Miriam speaks fluent Italian, so she could be very useful when you're dealing with our Italian customers. Also, she's very keen on skiing. So you two should have something in common.

H Oh, that's interesting. Have a seat, Miriam. Would you like a drink?

4 Change

4.1 (I = Interviewer, MM = Maggie Miller)

I You've introduced some major business changes at Sainsbury's. Why was it necessary to change?

MM Well, in the year two thousand we had a new Chief Executive join the company. Peter Davis joined a company that had been very, very successful in the past but had become rather complacent and had lost its business lead over its competitors. Peter analysed the situation and realised that we needed some major investments: firstly in our supply chain – that's our depots and logistics infrastructure; secondly in upgrading our stores, which were beginning to look very old and tired; and thirdly we needed to support the business in developing some new capabilities, for which we needed a very large investment in new IT systems – in fact, replacing all our IT systems over a period of four years. We reviewed the capabilities we had in our own IT team and realised we needed much greater depth and breadth of skills and we needed to inject some world-leading best practice, and therefore decided to use a third party.

I And what has happened since you introduced these changes?

MM Well, we haven't completely finished yet. I think it's fair to say we're eighty to ninety percent through the IT system change, but we still have a long way to go in changing all our business processes and all our ways of working and driving out the maximum benefits. We have

already seen some major changes in attitudes as people see the barriers eliminated. In the past, the IT systems stopped people improving the way they did things. Now those barriers have been eliminated and you find that many people feel released and able to embrace new ways of doing things. For some people that's more difficult. But we're already, we have already delivered over seven hundred million pounds in measurable benefits.

4.2 (I = Interviewer, MM = Maggie Miller)

I And which was the most successful change and why?

MM The whole programme has been very, very successful. The things that have been easier have been those where the change was limited to one division or one function. But the one initiative that I'm proudest of, probably, is the change in all our point-of-sale systems – and that's the tills at the front of the stores. We have about five hundred stores, each of which have up to fifty sales tills. And we embarked on a programme to replace all those tills, their associated cabling, system software and infrastructure in a very short time period. And a lot of people said we couldn't do it. In fact, we changed those tills at a rate of twenty-two stores per week. And that involved replacing the hardware and the software and the technical environments for fourteen thousand sales tills. We had to retrain a hundred thousand people, and it involved the installation of five hundred tonnes of equipment. That change happened very rapidly and didn't – for every store, we made the change overnight and we didn't have to delay the opening of any store on any day. That was a huge commitment and a huge achievement on the part of a very large number of people.

I And what advice would you give to businesses planning change?

MM I think it would be to plan very carefully, and especially if there's a lot of computer system change, to recognise that the computer system change is a tiny piece of what's required, that there are three pieces you need to focus on. One has to do with people – their attitudes, the culture and how they're rewarded. Another has to do with the business processes – how they have to change – and the third leg is the computer systems. It's important to focus on all three and plan very carefully. And I've heard someone from computer company HP say that in their change programme they put four times the amount of effort into the new way of working than the old because, by their very nature, people and companies will refer...revert to the old ways of working if you don't put a quite disproportionate amount of effort into doing things the new way.

4.3 (C = Carl, N = Nancy, M = Max, S = Stefan)

C Can we move on to the next point, the open-plan office? Nancy, would you like to begin?

N I like the idea. It's good for communication, people see each other at the office, it's, er, it's good for team spirit, too. There's more interaction between people, and people work harder when they're on display.

M I'm not sure I agree with you there. With open-plan offices, there's a problem of privacy.

C OK Max, thanks. Em, Stefan, what do you think?

S I agree with Max about privacy. What if you want to have a private conversation or make a private phone call?

C Well ... erm ... I suggest we use meeting rooms for private conversations or calls.

S Meeting rooms? Yes, that's true, I suppose ...

M Could I just say something? I don't think it works.

C Let Stefan finish please, Max...

M Well I'm not happy about it. I don't think we should have a vote about it now. I mean, I think we need a report or an extra survey done about this.

C How do you mean, 'an extra survey'? Are you saying we need to bring in a consultant?

M No, I was thinking of someone inside the company.

C OK, I think a report is probably better. I propose that someone prepares a report on the open-plan idea, by, say, the end of the month. Is everyone agreed?

All Yes, right, agreed.

C Right, can we move on to the next item on the agenda, 'hot-desking', Max?

M Frankly, I was shocked to see the proposal about hot-desking. I don't think it's a good idea at all. It will upset people and it just won't work.

C OK, how do you feel about it Nancy?

N I'm pretty sure hot-desking won't work unless we have an open-plan office. I don't think hot-desking works in closed offices.

S Sorry, I don't follow you, Nancy. What exactly are you saying?

N What I mean is, we could change to an open-plan system but I'm against introducing hot-desking now. It's not good to change everything too quickly. Staff need time to get used to changes.

🎧 4.4 (I = Interviewer, HW = Hugh Whitman)

I I imagine you'll be making some changes, Mr Whitman, now that you're in charge at Metrot.

HW Yes, there will certainly be some changes, there always are when you acquire another company. Metrot is a fine company, that's why we bought it. It has a skilled workforce and excellent products. We think we can help Metrot to become more dynamic and efficient. We want it to compete successfully in European markets where there are big opportunities for us.

I You say, more efficient. Does that mean reorganisation? Job losses? I believe that the staff at Metrot are worried about this.

HW It's too early to say. But there could be some staff cutbacks in the short term. We shall see. Our plan is to expand the company and create as many job opportunities as possible.

I What about the factories? Some people say you're thinking of relocating some of the factories and selling off some of the land you've acquired.

HW I don't want to comment on that. Our aim is to build Metrot and make it a strong company at the leading edge of technology, with an image for quality, reliability and good service.

I I see. Thank you, Mr Whitman. I wish you the best of luck in your new position.

5 Money

🎧 5.1

Yahoo has strengthened its European presence with the four hundred and seventy-five million euro acquisition (that's a five hundred and seventy-eight million dollar acquisition) of Kelkoo, the French-based on-line shopping service. The European on-line retail market is forecast to grow to one hundred and seven billion euros in the next three years.

The Nikkei two two five Average climbed nought point seven percent to eleven thousand, three hundred and sixty-four point nine nine while the Topix index rose one point two percent to one thousand, one hundred and forty-five point nine five. Banking shares benefited most, with Mizuho jumping five point six percent to four hundred and thirty-seven thousand yen, SMFG rising four point seven percent to seven hundred and fifty-two thousand yen, MTFG gaining seven point nine percent to close at one million and fifty thousand yen and UFJ up four point two percent to six hundred and forty-six thousand yen.

🎧 5.2 (I = Interviewer, HC = Hugh Campbell)

I What are the best ways for a new business to raise money?

HC Well, I think there are three key areas to look at if you're an entrepreneur. The first area is bank debt. The second area is private investors or, in the UK, 'business angels' is their colloquial term. And finally there's venture capitalists.

If you're an entrepreneur starting a business for the first time, then often bank debt is not an area which you're going to find very successful – mainly because, if you're a start-up business and you're an inexperienced entrepreneur, the banks won't want to lend to high-risk businesses. And if you don't have any trading history, then they will – are unlikely to provide you with bank debt or with an overdraft – that is, unless you want to provide a personal guarantee to the bank, perhaps putting your house at risk.

The second area, if you're a start-up business, is private investors or business angels. These are typically wealthy individuals that over their life have saved up a considerable amount of money which they want to invest in high-risk, high-return businesses. So this is…these are individuals that have decided not to invest in the stock market, which is large, lower-risk investments, but to really take up an opportunity to make ten times their money by investing in start-up businesses.

And the third area to look at is venture capital. Now venture capital is only appropriate for entrepreneurs that are looking to raise more than a million pounds. If it's less than a million pounds then you need to go down the private investor route. An example of a venture capitalist in the UK is a company called 3i.

So, if you're an established business looking to raise money then the bank debt route is probably the most appropriate. If it's under a million pounds then it's private investors, and if it's over a million pounds then it's venture capital.

🎧 5.3 (I = Interviewer, HC = Hugh Campbell)

I And how do venture capitalists select the best companies to invest in?

HC There's no real hard and fast rule here, and it's certainly more of an art than a science. However, there are three areas that a venture capitalist will look at. A venture capitalist will look at the market; it will look at the industry; and they will look at the management team. Now the market is an important area because, as an investor, I want to invest in a business which is selling product into a fast-growing market, a large and fast-growing market, because as an investor, if I invest a million pounds, I want to make five million pounds as my return. So, that means I need to invest in a market that is growing very quickly. And the market, it's important to note, is all about the buyers – so who is going to buy my product, at what price are they going to buy it?

The second area is industry and the industry is all about the sellers. So, it's all about the competition. So if you're Renault you're competing against Volkswagen, BMW, and er Mercedes Benz, for example. So, as an entrepreneur starting a business I need to make sure that I have a lot of competitive advantage. And in many cases I deal with technology companies. That means I need to have some intellectual property or some patents which protect my technological advantage.

So, the second area is industry, and the final area, which I think is the most important, is the area of the management team. And management teams are very difficult to assess, but venture capitalists look at three areas. They look at the experience of the management team – i.e. how well do they understand the market and the industry that they are going into. They look at the ability of the management team to execute on their business plan. So, if they've said they're going to turn a business – create a business – with revenues of ten million pounds, as an investor, how much do I trust that view? And finally, which is a very subjective area, is – does this individual manager have the personal commitment to deliver on this plan? Are they willing to work twenty-four hours a day to ensure that my one million pounds turns into five million pounds?

🎧 5.4 (I = Interviewer, HC = Hugh Campbell)

I Can you give us an example of a really good business proposal?

H Well, the most exciting business that we've worked with recently has been a spin-out from Oxford University. And, as you can imagine, from Oxford University they have a lot of intellectual property, so they have a lot of competitive advantage. Secondly, this business is focused on developing software for the computer games industry. The computer games industry is a very exciting market – it's been growing very, very strongly over the last few years, and will continue to do so with the success of people and games like Lara Croft. Now the management team was a difficult area because, although the management team were very technically strong, they didn't have a lot of management experience. But the investor decided to invest a million pounds and the first thing they did after investing was to hire a commercial director to run the company alongside the two founders with technical backgrounds.

🎧 5.5 (I = Interviewer, HC = Hugh Campbell)

I And have you ever missed investing in any big business opportunities?

HC I think there is one company in particular that I now kick myself about, and this is a company in the market of Internet advertising. And I missed out on this mainly because I didn't understand or I couldn't predict the market opportunity.

As you know the Internet bubble collapsed very publicly in 2000 and 2001. And this business that I met offered me an opportunity to invest a million pounds at a valuation of five million. But I decided to turn them down, even though the team was very good, mainly because I couldn't understand how anyone could make any money advertising on the Internet.

Now over the last two or three years, although the media have written a lot of negative things about the Internet, you and I and everybody around this table continues to spend more – more and more time – on the Internet. And so actually this business' business model started to look very exciting. And last year the business was sold to a US competitor for one hundred and sixty million pounds. So the numbers are, are very exciting. I was offered an opportunity to invest and take twenty percent of the business for five million pounds and it's now been sold, two years later, for a hundred and sixty million. So I think if I'd have taken up that opportunity I'd probably be on my yacht down in Monaco right now.

🎧 5.6

Unibrand

We plan to increase sales by at least ten percent this year. We have excellent sales opportunities in South America and Asia. We are opening twenty new sales offices in those areas and increasing our marketing effort. We have already launched a new perfume and we expect it to be very successful.

Technoprint

It's been another excellent year for our inkjet sales. They increased fourteen percent worldwide, even though prices generally for inkjets have fallen because of competition. Our sales of cartridges increased by over twelve percent. Our sales of laser printers remained steady. Our new laser printer has great potential. We expect it to dominate the market as it has several unique features. We will continue to reduce costs by sourcing components from low cost countries.

OLF

I am delighted to report another outstanding performance. Visits to our website have increased to 82,000 daily. We now have over 400,000 regular users. We are launching a multimedia advertising campaign to promote our new ranges of jewellery and travel accessories. We expect to increase our sales target by at least fifty percent and become the leading on-line designer clothing company.

AV

There are fantastic possibilities for our company. The Brazilian government have been very cooperative. They have helped to build a new road to our sites. The area is rich in diamonds. We expect to make profits of at least two hundred million euros this year, and to declare a dividend for the first time. We will issue new shares to finance the exploration of two new sites.

6 Advertising

🎧 6.1 (I = Interviewer, JTW = Jeremy Thorpe Woods)

I   What are the key elements of a really good advertising campaign?

JTW The most important thing nowadays is to be able to gain the consumer's attention. It is much more difficult than it has been in the past to get a share of their attention because there's so much competition out there. So, campaigns have to cut through all the competition and the competitive clutter and they have to be able to involve their target audience. You have to have a very clear point of view, you have to be very single-minded in what you need to say, and I think, certainly in the UK, you have to be able to be entertaining and involving in getting your point across. That is generally the key to a good advertising campaign. The other thing about a campaign is it demands consistency.

🎧 6.2 (I = Interviewer, JTW = Jeremy Thorpe Woods)

I   Can you talk us through the typical planning and launch stages of a campaign?

JTW Well, it starts way before you would ever see anything on television or hear it on the radio. The early stages are in discussion with your clients, where you are talking to them about the business objectives for their company and their brands. And in that process you would develop a marketing strategy. Once you've done that you then need to go and understand in some depth and detail your target audience. So, typically you would go through a research stage where you would observe them, get to know them through qualitative research and understand what motivates them, how they think and feel about the communication. Once that's been done, you pull all those pieces together and develop a creative brief where you start talking to your creative partners about idea generation and then that would take two to three weeks for them to come up with a communication idea, which you would then discuss with your client. But most importantly, you go back to your target audience and talk to them about the idea because it's very rare that you will get it right first time. You then go and make the communication campaign. A thing that's particularly important is that once you have your campaign in the market, is that you use further research to track how it's working in a real sense, to get some feedback for the next stage of the development. So that would be a typical process and, to be honest, each campaign is different and sometimes you can shortcut those, sometimes you have to do more.

🎧 6.3

Formal presentation

Could I have your attention please? Good morning everyone. On behalf of myself and Focus Advertising, I'd like to welcome you. My name's Sven Larsen, I'm Commercial Director.
This morning, I'd like to outline the campaign concept we've developed for you. I've divided my presentation into three parts. Firstly, I'll give you the background to the campaign. Secondly, I'll discuss the media we plan to use. Finally, I'll talk you through the storyboard for the TV commercial. If you have any questions, please don't hesitate to

interrupt me.

Informal presentation

Right let's get started. Hi everyone, I'm Dominique Lagrange. As you know, I'm Creative Director of DMK. Good to see you all. I'm going to tell you about the ideas we've come up with for the ad campaign. My talk is in three parts. I'll start with the background to the campaign, move on to the media we plan to use, and finish with the storyboard for the commercial. If there's anything you're not clear about, go ahead and ask any questions you want.

🎧 6.4

1   I wonder if any of you here know the answer to this question: What's the most popular holiday destination in Europe for people under the age of twenty-five?

2   When I was on holiday a few years ago in Greece, I remember talking to the owner of a taverna. He said to me that in twenty years' time, the little island where he lived would be a popular tourist resort.

3   Let me start by giving you a statistic: ninety-two percent of all Americans do not possess a passport. Think about that, and consider the opportunity it presents to the travel industry.

4   We're facing a crisis with our market share. What are we going to do about it?

5   Someone once said that 'travel broadens the mind'. What I hope to do in this presentation is to demonstrate how to convince the next generation of travellers that this is still true.

7 Cultures

🎧 7.1 (I = Interviewer, JT = Jeff Toms)

I   How do you prepare people to do business internationally?

JT How we prepare people to do business internationally really depends on the task that they're undertaking on behalf of their company or organisation. For example, if you're being sent by your company to live and work overseas for a period say of two or three years, as an assignee, then we would provide you either with a one- or two- day programme covering such issues as: cultural awareness, practical issues of living in, working in, as well as how to deal with culture shock, which everybody goes through when they go on assignment. We'll also deal with particular issues such as schooling, health care and, in particular parts of the world increasingly, with security. However, if, as is the case now, many more people are not actually going to live overseas but have international responsibility. You need a different set of learning tools and that is, first of all, a general cultural awareness and understanding of how you should really operate when dealing with people with other cultures; teaching you how to negotiate contracts; communication, just generally whether that's by telephone, by e-mail or even by the written word. The words that you choose have a very different effect on the recipient depending on which culture you're conversing with.
Another important area these days is presentation skills. In the past it has been assumed that you use the same presentation from your home country when presenting to a more multi-cultural audience. That's very much not the case, and we teach people even down to the kind of words you use on the slides, the colours you use, and indeed how to deal with questions and answers and manage your audience because of course in different cultures there's a different response. Finally, it's very important we believe here at Farnham Castle, to underpin all this with some ability to communicate in the host language. Whilst English is still very much regarded as the international language of business, it is increasingly expected that people will make at least some effort and attempt to learn the language of the people that they are dealing with, particularly in a social environment. It really demonstrates an interest and an affinity with the people that really you are trying to build relationships with and, of course, business is all about building relationships.

🎧 7.2 (I = Interviewer, JT = Jeff Toms)

I   And are there certain skills and techniques for doing business internationally, which can be applied in any culture?

JT I think rather than skills and techniques there are some very strong personality traits that those people who tend to be more successful in an international business environment tend to demonstrate. For example, flexibility and adaptability would be a particularly strong requirement, the ability to observe, participate in something and adapt your own set of skills and knowledge and your own way of doing things.
To actually listen more carefully would be another strong trait that you really ought to demonstrate.

Adaptability, listening and I think really to take an approach with a very positive attitude. I think anybody who approaches cultural issues with a very negative attitude will get a very negative response from the people they are trying to do business with.

🎧 7.3 (I = Interviewer, JT = Jeff Toms)

I And can you give us examples of typical cultural mistakes made by people doing business internationally?

JT There are lots of quoted examples and I think they are really to do with attitudes, particular facets of cultures. For example, time would be a very important cultural aspect that you really do have to learn if you are from a western culture then how you do approach time and how you do business. For example, in a country like Saudi Arabia would be very important.
Other examples are really attitudes to hierarchy. For example: there are many US corporations who have very young, high-flying business, very successful business executives. For example, if you send one of those individuals to meet and do business with a senior Asian businessperson, again Japan comes to mind, then they will be met with a very distinctively negative response, and what indeed will happen is that the senior Asian businessperson will see it very much as an insult, probably either leave the meeting or refuse to attend the meeting and will actually send somebody who they think is of equal status and age to negotiate with that individual and because that lower individual, more junior individual doesn't have the authority then you're very unlikely to achieve anything out of that meeting.

🎧 7.4

1 I was thrown in at the deep end when my company sent me to run the German office. I was only given two days' notice to prepare.
2 We don't really see eye to eye about relocating the factory. The Finance Director wants to move production to the Far East, but the rest of the board want it to remain in Spain.
3 I got into hot water with my boss for wearing casual clothes to the meeting with our Milanese customers.
4 Small talk is one way to break the ice when meeting someone for the first time.
5 I really put my foot in it when I met our Japanese partner. Because I was nervous, I said 'Who are you?' rather than 'How are you?'
6 I get on like a house on fire with our Polish agent; we like the same things and have the same sense of humour.
7 When I visited China for the first time I was like a fish out of water. Everything was so different, and I couldn't read any of the signs!
8 My first meeting with our overseas clients was a real eye-opener. I had not seen that style of negotiation before.

🎧 7.5

A So where did you go for your summer holiday?
B Italy.
A Did you have a good time?
B Yes. It was OK.
A And which part of Italy did you go to?
B Tuscany.
A I went to Pisa – really enjoyed it. What did you think of it?
B Nothing special.
A Oh right. So, … how's it going at work?
B We're really busy.
A That's really good, isn't it?
B I don't know about that.

🎧 7.6

1 I'm sorry. I didn't catch your name.
2 I'm sorry. I'm afraid I'm going to the opera on Tuesday.
3 Not for me thanks; I'm not very keen on fish.
4 I'm sorry. I really must get going. It was really nice talking to you.
5 Welcome to our headquarters.
6 Michael, can I introduce you to John Perry? John's over from the States. John, this is Michael Andrews, my boss.
7 Let me get this.
8 Here's to our future success.
9 I'm very sorry to hear about what happened.
10 I'm sorry I'm late. The traffic was terrible.

🎧 7.7

A Is this your first visit to the Far East?
B No, I come here quite often.
A Oh really. What do you do?
B I'm the Marketing Director for a small import–export company.
A How long have you been there?
B Nearly ten years.
A Have you been to Hong Kong before?

B No. This is my first trip.
A Business or pleasure?
B Business, I'm afraid.
A How long have you been here?
B A week.
A And how long are you staying?
B Till tomorrow night.
A Where are you staying?
B At the Peninsula Hotel.
A What's the food like?
B It's very good, but eating at the Peninsula can be quite expensive.
A So, what do you think of Hong Kong?
B I really like it. There's so much to do.

🎧 7.8 (CE = Catherine Eng)

CE I'll talk first about building relationships with the Chinese, then move on to suitable conversation topics. After that, I'll comment on gift-giving and, finally, mention a couple of points to think about when dealing with Chinese visitors.
It's important to remember that business relationships with the Chinese are built on personal trust and respect. Everything you do during visits must show that you consider your visitors to be important people. Developing a personal relationship and having a good social programme will often be more important than a business meeting.
Remember that status is important. The most senior person may not speak English as well as other, more junior, members of the group. However, you should pay careful attention to everything that person says.
Make an effort to learn and use a few words in Chinese. Your visitors will appreciate this. If there's someone in your company who speaks Chinese, it may be better to use that person instead of a professional interpreter. It will be cheaper and the Chinese may trust a company member of staff more quickly.
Be careful about topics for discussion at social events. Don't embarrass visitors by introducing 'difficult' topics. They will be eager to learn about life in your country and about its culture.
Now a word about gifts. Chinese people will often refuse a gift a number of times before finally accepting. Don't offer anything that's too expensive. Give similar gifts to people who are at the same level of importance. Wrap your gifts in red paper which is considered a lucky colour. Chinese people will appreciate any famous brands of the country they're visiting.
Punctuality is very important. They expect people to arrive on time for a meeting. To arrive late shows a lack of respect.
'Sincerity' is highly valued by the Chinese.

8 Employment

🎧 8.1

Well, what usually happens is that an employer will advertise a vacancy or new post – sometimes both inside and outside the company. Then, after they have received all the applications, they shortlist the candidates, choosing those who appear to meet their criteria. Next, they will assemble an interview panel and call the candidates to an interview. Some employers choose to check references at this stage to avoid delays later, while others wait until after the interview when they have chosen one of the candidates. Provided the panel are happy, the employer will make a job offer and the successful candidate starts work. Often they attend induction sessions or are given a mentor who helps to train new staff.

🎧 8.2 (I = Interviewer, SK = Dr Simon Kingston)

I How do you identify and attract the best candidates for a particular job?
SK Well, the most important thing for us at the beginning is to have clear and full briefing from our clients. So we spend a great deal of time talking to a range of people in the client organisation. And then, according to the sort of job that we are seeking to fill, we will use three different sorts of method for identifying candidates. One, the most obvious one, is advertisement in appropriate newspapers or journals. The second is by asking for nominations from within our client organisation of appropriate candidates. And the third, and most labour intensive for us, is our own, original research. And that will be derived from our database, from talking to authoritative sources in the relevant market place, and then from beginning to map the business sector in which we think we are most likely to find good candidates. All three of those different methods of identifying candidates will cross-reference, and ideally we'd like to find candidates who're sourced from each of the three areas. And

sometimes, when we're very fortunate, we will find an individual who comes referred from each of the three approaches.

In respect of our own research, it's always very valuable for us to be able to speak, at the beginning of a search, to experts in a given sector, perhaps people from the media, commentators, sometimes academics who have wide networks of their own, that are independent from any single client organisation but span a broad cross-section of companies and organisations. And on those occasions, frequently those people will have access to, may have met, rising stars in a given sector, and can offer us an autonomous, an independent view of the skills and abilities of some of those people. And furthermore they may frequently have ideas on the interests and likely level of availability of people. So that when we make an approach to someone we haven't spoken to before, we do it in an informed way.

🎧 8.3 (I = Interviewer, SK = Dr Simon Kingston)

I What advice would you give to someone planning an ambitious business career?

SK I think there isn't one single pattern for success in a business career. But there are one or two things that are apparent and common themes in the careers of a lot of successful people. One of those is an honest understanding of the individual's own strengths and weaknesses, and that allows them, I think, both to plan the sort of organisations in which they will work and which they are likely to succeed; but also, very importantly, allows them to react rapidly but appropriately to opportunities that are unplanned that present themselves. And I do think that's something that distinguishes really successful people from those who are average in their professions. I do think one of the other characteristics that is apparent amongst very successful business leaders is a curiosity that even thirty years in the same sort of business doesn't dilute or indeed destroy. At the very top of major organisations, people like Sir John Browne, now Lord Browne, at BP, demonstrates, even after a lifetime with a single company, which one might say has meant he has been engaged in a very similar sort of activity for the whole of his career – he demonstrates real interest in innovation and also an open-mindedness about the structure of the industry that he leads and how it ought to consider its role and indeed the very essence of what it does in the future. That ability to remain interested in the core essence of one's business is, I think, something that distinguishes the successful. Many of the rest of us lesser mortals get bored very easily, or lose the ability to spot the interest and to sustain motivation and momentum on the strength of it.

🎧 8.4 (A = Andrew, B = Bob, M = Maria)

A Good, everyone's here now. There's coffee if you want it. Right, can we start please? As you all know, Roberto's been working as assistant to Carla Nuñez for six months now. He's just finished his probationary period. How do you feel about offering him a full-time contract?

B I'm not sure we should do it really. It says in this report that he's been late to work a few times and he can be rather ...

M Oh, I don't think that's too important ...

A Could you let him finish, please?

M Oh, sorry ...

B Another thing about Roberto I'm not happy about. He leaves exactly on time every day. Also he doesn't have lunch with us very often, you know, he goes off on his own ...

A I'm not sure that's relevant.

B Mmm, maybe.

A I think we should move on now if we're going to finish by eleven o'clock ...

M What about his actual work? In my opinion, it's fine. He's contributed to several of the innovation projects.

A Well, I think we should discuss this a bit more. What exactly do you mean by 'contributed to the innovation projects'?

M By providing administrative support to the management team – sometimes beyond the call of duty. For example, he stayed behind one evening and typed up all of the results from the feedback seminars. I could go on. This shows he's motivated to go further in the company.

A Well, thanks very much, Maria. You've made your views very clear. OK, let's go over what we've agreed. Roberto will have a further probationary period of three months. After that ...

🎧 8.5 (I = Interviewer, GP = Guido Passerelli)

I Could you please tell me why you want to leave your present job, Mr Passerelli?

GP Certainly. I'm glad you asked me that. It's very well paid, as you know, organising stunts, and the people who do stunts are just great.

But the job needs a lot of planning skills and is very responsible. If you make a mistake, someone can get badly injured or even killed. To be honest, I don't want that level of responsibility any more. It's time to make way for a younger man.

I Right. You've told us about your experience and qualities, what would you say is your main weakness – something you lack and would like to put right, maybe?

GP My main weakness? Hmm. Let me think. Well ... I suppose some people would say I expect too much of people who work for me. I have high standards and I get impatient if people don't do their job properly. But I'm trying to learn to be more patient; nobody's perfect, are they?

I Finally, could you summarise why we should offer you this job?

GP I think I can offer you a lot. I've got energy – even though I'm fifty-two – I'm in excellent shape physically. I'm a brilliant planner and I've got lots of ideas for improving your profits. I've spent a month studying your organisation and visiting your clubs. I know what to do to get you back on your feet.

🎧 8.6 (I = Interviewer, ML = Martine Lemaire)

I Could you please tell me why you want to leave your present job?

ML Yes, I feel I have the ability to perform well in a more challenging job. I'm the Assistant Sales Manager but it doesn't seem that I'll get the opportunity to advance any further. Basically, I'm not fulfilling my potential. The job you offer is exciting and much better paid. It matches perfectly my interest in health and sports.

I You've told us about your experience and qualities, what would you say is your main weakness?

ML Oh, what a funny question ... I don't know, really. I'm not aware of any weakness, I mean I have lots of friends and get on well with everyone really. Sorry, I can't think of anything at the moment.

I Finally, could you summarise why we would offer you this job?

ML I think my training as a dietician could benefit Slim Gyms a lot. I could advise your members on their diet and help them to have a healthier lifestyle. I've got excellent interpersonal skills, and if I get the job, I'll build up a first class management team by ensuring regular team-building activities are part of their working week. This way I hope to encourage good communication. I am sure this strategy will make Slim Gyms profitable again.

🎧 8.7 (I = Interviewer, DC = David Chen)

I Could you please tell us why you want to leave your present job, Mr Chen?

DC Right. I suppose, basically, I need a new motivation. I've achieved everything I can in my present job. The work's no longer challenging. I'm not stimulated any more. I'm a member of Slim Gyms; I've been going to your club for several years. I really like the one in my area, but I feel it could be better managed. So, I like the idea of working for you – it's a very attractive job.

I OK. You've told us about your experience and qualities, what would you say is your main weakness?

DC That's a difficult question. I probably have many weaknesses. I try to be polite and helpful at all times, but maybe sometimes I should be more forceful, more assertive when I give my opinions. I try to be pleasant with everyone; I don't like having arguments with people, even if I'm right. Maybe this is my weakness, I don't know.

I Finally, could you summarise why we should offer you this job?

DC I'd say I have a good combination of business and sports experience – that'd be useful for Slim Gyms. And my knowledge of Chinese culture, and the language, would be a big advantage. There are a lot of Chinese people in this city who would join the clubs if I were in charge. I think people like me and respect me. I'm a very fair and honest person.

🎧 8.8 (I = Interviewer, GD = Gloria Daniels)

I Could you please tell me why you want to leave your present job, Mrs Daniels?

GD Why? Well quite frankly, I'm tired of all the travelling. It's such a stressful job, the money's pretty good but I need to spend more time at home, more time with my family. I think it's important to get the balance right between work and your personal life. I'm not sure I've got that right at the moment. So I think it's time to change my job.

I OK, you've told us about your experience and qualities, what would you say is your main weakness?

GD Oh dear, I've got so many! I am very competitive, I know. Too competitive. If I don't get what I want, I can get a little upset. I need to accept that you can't always win in life, but it's hard for me to do this. I think that's definitely my main weakness.

I Finally, could you summarise why we should offer you this job?

GD That's easy. I'm a people person; I'm a really good communicator. I love all sports. When I do a job, I give a hundred and ten percent. I'm a winner, and that's what you need now to turn Slim Gyms around. I can promise you, I'd do a really good job.

9 Trade

9.1 (I = Interviewer, IM = Ian McPherson)

I Perhaps you could summarise for our listeners the points you've made so far, Ian. You started by telling us what free trade is.

IM Right, I defined it as a situation in which goods come into and out of a country without any controls or taxes. Countries which truly believe in free trade try to liberalise their trade, that's to say, they take away barriers to trade, they remove things which stop people trading freely. They have open borders and few controls of goods at customs.

9.2 (I = Interviewer, IM = Ian McPherson)

I OK, then you gave several examples of barriers to trade.

IM Yes, I said that there are two main barriers: tariffs and subsidies. Tariffs are taxes on imported goods; so that the imports cannot compete so well against domestic products. Subsidies are money paid to domestic producers so that they can sell their goods more cheaply than foreign competitors. Tariffs and subsidies are barriers to trade because when people are given a choice, generally they will buy the cheapest product.

I You mentioned other barriers, less important ones, perhaps.

IM Uh huh. I talked about quotas, which limit the quantity of a product which can be imported, and I discussed other restrictions on trade, such as expensive licences for importers, which add greatly to costs; and regulations relating to documents which a company must have to export its goods to certain countries – the documents can be very complicated and difficult to complete, so they slow down trading.

9.3 (I = Interviewer, IM = Ian McPherson)

I I asked you if free trade was always a good thing.

IM And I answered, in principle, yes, it is a good thing, it's beneficial to countries.

I Why?

IM Countries which open their markets usually have a policy of deregulation, that's to say, they free their companies to compete in markets, without government control or subsidies. Because of this, consumers in free trade areas are offered a wider range of high-quality products at lower prices. People in those areas can move to the most productive parts of the economy and get better jobs with higher wages or salaries. OK?

I So why do so many countries protect their industries and not allow free markets?

IM I gave three reasons, if you remember.
Firstly, some people say, why should we practise free trade if other nations compete unfairly? For example, dumping is fairly common in international trade. When companies dump goods in overseas markets, they sell goods at very low prices, usually for less than it costs the company to produce the goods. Companies can usually only do that when they are heavily subsidised by their governments. Secondly, many people believe that strategic industries must be protected. These are industries that are very important to the economy: steel, power, communications, and so on. In the United States, many Americans think that the steel industry should be protected against cheap imports from Brazil and other countries. If the US depends too much on foreign-made steel, they argue, this could be bad in a time of war.
Finally, some say that in developing countries, industries need to be protected until they're strong enough to compete in world markets. This is the infant industry argument: certain industries have to be protected until they can stand on their own feet, as it were.
My final point was that throughout the world, there is a trend towards liberalising trade and removing trade barriers. The most successful economies tend to have open markets, and most of their industries have been deregulated.

9.4 (BF = Bella Ford, RdS = Ranjit de Silva)

BF If I order five thousand boxes of tea, what discount will you offer us?

RdS On five thousand nothing. But if you buy ten thousand boxes, then we'll offer you ten percent.

BF OK, I'll think about that. And tell me, if we placed a very large order, say fifteen thousand boxes, would you be able to despatch immediately?

RdS We can normally guarantee to despatch a large order within two weeks. But if you order at a peak time, like just before Christmas, it will be impossible to deliver that quickly.

BF I take it your price includes insurance?

RdS Actually, no. Usually, you'd be responsible for that. But if the order

were really large, that would be negotiable, I'm sure.

BF What about payment?

RdS To be honest we'd prefer cash on delivery, as this is our first contact with you. If you were a regular customer, we would offer you thirty days' credit, maybe even a little more.

BF That's alright. I quite understand.

RdS Look, how about having some lunch now, and continuing later this afternoon. Then we could meet for an evening meal.

BF Yes, let's continue after lunch. If I had more time, I would love to have dinner with you, but unfortunately my flight leaves at seven tonight.

9.5 (I = Interviewer, KW = Kevin Warren)

I When you go into a negotiation, do you always expect to win?

KW I guess the honest answer to that is I always have a clear expectation of what I expect to achieve, and I guess I would like to always win. Let me illustrate that for you. Something that was sort of shared with me very early in my career was the mnemonic L-I-M and that's Like, Intend, Must. What would I like to do, what would I intend to do, and what must I do? And this is probably well illustrated by a recent contract that we negotiated in the UK with a major leisure company. And, I guess our 'Like' was, we would like to win the business there and then, in the negotiation on that day. I guess our 'Intend' was that we must leave that group thinking we are a very professional and competent outfit who can best meet their needs. And I guess our 'Must' was, we must have done enough to keep the dialogue open and ensure that our competitor didn't win the business on that day. So, the short answer is, you don't always win. I always want to win, but I don't always expect to win – but I certainly expect to deliver the objective that we went in to achieve.

9.6 (I = Interviewer, KW = Kevin Warren)

I Could you give me some tips for negotiating?

KW Yes. I think everybody has their own tips. But these are things that have worked for myself and the people I've worked with, and it's more around avoiding classic errors. And I guess the first one is to identify who the decision maker is. I've lost count of the occasions at every level, from first-line salesman through to board director, board to board negotiations, where I've seen fantastic presentations, superb dialogue and the person that's been sitting across the table, so to speak, is not the decision maker. So that's the first tip, make sure you know who you're talking to.
The second one is that all salesmen, if they're good salesmen, tend to be very enthusiastic about what they're selling. That could be a product or a service, or even a social occasion, but it's all selling at the end of the day. And in their enthusiasm, they focus on their need, rather than the buyer's need. So, for example, in our own case I've seen on many, many occasions people basically go straight to the point – we're here to sell you Coca-Cola, it's the world's number one brand, you must want it. What they haven't done is establish the buyer's need. So, for example, the buyer's need may be in a grocery store that they want to supply the world's number one brand to encourage consumers to come in and purchase their range of products. The manager of a ball bearing factory might want a vending machine because if he supplies a free, or discounted refreshment service it keeps his union employees happy. So the important thing is to understand the buyer's need. Now, it's not impossible to sell without establishing that need. But it tends to mean you'll never have a long-term relationship. So, for example, again the workplace example, I could come in, bang, sell you a Coca-Cola vending machine, pay you maybe a small royalty. Because I never established your need, if another soft drinks supplier walks through the door and just offers you more money, you will probably switch. Whereas if we'd established the fact that all you were interested in was offering a service and you wanted it to be as hassle free as possible, we could have tailored our offering. So I think that's very important. My favourite one, and I'm probably in danger of doing it myself now, is once you've made the sale, shut up. I think it's very important: close the sale, reinforce the buyer's decision – everybody likes to feel they've made a good decision – and then leave.

9.7 (A = buyer A, B = buyer B, S = Supplier)

Extract 1

A OK, what do we want to get out of this meeting with Eastern Fabrics?

B I think our main aim should be to get a better deal on prices. I've been checking up on Eastern Fabrics, they've just built a new factory in China, they need to keep it working to full capacity. They'll be keen to get our business, so they'll lower their prices, if we play our cards right.

A Right, let's try to get ten percent off their list prices.

B Agreed.

Extract 2

S Can you tell us a little about your customers' needs and their buying habits? You know, what colours they like, what sizes are most popular, and what your main sales outlets are – that sort of thing?

Extract 3

B If you give us a discount on our first order, say ten percent, we can accept the end of May as a delivery date. We'd like to have the goods earlier, but we understand this would be difficult for you.

S A ten percent discount – mmm, that's more than we usually offer new customers, but it might be possible, especially if we can deliver some of the shirts early in June.

B Well, July and August are our peak selling months, so that would probably be OK.

Extract 4

S How about if we send the first consignment by air to make sure the goods arrive on time? And we'll send the rest by sea as soon as possible.

B Mmm, sounds like a good idea to me. As long as we get the first consignment by the end of May, we'll be happy.

S I can guarantee delivery by that date. OK?

Extract 5

S Normally we supply three colours only, black, blue and red, but with a variety of designs of course. If you wanted the T-shirt in other colours …

B What? You mean if we ordered other colours, the shirts would be more expensive.

S Exactly, we'd have to charge a little more.

Extract 6

S Good, we agree on price, quantity, discounts and, let's see … method of transport. I'll send you an e-mail confirming everything. Let me know if there are any problems.

Extract 7

S OK, I think we've covered everything. If there are any other points, I'll e-mail you.

B Great. That was a very good meeting. We covered a lot of ground. What time shall I meet you for dinner tonight?

10 Quality

🎧 **10.1 (I = Interviewer, MA = Mike Ashton)**

I How do you define quality in business? How important is it?

MA Delivering good quality is absolutely fundamentally important to any business. I believe the best way to define quality is to look very closely at customers expectations and then to look at the ability of a business to meet or exceed those expectations, consistently. Customers generally place great trust in the ability of their favourite brands or companies to address their requirements dependably, whether it be a soap powder, a hotel room, or a massive conference facility. Our job in our business is to make sure that our customers requirements are very clearly understood, and to ensure that at every stage in the guest's journey through our hotels, we are able to address our guest's needs smoothly, easily, and efficiently.

🎧 **10.2 (I = Interviewer, MA = Mike Ashton)**

I How should quality improvement be measured?

MA Well, as a general guide, I'd say quality improvement should be measured consistently over a period of time, and very accurately, so that everybody believes in the reports and the figures that are circulated round an organisation. But in three specific ways, we at Hilton measure the quality of our performance. Every year we contact thousands of guests to understand just how satisfied they are with all the important areas in our business, whether it be the way they arrive and depart from a hotel, or the quality of their bedroom and the food that they eat. We contact all of our team members, the people who work for us around the world to understand how satisfied they are with the experience of working for Hilton, their career development, and the training they receive. And finally we look at how efficiently and consistently we deliver our own operational standards. So, if we for example say that no-one should take longer than a couple of minutes in a queue to be checked into our hotel, are we delivering that consistently around the world? And we do that through mystery visits to all of our hotels. That gives us guest satisfaction, operational efficiency and the satisfaction of our team members, in all of our hotels around the world.

🎧 **10.3 (I = Interviewer, MA = Mike Ashton)**

I Does high quality mean high cost?

MA I guess it can do, but I think what's more important is, is investment in high quality, something which will pay dividends to a company, will it help to build profitability? Certainly delivering good quality consistently is not something that can be done without any cost to an organisation. Investment in good people, in good training, in efficient practices and processes will always mean that there is investment required. However, it should also be at the heart of delivering what any organisations' customers are looking for, and if they are satisfied, and if they keep coming back as a result, then what should follow, is healthy revenues, and even healthier profits, and that for me makes investment in quality something that's very affordable, in fact it's absolutely essential.

🎧 **10.4 (CSR = Customer Service Representative, TG = Teresa Green)**

CSR Good afternoon. Electrical Goods Department.

TG Hello. This is Teresa Green. I'm calling about the DVD player I bought from you a few weeks ago. Unfortunately there's a problem with it.

CSR I'm sorry to hear that. What seems to be the problem?

TG It doesn't work.

CSR Could you give me some details, please?

TG Well, the eject mechanism's not reliable. Sometimes it works, and sometimes it doesn't.

CSR Can you bring it in? Then we can look into the matter and we'll probably send the machine back to the manufacturer.

TG I'm sorry but I'd prefer to exchange it.

CSR I'm afraid it's not our policy to replace items. We'll send it back to the manufacturer for repair.

TG Well, that's not really good enough. I'd like a different make and I don't mind paying a little more for a better model.

CSR All right then. Bring the machine in and we'll see what we can do for you.

🎧 **10.5**

1 The worst time is seven to eleven in the morning. There are always big queues at the check-in desk, and it's very disorganised. I also missed a flight because of the long line at passport control – there are always huge queues there.

2 It's just like the airports back home for us smokers. I had to go right outside the terminal to have a cigarette before my flight. And I wasn't the only person there, I can tell you. I hoped you British would be a bit more understanding about smoking. We're not criminals, are we?

3 There's a huge duty-free shop – that's good. But the staff are too keen to get you to spend your money. They follow you round the shop offering special promotions. They really hassle you. The other services are poor. They need more dispensers for candy bars, beverages, magazines and so on in the waiting areas. Such things are useful when your flight is delayed.

4 It's difficult to get information about flights. The public announcements are either non-existent or so quiet you can't hear them above people talking. The TV screens could provide updates on a regular basis but the information is very vague. A few weeks ago, my flight was delayed four hours. Engine trouble. Noone told us anything. There should be more airport staff to deal with emergencies.

5 You need to provide guards or officials to watch passengers and their belongings. I put my briefcase down when I was getting money out of a cash machine. It was gone in a flash, never saw who took it. I had my laptop in it, and I wasn't insured. I talked to another passenger; he'd had small things stolen from his luggage on three occasions.

6 I find the worst service is at the point where I pick up my suitcase as it comes off the plane. There's this huge room but it only has two conveyor belts and they break down all the time. You often wait about twenty minutes for the first bags to appear. So now I expect to wait at least thirty minutes before I pass through customs. Oh and another thing, you need more trolleys, all over the airport, not just at the point where you pick up your luggage.

7 The facilities for disabled people like me could be better. I had to pay eighteen pounds to use a wheelchair to get to the plane. I think it's outrageous. I don't know whose responsibility it is.

8 Well, my complaint is that there is nowhere to park. I travel everywhere by car. Your car park is much too small. The other day I spent forty minutes driving around until I found a space. It was only my good luck that someone was leaving. This is the twenty-first century, isn't it? You'd think airports of all places would be prepared for the increased traffic!

11 Ethics

🎧 11.1 (I = Interviewer, AH = Andy Hammerton)

I What is the bank's ethical policy?

AH Our ethical policy is a clear set of promises to our customers about how we will and won't invest their money. It's important, though, to understand that the promises we make are based on the views of the customers.

Firstly, it's worth explaining the development of the policy, which was introduced in 1992 after consultation with our customers. We now consult them regularly, to ensure that the investment guidelines we follow continue to reflect their views.

We implement the policy by publishing the types of business activities that are of such concern to our customers. They don't want the bank to provide banking services to these types of business. For example, we will not invest in a business involved in the manufacture or transfer of armaments to oppressive regimes.

The policy also contains a number of positive statements that commit the bank to do business with customers involved in social or environmentally beneficial activities, such as renewable energy and energy efficiency.

To show customers we are keeping our promises, our selection procedure is independently audited; the results are published in our annual report.

🎧 11.2 (I = Interviewer, AH = Andy Hammerton)

I Is it really the job of business to provide a lead in ethical standards?

AH Businesses don't operate in isolation. Businesses are part of the wider community, through their staff and their suppliers, for example. Business activities will inevitably lead to a series of ecological and social effects. The nature of some industries has huge and very obvious effects on the environment and society, whilst the effect of others, such as the financial services industry, is not always so apparent.

The bank chose to base its policy on the concerns of its customers, because it is their money that is being used, and they should have a say in how it is used.

We also campaign for change on issues that our customers feel strongly about. One of our first campaigns called for a ban on the use of landmines – now banned in a hundred and forty-two countries. Since then we've campaigned on other issues from third world debt, human rights, fair trade and youth poverty. Customers can get as involved as they want and, because the bank represents them, it means their view is more likely to be heard.

🎧 11.3 (I = Interviewer, AH = Andy Hammerton)

I Can successful businesses always behave ethically?

AH We believe they can. In fact, we believe that, in the years to come, the only truly successful businesses will be those that achieve a lasting balance between their own interests and those of society and the natural world.

Therefore businesses cannot just have a self-interest; they must play a social role. Our position has enabled us to build trust, develop our brand and have a positive impact on the bank's bottom line.

On the issue of trust, research shows that trust in business has been declining for a number of years and the general public feel that businesses don't take them seriously. Higher trust creates higher loyalty. First, because customers trust you, they are less likely to look elsewhere in the first place. Second, if you do make a mistake, they are more likely to forgive you.

🎧 11.4

A I'll never forget the trouble we had with that face cream. We launched it and, you know, it was a real winner. I mean, it was going really well.

B Hmm, great.

A When suddenly people started phoning and complaining it was burning their skin.

B Burning their skin? You mean, like a kind of allergy.

A Yeah, it was making red marks on their faces. The newspapers heard about it and wanted to know what we were doing about it.

B Huh, typical. They don't exactly help, do they? So what did you do?

A We didn't know what to do. You see, we'd tested it for over six months, and, you know, there'd been no bad reaction to it.

B Well, so what was the problem?

A Well, we'd invested a lot in the product and the launch. I mean, you know what advertising costs are these days, then suddenly the number of complaints doubled in the space of a week or so.

B Doubled? Incredible! Did you manage to keep it quiet?

A No, our Managing Director got more than a bit worried. Said all this was harming the company's image. So we recalled the product and lost a lot of money. I tell you, the only people with red faces were us. Since then, we've kept away from skin-care products.

🎧 11.5

A We've got to do something about it. People are taking too many days off sick. Sick leave increased by twelve percent last year. I got the figures today. On average staff took fourteen days off sick – that's far too many.

B Absolutely, it's really damaging for us. It's affecting the service we give our customers and it's costing us a lot of money each year. It can't go on.

A OK, well, as I see it, there are several ways we could deal with this. We could get tough and simply say, no paid leave at all for the first three days someone is sick. Or we could do it another way er ... offer staff a bonus at the end of the year if they don't take much sick leave. And there's a third option, we could bring in a doctor and physiotherapist for staff, and free health tests and counselling. They could check up on staff who are taking far too much sick leave, the ones who think it's extra holidays for them.

B Let's look at the pros and cons of the first option: no paid leave for the first three days staff are sick. On the one hand, I think it will reduce the amount of sick leave because people will lose pay when they're off work. On the other hand, it's very unfair to people who are genuinely sick, you know if they're suffering from a bad cold or flu, for example. It wouldn't be popular with the staff, or with the unions ...

A Well, let's look at this from another angle. It might be worth using a completely different approach. We could try sending a questionnaire to all staff, asking them to suggest ideas for reducing absenteeism, because of sickness. Of course, we'd explain why the present policy isn't working.

B Good idea. If we do this, then they're more likely to buy into any new scheme. Yes, it should work well.

A Right. So, ... the best way forward is to sound out staff and get their opinions. A survey will give us all the data we need.

B And the next thing to do is to prepare a questionnaire. I take it you want my department to do that?

A Yes, if you would. Could you have a draft questionnaire ready by next Monday, for our meeting?

B Yes, I think we can manage that. I'll let you know when it's ready.

🎧 11.6 (BD = Bob Dexter, NT = Nikos Takakis)

BD A bit of information now, Nikos, I think you ought to know. Carl often has lunches with Monica Kaminsky, the Design Manager of Rochester Electronics, our main competitor.

NT Monica Kaminsky? Really? That's something I didn't know.

BD Yes, and she often phones him at work. She has long chats with him; I've no idea what they talk about.

NT Am I reading you right? Are you saying ... there's something going on between them? You know...

BD Well, since you ask ... You know Carl got divorced last year ... There's a rumour going round, Monica's more than just an acquaintance, I thought you might like to know that. Someone saw them together at a cinema last Saturday. It looked as if they ...

NT Thanks Bob, I've heard enough. I won't be saying anything to Carl about this. It's his business. I trust him to keep his personal and business life separate.

NT OK, I won't say anything more then. What are you having for lunch?

🎧 11.7 (MK = Monica Kaminsky, CT = Carl Thomson)

MK I can't believe what you're saying, Carl. I'm really shocked. I thought we had a good relationship. Why on earth do you want us to break up? I don't get it.

CT It's ... well, we've had some good times together, I know, but ...

MK But?

CT Well, it's about work really. I mean, we work for rival companies, and that's a problem. A very big problem, actually.

MK Oh, what do you mean? Problem?

CT Think about it. We often talk about things that happen at work. You can't help it. But I think we talk too much about work sometimes. And that's not good.

MK I don't know, I think we talk about all kinds of things. Not just work, that'd be boring.

CT Yes, but I still feel I talked too much about work in the past ...

MK Ah, I see. You're referring to ...

CT Yeah, the DC01 can opener. I seem to remember I told you quite a lot about the problems we'd had designing it. And how we solved them. That information could have been very useful to your company, let's face it.

MK Listen Carl, are you accusing me of using that information to help us design our can opener? Because if you are …oh, that's so unfair.

CT I'm not accusing you of anything, but some of my colleagues are sure I leaked information to you. They don't think I'm trustworthy and that's making life very difficult for me.

MK Sorry Carl, I can't stop people talking – should I say gossiping. Anyway, you didn't have to sign a confidentiality agreement, so what are you worrying about?

CT No, I didn't, but I don't want to get a reputation. I think we need to separate for a while; at least until people have forgotten about the DC01 can opener.

MK I see … I'm disappointed with you, Carl. I get the feeling you don't trust me any more. I didn't think you were such a weak person, so easily influenced by people. Maybe you're right; maybe we should go our own ways for a while.

12 Leadership

🎧 **12.1 (I = Interviewer, ML = Max Landsberg)**

I What qualities are needed to run a large company effectively?

ML The leader of a large company needs to do three things. Firstly, to create a picture of where the whole team is meant to be going. What is this journey, the change and the way forward and particularly what is my role or your role going to be in that journey. So, that's vision.
The second thing is inspiration, which is a very personal thing, but great leaders manage to inspire the people that they work with. And thirdly, because all businesses need to move forward and make money – momentum. They manage to create momentum and make sure that people are moving forward with the various projects that are under their control.

🎧 **12.2 (I = Interviewer, ML = Max Landsberg)**

I And how do you help leaders to develop their skills?

ML We think that the way that people develop is seventy, twenty, ten, which means that seventy percent of the way they develop is on the job; twenty percent is through coaching by somebody else and only ten percent is by training. So, the vast majority of how somebody learns anything, and particularly how they learn to be a better leader, is on-the-job training. And what that means for the career of somebody is that they need to experience a lot of different types of activity, lots of different roles and lots of different challenges, and only then can they start to build up a range of experiences and a range of skills in leading people in different situations.

🎧 **12.3 (I = Interviewer, ML = Max Landsberg)**

I Which leaders have influenced or impressed you?

ML This is always a very difficult question because the people who have influenced me may be people that nobody else has ever heard of. So, whenever I'm asked this question, I always have to give the examples of very famous people but unfortunately, these are people that I haven't personally worked with. So, there is a bit of a problem always with this question. However, Nelson Mandela is someone who has always impressed me. In addition to the vision and inspiration and momentum that we mentioned earlier, he also has some magical charisma, even via the television screen, and is clearly able to move people to action.
The second would be Winston Churchill because I think he is a very interesting example of somebody who was a very good leader for one era in England – Britain's – history. Although he was not seen to be a very good leader at a different era. So, I think he's a good example of a man who was good for one time but not for another.
And then I have Bernie Ellis, who was a postman who coached our rowing boat when I was at University. Nobody else will have heard of him except the eight people in the boat, but he was a brilliant leader because he was very down to earth and he managed to inspire us to row very fast.

🎧 **12.4 (C = Chairperson, M = Michel, P = Paula, T = Tom, S = Susan)**

C OK, the main item on the agenda is whether we should sell our store in Paris. I'd like to hear your opinions about this. But first of all, can you give us the background, Michel?

M Yes. As you all know, we opened the store in Boulevard Jordan five years ago. We hoped it would be a base for expansion into other areas of France. But it hasn't been a success. It hasn't attracted enough customers and it's made losses every year. As I see it, it's going to be very difficult to get a return on our investment.

P I agree. There's no possibility it'll make a profit. It's in the wrong location, there's too much competition, and our products don't seem to appeal to French people. We should never have entered the

market – it was a mistake. We should sell out as soon as possible.

T I don't agree with that at all. Things have gone wrong there, it's obvious. The management's let us down badly, they haven't adapted enough to market conditions. But it's far too early to close the business down. I suggest we bring in some marketing consultants – a French firm, if possible – and get them to review the business. We need more information about where we're going wrong.

S I totally agree with you. It's too early to close down the store, but I am worried about the store's location. We're an up-market business, but most of the stores in the area have moved down-market, selling in the lower price ranges. That's a problem. I think we have to make changes – very soon. I mean, our losses are increasing every year, we just can't go on like this. We may have to revise our strategy. Maybe we made a mistake in choosing France for expansion.

C Well, thanks for your opinions. I think, on balance, we feel we should keep the store going for a while. So, the next thing to do is to appoint a suitable firm of marketing consultants to find out what our problems are and make recommendations. Personally, I'm convinced the store will be a success if we get the marketing mix right. We've got to get the store back into profit, we've invested a lot of money in it.

🎧 **12.5**

I don't think it will be too difficult to improve the store's performance. I suggest you review your product ranges as soon as possible and stop promoting those items which aren't making any money.
What you need is more knowledge of the youth market – they're the consumers who are spending most money on clothes. You should target that segment of the market.
Also, I think you should hire a top executive to run that part of the business. Someone with a really good track record in the retail fashion trade. I could suggest names, if you wish.
You need to take a hard look at other parts of the business. I'm not happy with the furniture department in the store. It takes up a lot of space and isn't making any money. To be honest, I just don't think it will ever make much money. I also have doubts about your stationery department. Is it really worth keeping?
The answer to your problems is to do something quickly, to stop profits falling and turn the store around. So, this is what you should do now, in my opinion: reduce your range of products, cut out the loss makers; hire a new executive with experience of the fashion clothing business. Close down Furniture and possibly Stationery. OK, any questions?

🎧 **12.6**

Here are some ideas, in no particular order that we can think about. Some of them you may think are a bit crazy or not practical, but hear me out …
I know of one CEO who sends out birthday cards with his signature and a personal message to every employee. We could try that. We could also start a company magazine. It may be a bit expensive but I think it could really help.
I know one of our competitors has an employee of the month scheme. It's very popular. Staff nominate a colleague who has done well in some way. The employee selected gets a company gift.
I would also like to get out of my office frequently this year and drop in on staff at the different stores. And should we have an open-door policy in every store? Employees can then see the manager when they want to.
Now this sounds crazy, but what about having a company uniform? This type of thing seems to work well in Asian countries – it creates loyalty and good team spirit.
Another thing I've been thinking about is to cancel the end-of-year bonus scheme – it's very expensive – and spend the money instead on Christmas parties at top hotels.
Finally, I'd like to see a new appraisal scheme. I haven't thought about the details, but it should reward high achievers generously.

13 Innovation

🎧 **13.1**

The idea of a lone inventor who makes a discovery or has a sudden clever idea or brainwave, is maybe a little out of date today. While these types of pioneers do still exist, these days companies often have large R & D departments – teams of people who are constantly innovating and perfecting designs. Perhaps they begin with a concept and then build a prototype, or working model. Sometimes during testing there is a setback when it becomes clear the design has a fault. At this point maybe it is time to start again, or go back to the drawing board. More work is done and there is a breakthrough – a solution is found. The product can be retested and then, hopefully, manufactured. The company will apply for a patent for the design so that others cannot copy it and steal the idea.

13.2 (EJ = Eve Jones)

EJ When you make a presentation, the first stage is to plan it. You should start by thinking about your audience – who they are, what they know about the subject and what they expect from you. Think also about what their attitude will be to you. Will they be interested, enthusiastic, cooperative or perhaps critical? Are you presenting to a group from your own culture or to people of different cultures? All these factors will influence the way you approach the presentation. If possible, try to visit the room where you're going to give the talk. Check the equipment and make sure your voice carries to the back of the room if you don't use a microphone. Look at the seating arrangements and make sure they are what you want.

You also want to feel comfortable and relaxed when you're presenting.

You're now ready to prepare what you are going to say. Stage one is the opening. A good opening is essential as you will be nervous and you need to grab the attention of the audience. You start by introducing yourself and then you use a technique to get the audience's interest. We call this the 'hook' which focuses the audience's attention on what you're saying. You can do this in various ways. You can: ask a question; use a famous quotation; use a striking visual image; appeal directly to the audience's interests or needs.

Once you have the audience's attention, you should tell them the structure of your presentation. You give them a map of the talk, with signposts along the route, so they know what you will cover in your talk.

After the opening and a brief introduction of your subject, you come to the main body of your presentation. Then you have a conclusion during which you summarise your key points, and give your final opinion and recommendations. After that, it's the question and answer session.

13.3 (EJ = Eve Jones)

- Some tips now about how you deliver the presentation. How you actually perform it.
- Firstly, what about the opening two minutes? You'll be very nervous, almost everyone is. Some people deal with this by writing down the opening two minutes, marking the stresses and pauses, and practising it again and again. They memorise the opening and that helps to calm their nerves.
- Rehearse your presentation, using the equipment you will use when you do the real thing.
- Have a back-up plan. What will you do if your projector doesn't work? If your computer crashes? If you cannot find your slide tray because you left it at the hotel?
- Keep good eye contact with your audience at all times, even when you use Powerpoint or the OHP for visual effects. Eye contact will help you show that you are speaking to the audience, not at them.
- You need to build a rapport with the audience, and to develop a warm and friendly relationship with them. Enthusiasm is important. If you are enthusiastic, your audience will be too.
- The right body language is important. Generally speaking, it's better to stand than sit when making your presentation.
- Avoid repetitive, annoying gestures. But dramatic gestures can be effective when you make key points.
- Vary the speed of your voice – a pause is often very effective.
- Vary your intonation – change the pitch of your voice, by using a high or low tone.
- Vary the volume of your voice – you can speak loudly or quietly to attract your audience's attention.
- Follow the KISS principle – keep it short and simple.
- Use short words and sentences.
- Don't use jargon unless your audience understand it.
- Generally present concrete facts rather than abstract ideas.
- Give examples to support your points.
- Use visuals which can be seen by all the audience. Don't put too much on a single transparency or slide. Visuals add variety and interest to your talk.
- Finally, end with a BANG!
- Give the audience some memorable words or phrases which sum up your key messages. Or use a visual or slide which will remain in the memory of your audience.
- Thank them for giving up their time to attend your presentation and ask the audience if they have any questions.

- Remember, a presentation is a performance. What you say is important, but how you say it is even more important.

13.4

Good morning everyone, thanks for coming to my presentation. I know you're all very busy, so I'll be as brief as possible.

OK then, I'm going to talk about the new chocolate bar we're putting on the market, the Frejus premium bar. I'll tell you about the test launch we carried out in the southwest of England a few weeks ago.

My presentation is divided into three parts. First, I'll give you some background about the launch. After that, I'll tell you how we got on and assess its effectiveness. Finally, I'll outline our future plans for the product. If you have any questions, don't hesitate to ask.

Right, let's start with the background to the launch. As you know, Frejus is an orange and nut bar with a distinctive taste. It's been thoroughly tested in focus groups and special attention was paid to packaging. It's wrapped in a metallic foil. The colours are rich, strong, to give high visual impact. OK everyone? Yes, Johan, you have a question.

So, that's the background. Right, let's now move on to the test launch. How successful was it? Well, in two words, very successful. If you look at the graph, you'll see the bar's actual sales compared with forecast sales. Quite a difference isn't there? The sales were over twenty percent higher than we predicted. In other words a really good result. Well above our expectations. The sales show that the pricing of the product was correct. And they show that, as a premium line, the Frejus bar should be successful nationwide.

To sum up, a very promising test launch. I believe the bar has great potential in the market. Right, where do we go from here? Obviously, we'll move on to stage two and have a national advertising and marketing campaign. In a few months, you'll be visiting our sales outlets and taking orders, I hope, for the new product.

Thanks very much. Any questions?

14 Competition

14.1 (I = Interviewer, IB = Ian Barber)

I The credit card business is highly competitive. How do you stay ahead of your competitors?

IB Well, it's certainly true to say that in the UK especially, the credit card market these days is hugely competitive. When Barclaycard launched in 1966 we were the only credit card in the UK and it took some ten or twelve years before we even saw one other competitor in the UK market. Today, if you apply for a credit card in the UK, you can choose between maybe one thousand, one and a half thousand different cards from different providers. So there is a huge amount of competition out there. The way that Barclaycard tries to maintain a difference to all the rest and tries to stay competitive, er, we do that in a number of ways. Firstly, we have a brand – a very strong brand in the UK market – which is fairly unique for the credit card market. We've invested in that brand over a long period of time and certainly it has a level of recognition and stature that our competitors just don't have. We also obviously need to compete on price. We need to make sure that we're always competitive on price. That doesn't necessarily always mean being the very cheapest. We have a tradition of providing our customers with extra value features and services on their cards, er, which we will continue to do. And we need to innovate. We need to make sure that when things change in the credit card market – people always want what's new and what's exciting – and if you can be the company that provides that for them, er, then you're going to succeed. But ultimately, er, the way that we stay competitive is to keep hold of our customers, and the way that you do that is by offering them good service. Most people are very happy to have a credit card and to pay a reasonable sum for that credit card. The reason they will leave you is if you annoy them. So the more we can do to provide good service, look after our customers when they're with us, the more competitive we stay.

14.2 (I = Interviewer, IB = Ian Barber)

I Does competition always lead to better goods and services, and to better value for customers?

IB I think that broadly, yes, competition does provide more services and more goods for customers, and it's really a question of choice. When you look in the credit card market for example, we're seeing that customers increasingly don't always want to borrow on a credit card. They may look to other forms of borrowing, whether that's a straightforward loan, whether that's some finance from a store, from a shop, when they walk into a store, or whether they want to draw down equity against their house – that's to say, to use the value in their house to borrow perhaps at cheaper rates. So, customers are getting more and more choice in terms of the way that they borrow. When you look at the credit card market in particular, certainly the quality of goods and services has expanded rapidly in recent years. We have offers in the market today where you can borrow at interest rates as low as nought percent, for example – zero interest. When you look back two or three years, those offers were available for maybe two or three months. Barclaycard has just released, or just launched, an offer giving customers nought percent interest for twelve months. So, free money for twelve months is an incredibly competitive deal! You also see features such as cashback, where you're rewarded for spending on your card with a cash rebate once a year. So ultimately, yes, the market has seen vastly increased competition in recent years, and with that, a lot wider choice for customers. Ultimately not just more choice but more choice, more cheaply.

🎧 14.3 (I = Interviewer, IB = Ian Barber)

I How do you see competition affecting the way your business operates in the future?

IB What we're seeing is a number of different reasons why our customers choose to borrow money. And what we're seeing is a number of different businesses willing to offer them that lending. For example, it's not unusual now for customers to borrow from their supermarket, for example. So we need to make sure that, however or why ever our customers want to borrow money, we're able to provide that to them. And that won't always mean borrowing on a credit card. Broadly speaking, people borrow for one of three reasons. They borrow to buy major items: a car or holiday, something like that. They borrow to consolidate other debts – so they put all their debts in one place, so as it's more manageable and they have to make just one monthly payment. Or they borrow in a more traditional way, if you like, for credit cards: they borrow for everyday purchases, simply to spread the cost of their monthly spending in a more manageable way. So we need to recognise that customers are borrowing in these three different ways, and we need to make sure that we have the right products and services for them when they choose to do that, and that we're not simply asking them to always borrow on a credit card. That won't always be the right way. So competition is really about providing our customers with increased choice and increased flexibility. And we are becoming much more of a lending business rather than simply a credit card business.

🎧 14.4 (M = Manufacturer, A = Agent)

M OK, perhaps we could start, as we agreed, by discussing the kind of relationship we want.

A OK.

M Usually with a major distributor or agent, we don't offer an exclusive agency agreement, because they don't want it. They like to use and distribute the products of most of the top companies. They make more money that way.

A Yes, a non-exclusive contract would be perfect for us, too. As you know, we represent many famous brands and will be happy to add your product lines to our list.

M Right. Now, prices: we like to recommend prices for each overseas market – we advise on minimum and maximum prices for each of our models.

A No, that's no good for us. We prefer to set the prices for all the products we offer. We know the conditions of the market far better than you, we would set the correct prices to maximise profits, of course.

M OK, it's not really a problem if you prefer it that way – I won't argue with you. Now the commission: I suggest a rate of fifteen percent on all the revenue you obtain, either directly or indirectly. Is that OK?

A Fifteen percent is too low. We want at least twenty percent. The market is very competitive. We'll have to spend a lot on advertising and promoting your products.

M Yes, but we could help with this.

A How much will you pay us?

M Well, we might go fifty, fifty up to an agreed limit. We can talk about the exact figures later.

A I'll have to think about it. We will talk about the commission later.

M Let's discuss the length of the contract. Normally we offer two years and to be honest, with a new distributor we prefer a shorter period. Either side can terminate with sixty days' notice.

A Well, it must be at least three years for it to be profitable for us.

M Well, we can talk about it later. I suggest we break for lunch now.

🎧 14.5

1 A non-exclusive contract would be perfect for us, too.
2 No, that's no good for us.
3 We know the conditions of the market far better than you.
4 I suggest a rate of fifteen percent on all the revenue you obtain.
5 Fifteen percent is too low. We want at least twenty percent.
6 We could help with this.
7 How much will you pay us?
8 We will talk about the commission later.
9 To be honest, with a new distributor we prefer a shorter period.
10 It must be at least three years.

Vocabulary file

Numbers following the words indicate which unit the word first appeared in.

Products

Products can be ...

affordable 12	exciting 1	inexpensive 1	stylish 1
cool 1	fashionable 1	luxurious 1	timeless 1
defective 10	good quality 1	produced under licence 1	value for money 1
durable 1	high priced 1	reliable 1	well-made 1

You can ...

develop 1	outsource 1	redesign 10	replace 10
endorse 1	place 1	relaunch 4	replacement 10
launch 1	promote 1	reposition 1	roll-out 13
modify 4	recall 10	test 10	lifecycle of a product 1
		... a product	range of products 1

We have expanded our **product range**. 4
Our company has developed **a distinctive new brand** which stands out from the competition.
They withdrew the **faulty product** from sale.

People involved in business

bidder 10	distributor 5	importer 9	shareholder 5
brand owner 1	entrepreneur 1	investor 5	shipping agent 14
competitor 3	executives 1	manufacturers 1	supplier 7
consumers 1	exporter 9	retailer 4	wholesaler 4
contractor 10			

Jobs

accountant 11
Account Manager 2
Assistant Sales Manager 8
auditor 11
Brand Manager 1
CEO (Chief Executive Officer) 4
civil servant 11

Commercial Director 6
dietician 8
director 1
estate agent 11
Finance Director 7
lawyer 11
Marketing Consultant 12

Marketing Manager 1
PA (Personal Assistant) to somebody 11
Sales Director 1
secretary 3
Warehouse Manager 7

*I'm **in** (sales). 3*
*I'm **in charge of** (about 30) people. 3*
*I'm responsible **for** (local contracts). 3*
*I work **for** (SFD).*

Work

Nouns	Verbs
applicant 8	advertise a vacancy 8
appraisal scheme 12	apply for a job 8
covering letter 8	create job opportunities 4
(good) financial package 8	fast-track 8
high performer 8	fill in an application form 8
interview panel 8	fire somebody 11
labour force 3	headhunt / to be headhunted 8
overtime 9	make somebody redundant 4
perk 3	phone in sick 11
permanent post 8	recruit 1
probationary period 8	resign 12
recruitment 8	retrain staff 4
sick leave 11	shortlist (candidates) 8
temporary post	subcontract work 1
vacancy 8	take a day / days off sick 11

*Do you have to **clock in** when you arrive? 3*
*She doesn't like **working to deadlines**. 11*
*She is **on a work placement** with SFD. 3*
*There could be some **staff cutbacks** in the short term. 4*
*In our company, there is now more **opportunity for promotion** than before. 4*
*My **application** was unsuccessful. 11*
*The successful applicant will have **a good track record in** accounting. 8*
*The job has no clear **career structure**. 13*

Describing people

adaptable 8	decisive 12	impulsive 12	patient / impatient 8
adventurous 12	dedicated 8	informal 12	persuasive 12
aggressive 12	determined 8	intuitive 13	proud 8
ambitious 1	dynamic 8	law-abiding 11	reliable 8
assertive 8	energetic 12	loyal 1	self-confident 8
charismatic 8	enthusiastic 8	motivated 8	selfish 12
competitive 8	flexible 8	motivating 12	shy 8
confident 5	forceful 8	outspoken 2	trustworthy 11
corrupt 11	honest 8	passionate 12	

Places and buildings

department store 1	headquarters 1
factory 1	hotel lounge 2
fitness club 8	pedestrian zone 2
flagship store 1	plant 1
gym 8	premises 14
	warehouse 3

American / British English

billboard / hoarding 6	freeway / motorway 2	round trip / return (ticket) 2
carry on baggage / hand luggage 2	parking lot / car park 2	schedule / timetable 2
coach class / economy class 2	résumé / CV 8 2	subway / underground 2
downtown / city centre 2		
elevator / lift 2		

Companies and organisations

Nouns	Verbs
branch 3	control a company 1
fast-growing company 12	decentralise 4
head office 3	downsize 4
highly profitable organisation 11	relocate 4
loss-making company 11	restructure 4
merger 4	run a company 3
outlet 3	
parent company 3	
start-up 5	
subsidiary 3	

Things you can say about your company or organisation:
*Our company is **well-established.*** 3
*Our company was **founded** (12 years ago).* 3
*Our company is **organised into** (3 departments).* 3
SFD **merged with** Reid International 4

*Our firm has an **excellent reputation** for reliability and good service. 3*
*Our company is **expanding** fast. 3*
*Our company is **renowned** for (its high manufacturing standards). 10*
*Our CEO has a **clear vision** of where the company is going. 12*
*We are looking at ways of **improving our image** as an ethical company. 11*
*Our company has **decentralised** responsibility and authority. 3*
*Our CEO believes in **autonomy**, but she's also keen on **accountability**. 3*
*Following the bankruptcy of our main competitor, we regained our position as **market leader**. 14*

Nouns	Verbs
market follower 6	implement a policy 11
market leader 5	introduce / launch a policy 11

An organisation can be...

bureaucratic 3	hierarchical 3
centralised / decentralised 3	market-driven 3
democratic 3	slow to respond 3

Travel

baggage reclaim 10	luggage 2
cancellation 2	overbooking 2
check-in desk 10	runway 10
jet-lag 2	terminal 10

*My plane was **delayed**. 2*
*She flies **business class**. 3*
*Several **budget airlines** offer **cheap flight**s to European destinations. 10*
*I missed my flight because of the huge queue at **passport control**. 10*

Business meetings

attend a seminar 2	second 8
call a meeting 4	send your apologies 8
chair a meeting	take part in a meeting 1

hold a meeting 1	action points 8
propose 8	AOB (any other business) 8
schedule a meeting 7	

*When will the meeting **take place**? 7*
*Can we move on to the next **item** on the **agenda**? 4*
*Will someone **take the minutes**? 8*
*The scheme, which was **proposed** by Ms Roberts, was **seconded** by Mr Todd. 4, 8*
*I think we should **have a vote on** that. 8*

Documents

draft (letter / report, etc.) 11   memo 1
letter of credit 3   the minutes of a meeting 4
licence 1

Markets, the economy and trade

Nouns
commodity markets 9
low-cost market 1
market segment 1
niche market 9

Its **market share** has declined. 1
Its market is **shrinking**. 1
After buying their largest competitor they totally **dominated the market**. 14

Nouns
economic downturn 4
recession 5
recovery 5

Verbs
break into a market 9
carry out a market survey 9
liberalise 9
subsidise 9

Nouns
barriers to trade / trade barriers 9
customs 9
deregulation 9
developing industries 9
fair trade 9

free port 9
laisser-faire 9
open borders 9
protectionism 9
quotas 9

regulations 9
restrictions 9
tariffs 9
strategic industries 9

Marketing and advertising

Nouns
advertising agency 6
advertising campaign 1
brand image 1
celebrity endorsement 6
differentiation 9
free sample 6
focus group 1
leaflet 6
luxury brand 1

mailshot 6
point-of-sale advertising 6
slogan 6
target audience 6
target consumer 6
TV commercial 3
USP (unique selling point) 6
word-of-mouth advertising 6

Verbs
develop brand awareness 1
differentiate 6
stretch a brand 1

We are launching a multi-media advertising campaign to promote our new products. 5
Advertisements can be ...

attention-grabbing 6
eye-catching 6
funny 6

humorous 6
inspiring 6
informative 6

shocking 6

Finance and money

Nouns

banker's draft / bank draft 9	earnings per share 5	
bonus 11	gross margin 1	
bribe 11	letter of credit 9	
cash flow 9	licensing fee 1	
commission 11	pre-tax profit 5	
consumer spending 5	profit margin 9	
cost-cutting practices 2	royalty 9	
dividend 5	sales revenues 5	
	tax refunds 5	
	turnover 4	

Verbs

claim expenses 11	make a profit 5
get a return on an investment 12	offer a discount 2
	pay a deposit 9
go bankrupt 4	raise money to start a business 5
increase profits 1	
lose money 1	cost consciousness 12
make a loss 1	

*Most of the store's **revenue** comes from clothing. 1*
*They spend a lot of money **on** advertising. 1*
*(That hotel) is **value for money**. 2*
*We **can't afford** to give him a 5% salary increase. 1*
*Many firms **cut costs** by outsourcing to India. 3*
*SFD will not be able to **reduce** the prices it **charges** its customers. 3*
*SFD needs to **boost** its profits and share price. 3*
*We will use any surplus cash to **reduce** the level of our debt. 5*

Doing business

negotiate a deal 3	set up a joint venture 7
place an order 9	underwrite a deal 12
quote (somebody) a price (for something) 9	win a contract 14

*We want **payment on delivery**. 14*
*We don't give a **discount** for orders of less than 100 items. 14*
*We expect **30 days' credit**. 14*
*Can you **deliver** in two weeks? 14*
*Unsold goods may be **returned**. The amount will be **credited** to the **customer's account**. 14*

Nouns

decrease in sales 5
increase in profits 5

Verbs

level off 5
plummet 5

*Sales **soared** to $18m. 5*
*Profits **rose** from $2.1 to 2.8 billion. 5*
*Our business **grew** by 15% last year. 5*

*Sales **reached a peak** of $20m. 5*
*Sales **reached a low point** of $5m. 5*
*We are unlikely to meet our **sales target** this year. 5*

Competition can be ...	**You can ...**		
fierce 14	adapt to 14	ignore 14	*We **faced** strong competition from (supermarkets). 4*
intense 14	catch up with 14	keep up with 4	
strong 14	cope with 14	overtake 14	*It is difficult for us **to compete with** the big multinationals. 14*
tough 14	crush 14	**... the competition.**	
unfair 14			

Difficulties and problems

Nouns

disorientation 2

disruptive and dangerous behaviour 2

irritability 2

misbehaviour 2

personality clash with somebody 4

setback 13

Verbs

blame somebody for (a problem / a mistake, etc.) 11

complain about something 3

correct a fault 10

deal with (a problem / a difficult situation, etc.) 4

discuss a problem 2

harm 2

have difficulties (doing something) 11

identify a fault 10

solve a problem 1

tackle (an issue / a problem, etc) 11

*My computer's just **crashed**. 2*

*They expressed their dissatisfaction **with** the service. 2*

*We're **facing a crisis** (with our market share). 6*

*The number of passenger **complaints** is soaring. 2*

*The company must decide how to deal with the complaints and **consider what action to take**. 10*

*Unfortunately, the redesigned product **failed** due to **lack of** consumer confidence caused by **bad publicity**. 10*

*During the inspection, a number of serious production **flaws** were found. 10*

*The product had a number of **defects**. 10*

*The product was not **up to standard**. 10*

*It all **went wrong**. 11*

*Our company **is having problems** innovat**ing**. 13*

Telephone language

Caller

Good (morning + name of company).

How may I help you? 2

I'd like to speak to ... 2

Who's calling please? 2

I'm calling because ... 2

Could you put me through to (extension 123), please? 2

Recipient

I'm afraid (he / she) is engaged at the moment. 2

Can I take a message? 2

Hold on a minute, please, I'll just transfer you to (a supervisor). 3

Would you like to call back later? 2

Could you ask (him / her) to call me back (tomorrow)? 2